FOSTERING FAITH

A Minister's Guide to Faith Development

Gary L. Chamberlain

PAULIST PRESS  *New York* / *Mahwah*

Text design by Ellen Whitney

Library of Congress Cataloging-in-Publication Data

Chamberlain, Gary.
    Fostering faith.

    Bibliography: p.
    1. Faith. 2. Christian life—1960-   . 3. Pastoral
theology. 4. Fowler, James W., 1940-   . I. Title.
II. Series.
BV4637.C424   1989   253   88-25383
ISBN 0-8091-3028-9 (pbk.)

Published by Paulist Press
997 Macarthur Boulevard
Mahwah, NJ 07430

Printed and bound in the
United States of America

TABLE OF CONTENTS

Dedicated to
Sharon A. Chamberlain
and
Michael and Benjamin Chamberlain
for their inspiration, humor
and earthy patience

PREFACE

Again and again in the gospels, Jesus reminds those whom he heals that it is their faith that has saved (healed) them (Lk 7:50). For us too as Christians our faith saves us. However, that simple statement does not reflect the full mystery and depth of the faith we all profess. For as we grow in size, maturity, wisdom and hopefully grace, *our* faith precisely as a basic aspect of our own persons grows or diminishes as we wrestle with understandings of ourselves and our God in new ways. We know that somehow our faith guides us in times of confusion, sustains us in times of doubt, comforts us in times of sorrow and celebrates us in times of joy. Yet the shape of our faith often eludes us. As a gift faith retains a mysterious force in our lives; as part of our persons faith takes its shape from the contours of our daily encounters.

Our faith in its mystery and its patterns is the very subject of this book. Using the pioneering work of James W. Fowler in faith development theory, we can examine some, but only some, of the unfolding textures and colors which faith takes in the patterns of our lives. Fowler's work first appeared in the early 1970's. In those early years he and his associates interviewed hundreds of people across a wide spectrum of age, faith traditions and cultures to hone the theoretical model so that it might adequately reflect the myriad and marvelous faith as actually expressed in daily living. Today as research and writing continues in the area of faith development, we are witnessing some truly exciting undertakings as theologians, educators and others consider the practical implications and applications of the theory.

The following discussion reflects a modest attempt to continue those efforts with a particular focus. The work emerged originally in my efforts at teaching graduate students in ministry education. And now as director of a graduate program for ministers and educators I am more firmly convinced not only of the usefulness of faith development theory as a tool in a variety of ministries but also of the essential dimension that growth in faith plays in the life formation of the minister. Personal growth in com-

munities of faith serves as the heart of education in ministry and professional development. In this educational process faith development
becomes a strong yet playful ally by assisting the minister to chart his or
her hidden, sometimes arduous journey of faith.

The central belief supporting the discussion here is that unless the
minister has understood his or her own faith growth, he or she cannot carry
out effective ministry. Given the times in which we live, ministry does not
mean the exhibition of professional skills in education, administration,
counseling or community development. The Christian churches certainly
need all these abilities in carrying out the tasks of church life. But most
fundamentally in our highly technical, consumptive, bureaucratic and
competitive society, the minister must point to the sacramental signs of
God's presence in the world. A tall order.

In this conception, the minister is a professional in every way and
exhibits primarily the imaginative capacity to "see" and "hear" God's
active love in the lives of ordinary people and in the structures, or more
probably in the prophetic anti-structures, of contemporary society. Imagination—the heart of a living faith in a transcendent God active in our personal and social histories, our stories—becomes the central dimension of
the following discussions of faith development theory through the exploration of symbols and images and in the ability to step into, to participate
in the worlds of other people and groups.

Our initial explorations in the following chapters penetrate the patterned skein of faith, imagination and ministry. Then after a brief discussion of faith development theory and the particular dimensions involved
in faith growth, we approach the implications for a variety of ministries
in the lives of today's Christian communities. First, the internal life of the
church community draws our attention—Christian education, family and
parish life. Then we follow Christian ministry as it breaks out into the
larger community, carrying the mission of the church to the world in efforts toward transformation around the sick, the elderly and those in
prison. And finally, we reflect on the broad areas of justice, spirituality
and worship as the concrete embodiment of the Spirit which animates our
lives, hopes, and visions of gospel realities.

While this book is meant as a resource for people engaged in some
form of ministry, whether full or part-time, paid or volunteer, I hope that
others will find its discussions and suggestions helpful in their own struggles to lead faith-filled and faithful lives. Parents, students, teachers, the
sick, elderly, imprisoned, doctors, wardens, counselors, managers—all
are ministers by reason of their baptism. All travel the paths of faith in

some way. All are capable of imaginative transformations of their own lives and of society. Faith can indeed move mountains, but only if the possibilities are imaged as real. The development of our faith calls us to such imaginative "faithings."

Finally I would like to express my deep appreciation to all those who have helped in the preparation of this work. My wife, Sharon, and my sons, Mike and Ben, endured my absences from their lives and my use of our shared computer while testing the theory in our daily life together. Larry Kohlberg, recently deceased, first introduced me to the work of faith development, and Jim Fowler generously has shared his work and his "imaginings" during my study with him and ever since. My colleagues at the Institute for Theological Studies, Margaret Lead and Leo Stanford, shared their own insights and concerns in ministry education, while Fr. Richard Ahler, S.J., chair of the Theology Department, supported my efforts at this writing in myriad ways. Typists Kathy Corneloup and Gary Dillon endured the frustrations of making sense of much of my notations and zig-zags. And most of all, I want to thank the students, faculty and associates of the SUMORE Program whose work and study in religious education and ministry were the inspiration for this enterprise, in particular, Cissy McLane, Kathleen Fischer, Suzanne Jabro, Peggy McGurn, Jean Durel, Mike Hays, Ether Vesper, Katherine Dyckman and Brennan Hill among so many. Without their support I would not have imagined nor completed this work.

FOREWORD

Till now no one has written a book quite like *Fostering Faith*. Gary Chamberlain has undertaken the creative task of leading his readers in the rethinking of a number of dimensions of Christian ministry in dialogue with faith development theory and research. His book, a welcome addition to faith development literature, makes a number of unique contributions.

First, he offers a conception of ministry that grows out of the spiritual revolution constituted by Vatican II. Inclusive of lay as well as consecrated or ordained ministries, Chamberlain's approach to ministry sees it as the calling of all the people of God. As such, ministry calls men and women to be "priests at every elbow," carrying and representing the love and redeeming power of Christ into all the institutional settings in which people live and work, hurt and aspire, suffer and serve, with each other.

Second, Chamberlain's treatment of faith development theory does not limit it to the formal structural-developmental characterization of stages of faith. While making thoughtful use of the stage descriptions, and even extending them from merely describing persons to depicting the patterns of faith in communities, Chamberlain is clear that faith development must also deal with the "contents" of faith. Part of what makes his work strong and original is its attention to the images and symbols that either support or assault the faith of persons in such settings as hospitals, prisons, and retirement homes, as well as in churches and schools.

Third, Chamberlain's work falls in the category of "prophetic inquiry." A passion for encouraging and informing ministry with the "marginated" persons in our society animates Chamberlain's book throughout. It takes a widely experienced as well as a committed and compassionate author to generate creative and relevant implications of the faith development perspectives for ministry to the sick and dying, to the elderly, and to prisoners. While Chamberlain also brings creativity to the more usual task of showing how faith development research illumines ministries with children, adolescents, young adults and adults, his most spirited chapters, in my reading, are those devoted to ministries among the marginated.

Finally, this book arises from and culminates in a spirituality for justice and peacemaking. Chamberlain concretely shows how continuing development in faith, if authentically Christian, must manifest a widening of effective social perspective-taking and a commitment to the extension of justice in society and the world. His remarks about spirituality and liturgy as contexts for the nurture and encouragement of justice ministries are richly informative.

As director for the last several years of the summer ministry education program of the Jesuit Seattle University, Gary Chamberlain has been in the thick of training women and men from all over this country, and, indeed, the world, in ministry. His training as a philosophical theologian, his years as a creative teacher of undergraduates, his research in faith development, and his own involvements with ministries to marginated peoples all come together in this rich book to give it integrity and relevance. Though it is Catholic in idiom and frequent reference, it is truly ecumenical in its generative approach to ministry. It deserves a wide reading, and Chamberlain deserves our thanks.

James W. Fowler
Emory University

1. Ministry, Faith and Imagination

There is a variety of gifts but always the same Spirit; there are all sorts of service to be done, but always the same Lord; working in all sorts of different ways in different people, it is the same God who is working in all of them.

1 Corinthians 12:4–6

And to some his gift was that they should be apostles; to some, prophets; to some, evangelists; to some, pastors and teachers; so that the saints together make a unity in the work of service, building up the body of Christ. . . . So the body grows full until it has built itself up, in love.

Ephesians 4:11–13, 16b[1]

Captain Robert de Baudercourt: "How do you mean, voices."
St. Joan: "I hear voices telling me what to do. They come from God."
De Baudercourt: "They come from your imagination."
St. Joan: "Of course. That is how messages of God come to us."

George Bernard Shaw,
"St. Joan"[2]

If I approach a man with the paradigms of faith, I compose his actions accordingly. . . . But this is a two way street. For not only does each one of us approach the world with or without faith; it is also necessary that each one of us *be approached* with faith; we have to be believed in by somebody, by man and/or by God.

Not only is faith a gift. So it is a gift *to be believed in*. We are created and patterned by the faith of others.[3]

William Lynch,
Images of Faith

Ethel teaches a heavy load at the rural community college, but her keenest interest centers on her ministry to men at the maximum security prison. Ever since her days in ministry studies, this energetic laywoman has served as lobbyist, volunteer organizer, go-between and friend to the "lifers" in the prison. Annette journeyed from the security of teaching elementary school as a woman religious to supporting and working with native Indians in North Dakota and Oklahoma, while Kay, her fellow religious, moved out of the classroom to the role of pastor for the people of a small town in Minnesota. Dan, married with two small children, emerged from the business world to delve into high school religion classes and then parish work, managing to express his own spirituality in dozens of poems. Joe, bank vice-president, took up his work with street people with renewed zeal as the plight of the homeless increased in recent years, and Betsey expresses her gifts and spirituality in classes and workshops utilizing dance as therapy.

What unites these people in the multiplicity of endeavors is their understanding of themselves as ministers, bringing the reality of the gospel message to a troubled yet expectant world. But Ethel, Annette, Kay, Dan, Joe, and Betsey are only one small example of the explosion of ministry in the Christian churches today. From parish to school, from families to prisoners, concerned, caring, and competent people are carrying out their ministries in times and places unheard of three decades ago.

At that time the world of "ministry," at least among Roman Catholics, was securely in the hands of the local parish priest and his assistants. "Monsignor," as he might have been titled, usually made the monthly appearances at the grade school or taught religion class at the high school administered by the sisters, celebrated Mass on Sunday, visited the sick, administered the large parish, and attended to sundry other duties during the rest of the week, perhaps taking a day out for rest, returning to hear confessions on Saturday. Through his ministrations, the "faithful" were secured in their faith, and the life of the parish in the closed world of the American Roman Catholic Church went on with only a few reminders of external threats to the "deposit of faith" passed on from the days of the apostles. The word "minister" was heard only in relation to "those Protestants."

Not only were the essential works of "ministry" focused on the parish pastor and his associates, the primary role of the pastor was sacramental, expressed through his priestly powers in exercising such sacraments as Eucharist, confession, baptism, marriage, and so on. Lay people might participate in this priestly work, but only by extension through direct assistance in the parish or through various "lay apostolates" in works of charity. Ministry centered on one person and primarily in his sacramental role.

Today we are experiencing an expansion of ministries. As the numbers of priests and religious decline, lay people take up the role of minister in myriad directions, extending from religious education coordinators, to youth ministry and campus ministry, peace and justice ministries, community organizing, spiritual direction, ministries to the divorced, sick, elders, dying, and imprisoned. These new directions reflect the church's mission to the world, a new self-understanding which not only provides radical experiences in the local church but extends to new ministries around the world.

Central to an understanding of these developments is the realization of ministry as a response to the gospel's call to all baptized people to carry out service to others utilizing the gifts unique to each. Such developments demand greater maturity of Christian faith for those who enter ministry than ever before. And the key to developing an active and responsive faith life lies in exploring the place of imagination in shaping our fundamental posture toward the world as Christians and as ministers. Upon that foundational link of *ministry* emerging from a commitment of *faith* resting upon our *images* of self and God, we can then explore how faith development theory provides a useful framework and tool for the personal growth of ministers and their ministry to others.

Ministry: The Past as Dynamic Present ——

The eruption of ministry in our times represents a culmination of several historical and social developments. Certainly the decline in the number of priests and religious has meant the need for more lay people to step into the tasks of church ministry. But more importantly, fundamental changes have occurred in lay people's perceptions of themselves, of their role in the church, and of the church's mission to the world. The Second Vatican Council unleashed a new self-understanding of church as *all* the people of God which a ready and educated lay people took seriously. Then too the sense of "vocation" or "call" as a personal response to God's word in faith through each person's unique gifts has led to a recognition of everyone's call to "ministry" through baptism. The rise of the charismatic movement with its central emphasis upon the movement of the Spirit coupled with a thirst for a spirituality suited to individual needs rather than a "lay spirituality" molded for all means a developing readiness to respond to that call for service in the church's mission.

In addition, the movement toward collegiality among bishops called for new collegiality between clergy and lay people in ministry. And finally emphasis upon local church and a new sense of the church's mission to the world rather than just to its own life brought about a focus upon the many needs in church and society which demanded responses from the faithful people who are church. These emphases upon functions of ministry rather than the ''offices'' of the minister have led to a willingness to go beyond the ''official'' categories of ministry sanctioned by the church to new undertakings of service in the Gospel's name.

Our sense of ministry today reflects the rediscovery of the church's past approaches to ministry. Through the research of theologians such as Edward Schillebeeckx, Thomas O'Meara, and others, the picture emerging from the earliest Christian churches attests to a wide variety of ministries, centered not upon liturgical celebration but rather upon the dynamic messages of itinerant prophets and evangelizers, teachers, and healers. In Paul's earliest writings we have a list of ministers which covers, in addition to those already mentioned, apostles, miracle workers, givers of support, community leaders, those speaking in tongues, and interpreters. There seemed to be no special procedures, not even a worship structure, which led to the selection and appointment of these leaders.[4] A review of the early church leads to the conclusion: ''There were, then, a variety of agents and officers who engaged in ministering to the small communities and house-churches of the first century. All arose as the needs of the community demanded.''[5]

Over the next centuries this great variety and outpouring of the Spirit responded to the challenges of organizing the community's life in view of heretical teachings, schisms, and the need for discipline against persecution. Gradually local authorities consolidated leadership of the community, and the emerging roles of presbyters and bishops appropriated the roles of the dynamic, spirit-filled prophets, preachers, and teachers. Adopting the model of the surrounding culture when thrust onto the center stage of the Roman Empire following Constantine's conversion, church leaders adopted the trappings of Roman rule, and the clerical hierarchy of the church emerged. This meant that the earlier outpouring of the Spirit upon a variety of persons was now channeled toward only a few. And the primary ministry of these few, the ordained clerics, focused upon their powers at the sacred rituals. Thus the apostolic building up of community through preaching, teaching, and leadership narrowed to a community ''built up'' around eucharistic liturgy and sacramental powers.

> Ministry evolved from being an ordered and effective diversity of services from the Spirit for the kingdom to being a sacral, liturgical administration. . . . As one ministry had absorbed the plurality of ministries, it soon returned to redistribute parcels of ministry out of its

own fulness. . . . All other Christians, including the ones to be com-
missioned to ministry, own a highly passive role.[6]

These explorations reveal a dynamic period in Christian history when
ministry rested in the faith of individual Christians called to exercise their
gifts in a variety of ways. This historical understanding of ministry vali-
dates the manifold expressions of ministry today and supports those calls
for ministries which may even challenge the "official" authorization of
ministry. As theologian Edward Schillebeeckx says in looking at the
church today in relation to ministry in the early church, "against the background of existing church order new and perhaps urgently necessary alternative possibilities can usually be seen only through the medium of
what must provisionally be called 'illegality.' "[7] This evolution of "alternative possibilities" in ministry will necessarily involve us in the development of the creative imagination.

Out of the very varieties of ministries we witness today as well as
from the historical witness, we can develop a definition of ministry which
at least brings us to clearer understandings of the limits as well as the reach
of ministry. Theologian Thomas O'Meara defines Christian ministry as
"public activity of a baptized follower of Jesus Christ flowing from the
Spirit's charism and an individual personality on behalf of a Christian
community to witness to, serve and realize the kingdom of God."[8] The
merits of O'Meara's terms lie in underscoring the roots of ministry in
Christian baptism, understanding that all Christians have a call to ministry. However, ministry must have a public dimension to it which leads to
"building up the body of the Lord" (Eph 4:12). And it is precisely at the
intersection of the Spirit's outpouring and the individual's expression of
gifts that ministry is experienced as a call *out of the community* in response
to the needs of the community. Urban Holmes expands the sense of community here when he sees the function of ministry "to make explicit, in a
given culture, the church as the primal sacrament of Christ."[9] In meeting
the challenges of that cultural setting ministry will be called on to exert its
imaginative character in penetrating the dominant cultural symbols and
images.

Key for ministry today is the sense in which the very person of the
minister becomes an essential dimension of each ministry in particular. In
his or her role as enabler, interpreter, or servant the minister's personal
responses shape the attendant response of the person or group where ministry is taking place. Thus while a shift has occurred away from the *office*

of priest-as-minister to the public activity involved in ministry, a renewed emphasis rests upon the very person of the minister. Recognizing this "sacramental" character of the minister, Fr. Dennis Geaney writes:

> If contact with the spiritual is made through an interpersonal relationship with the minister rather than what he or she symbolizes externally, some inner qualities that shine through tell the other whether this person is reaching out in love. . . . In a time of rapid cultural change like our own, cultural religious symbols do not carry the weight of the deeper gospel message with the result that the love must be fleshed out in very human ways if the message of Jesus is to be transmitted to another generation.[10]

In this empathetic role the minister is challenged to take the perspective of the other in an imaginative leap into the other's world. But also as cultural interpreter of the gospel's message for our times, the minister must employ images and symbols which can translate the realities of God's meanings into our own understandings. This important dimension of ministry which crystallizes around imagination lies in what Holmes sees as *the* "fundamental issue in ministry," namely, "the recovery of a sense of enchantment and the ability to be enchanting."[11] In addition to personal empathy, the minister today must serve as interpreter of a uniquely Christian understanding of reality in the midst of an unreceptive culture.

Obstacles to this general task of ministry emerge from our very inability to "see" God's presence in our own experience and in the world around us. Inasmuch as ministry is an action which expresses meanings in people's lives around themes of death and resurrection, redemption and liberation, sin and forgiveness, the challenge of ministry is precisely to create atmospheres in which the gospel's reality can be understood and embodied in the daily lives of ordinary people. At the same time in our technical, rationalistic, bureaucratic society ministry must enable the Christian community and the larger society to "filter in" those God-breathing experiences in our lives which identify God's presence. For only in this way will ministry as Christian activity in the world create a meaningful reality of what the kingdom is.

By identifying God as the source, heart, and author of created reality, the minister necessarily redefines or rather reimages reality. Thus when we assemble as community for worship we reimage ourselves as "brothers and sisters in Christ," an imaginative relationship which challenges our usual sense of self and other as clerk-manager, lay-priest, parents-children, male-female, worker-boss, aged-young, infirm-well, and so on. In our times the power of the gospel message to reimage ourselves is overshadowed by the pull of appearances in the very images of advertising, the dominance of television and video, and other institutional forms of image-making. "Our contemporary image life is beset with distorted and perverse images of human being. . . . The mirrors of the media distort our human worth, reflecting us as ugly if we do not look like movie stars."[12] Amid the noise, multiple images, and rapid texture of modern life, the minister must continually challenge the dominance of such images while creating "filters" of God's presence in people's lives.

Once we recognize that our knowledge of what is real and thus reality itself is formed by images from our social settings, then one of the central tasks of ministry is to continually challenge the existing structures of society and even of the church. In order to meet the needs of the community for full human expression and to provide interpretative images of God's presence among us, ministry must create alternatives to what already is. In that sense, ministry is always counter-cultural. Ministry does not "fit in" but is a little "weird," calling for the creativity of the artist even more fundamentally than other ministerial forms such as sensitive counselor or efficient manager.[13]

This critical, imaginative challenge and reimaging reflects the sense of "prophetic imagination" developed by biblical scholar Walter Brueggemann who writes: "Prophetic ministry consists of offering an alternative perception of reality and in letting people see their own history in light of God's freedom and his will for justice."[14] Prophetic ministry means not only to criticize what is but also to energize the community for the future by evoking from the biblical witness the power to transform suffering and despair while revealing new life and hope.

This role of the minister as imaginative interpreter of God's kingdom in our daily lives calls for expression of "prophetic ministry" through service in personal and public life. For too long the church's mission has centered predominantly around liturgy and cult. Important as worship is to the life of the community,

> Only with an expanded ministry, with new ministries realizing the old services of prophet, teacher, evangelist and deacon in the public sector can the tension between liturgical and communal leader and social evangelist be eased. . . . The movement by which Christians withdrew from public ministry to liturgical attendance must now be reversed.[15]

If "Early Christianity was clearly one of interpretation and service, not of cult and priesthood,"[16] our rediscovery of this history calls us to reclaim new areas for ministry. This call provides the basis for the forms of ministry which we will examine later in this discussion.

Ministry then is the interface of the Spirit's expression in the self-conscious "call" of each minister and of the demands of the community in particular social situations. The community's discernment provides the context for the expression of the minister's gifts, and that expression may or may not be "authenticated" by the official church. Yet it will be "authentic" in gospel terms as it expresses the needs and rights of the Christian community's mission to the world. This task involves the exciting development of imaginative visions through which ministers create and enable others to create alternative patterns of relationships in love, care, and just service.

Good ministry today demands growth in faith: ministers "must have grown in sufficient depth in faith and moral living to be able to help others do the same."[17] Such maturity entails understandings of self and one's role or roles which no longer reflect the obedient, dependent servant of the church, responsive to the authority of others. Rather mature ministry involves elements of risk and trust where mutuality and interdependence provide the basis for sharing one's gifts and enabling others to best express their own gifts. As a leader in the community the minister must rely on others, trust their strengths and gifts in order to delegate responsibilities and work in genuine collaboration. At the same time a genuinely mature faith calls for a recognition of personal weaknesses and a willingness to share those with others.[18] These personal qualities reflect different stages of faith growth, which we shall see later, as they define and shape the particular roles, offices, and forms of ministry we experience in today's church and society.

In addition, if ministry involves an awakening of the minister and others to the service of gospel faith, then understanding the meaning and development of faith itself becomes central to the understanding of ministry. When we visualize ministry as the unfolding of personal gift in response to a gospel call within the particular needs of church and society (call, concern, and context), the centrality of faith would seem obvious. What our discussion to this point has attempted to underscore lies in the imaging and visioning dimensions of ministry called for in our times. The faith roots of the minister as enabler, interpreter, and servant will be expressed in the imaginative capacities for "seeing" God's presence in the world and envisioning realities which incorporate that presence for others.

We will now turn to the very dynamics of faith to unfold this essential aspect of ministry.

Faith as Root of Ministry

While ministry begins in baptism and takes shape through the mature adult's response to God's call in a particular time and place, the awareness and expression of that call depends most centrally upon the dynamic process we are calling faith. In the past, many Christian traditions, and especially the Roman Catholic tradition, have understood faith as either an intellectual process or a non-rational leap beyond evidence. As a young Roman Catholic I was taught that faith was the intellectual assent to the truth of a proposition based upon the authority of the one revealing the proposition. Besides the circularity of this argument, the statement led to a separation of matters of faith from the rest of my life. Here "faith" was equated with "belief" in the truth of propositions.

Fortunately today we have appropriated a much richer understanding of faith. For theologian Gregory Baum faith "involves the whole person. . . . In faith [the person] is delivered from the confines of his own existence and passes beyond himself to the One who approaches him in grace."[19] In Karl Rahner's understanding faith, as God's free gift, is "an abiding feature of man's mode of existence as person."[20] In the words of James Fowler, whose theory concerns us here, "Faith is an orientation of the total person, giving purpose and goal to one's hopes and strivings, thoughts and actions."[21] In these understandings faith is the very mode through which the person shapes new self-understandings and new orientations toward the world. In this way, faith becomes a constitutive dimension of the human person, and the person's beliefs, values, and actions reveal an understanding of the self and the world which serves as the basic metaphor for life.

William Lynch provides a helpful understanding of this aspect of faith, so important to ministry, when he interprets faith as "a great primal and primitive force that precedes or even constructs knowledge itself."[22] In such a view faith emerges as an expression of knowing which animates the infant as thoroughly as the sage, providing the basis for our very interaction with all the various environments of our lives. And so this kind of knowing is primarily relational, passionate, and participatory. That is, we find ourselves related in faith to others and to God in ways which surpass rational categories. People in love "know" one another in ways which defy the understanding of those who would say "What can she see in him?" or "Knowing what he does about her, why does he still stay in the relationship?" Whether expressed in pathological or fully healthy forms, faith provides a kind of knowledge which emerges from being-in-relation. This knowledge pulls us passionately into the world of others, and in the process we feel about them in a variety of ways. Faith does not allow for intellectual distancing.

Faith exhibits a communitarian and participatory nature as well. That is, in faith we are bound together with another, a group, our God, in webs of relationships. We share meanings, languages, trusts, and we forge alliances or break agreements all on the basis of some sense of a shared goal or purpose. Marriage, for example, is never just a matter of two people. There is always a third reality present in which both parties participate, the relationship itself, the covenantal dimension as Fowler calls it.[23] In short, we are shaped and formed in our very persons by the communities to which we bind ourselves and by which others are bound to us.

The shape of our faith in a transcendent God reveals yet another aspect of every form of faith, its shaping or imaging factor. In calling ourselves a people of God, in addressing one another as brothers and sisters in Christ, or by responding to God as personal, we are dependent upon images of reality which we borrow from the Christian tradition. Precisely as a response to God's word faith composes and shapes our understandings of our surrounding worlds. For one person and community that shaping may take the form of the Ku Klux Klan without any sense of contradiction between the gospel and prejudice toward blacks, Catholics, and Jews. For another such shaping images lead to intense prayer to a God of love discovered deep within the very structures of the universe. Whatever the form, the shaping nature of faith is unmistakable, preceding conscious knowing. Faith composes or "recomposes the world according to its terms."[24] Such recomposing is the very heart of "prophetic ministry," indeed of any form of ministry since ministry is precisely the power of envisioning realities not yet seen. "Only faith can guarantee the blessings that we hope for or prove the existence of the realities that at present remain unseen" (Heb 11:1).

Faith as primal force, a form of knowing derived from being in relation, participatory, communal, and compositional—these provide the sense in which faith is constitutive of the person and the world. Yet the way in which faith develops such basic patterns within the person and society exhibits the fundamental place of imagination as the form by which we in faith experience the world and expresse our faith-filled responses to the world.

Imagination: The Heart of Faith

When we reflect upon the kind of knowing which faith involves, we notice that faith is our way of being in relation to others, to the world, and to God. Any change or new development in those relationships constitutes a change or new development in our own self-understanding. Furthermore, in these relationships our knowing rests upon the shaping, composing or imaging which best reflects the relationship. Whether the image is friend, sister, lover, enemy, each such faith-knowing-in-relation involves an image or set of images which go to shape a whole. The very order and fabric of our lives depend upon the ways in which images are integrated to form a sense of "wholeness" in our universe of meaning.

Just as dramatically our existing "wholeness" can yield to new possibilities for creative change through new images of reality. For millions of Americans in the 1960's and 1970's, the images of Bull Conner's dogs unleashed on non-violent black protesters, of the shooting of a Vietcong prisoner, or of student deaths at Kent State and Jackson State framed on the nightly news galvanized responses to the civil rights movement and the war in Vietnam in ways in which argument and analysis had failed to do. Our faith in justice in the south or in our government's conduct of the war in Vietnam was broken into irreparable shards of disillusionment, anger, and frustration. The universe of meaning changed, and new "wholes" began to emerge, images of whites joining blacks to achieve a more just society or of a peace movement supported by Americans from every sector of society.

When we think of faith as a response to God's self-revelation, our understanding of that revelation takes the form of symbols, myths, narratives which rely on images to express not an abstract truth but truth experienced concretely in our lives. The central truths in the Christian tradition enter our daily worlds precisely inasmuch as they are expressed in images and stories which make up a meaningful whole. If our understanding of God as transcendent reality is imaged as "Father," then our fundamental self-consciousness rests in a relationship of familial trust. Such basic trust in God as Father shapes a profound conviction of a friendly and responsive universe, a "felt whole" which is very different from an abstract belief that God is Father. The image demands a transformation of our consciousness.

Likewise whatever meaning we each give to such truths as incarnation and redemption rests primarily in our images of the birth of Jesus and his death upon the cross. Without those images incarnation and redemption become abstract artifacts, interesting to discuss perhaps but empty of any power to generate new realities in our lives. It is in this sense that Fowler sees faith *as* the imagination inasmuch as it composes a felt image of an ultimate environment in which we move and live.[25]

Through imagination we too are shaped by the very images we have composed or which have been composed for us by our tradition. Through our words such as "altar" for "table," "Eucharist" for bread, "church" for building, "people of God" for organization, we constitute a reality not seen with the naked eye. In one fundamental sense all language involves an imaging of reality, a basic faith. Upon this foundation Christian faith builds a new or deeper understanding of all our relationships in light of our fundamental relationship with God as Father, Son and Spirit. If God is Father, then we are sons and daughters. If God is Word, then we are listeners; if God is Spirit, then we are alive with a mysterious depth that carves hope out of despair, liberation out of guilt and oppression.[26]

We move through life from an early "bathing" in communities of shared images toward a time when we critically compose our personal and social worlds in new images. Thus we find ourselves caught up in a continuous spirit of faith unfolding as new relationships form new images out of the "stuff" of our experiences and understandings. This dynamic unfolding of faith in our lives is the very process which faith development theory examines.

In much the same way, Jesus' parables and deeds were an imaginative invitation in faith growth to those who heard and saw him. The gospels were, and still are, an invitation, a gift to the imagination. "Let those who have eyes to see see, and those who have ears to hear hear" (Mk 4:9). As Fowler notes, there are three movements of the imagination in Jesus' words and deeds. First the prevailing images are broken, cracked so that a new possibility can emerge. A withered hand was healed; a prostitute was pronounced blessed; a dead girl was given life; a blind man saw again; Pharisees and Sadducees were declared hypocrites—all new ways for people to "see" and "hear" different realities.

Then new images are formed which crystallize dynamic relationships involving self, God and the neighbor. "Happy are those who mourn; they shall be comforted" (Mt 5:5). "When you fast, put oil on your head and wash your face" (Mt 6:17). "The kingdom of heaven is like a mustard seed" (Mk 4:31). "Leave the dead to bury the dead; your duty is to go and spead the news of the kingdom of God" (Lk 9:60). Through his words and deeds Jesus gave those who followed him new images with which to understand God's dramatic action in their lives.

Finally, in a third movement of imagination, Jesus demands that those who follow him act in accordance with their new images of reality: "Go, therefore, and make disciples of all nations" (Mt 2:19).

> Under the impact of revelatory event, imagination dissolves the old and responds with new images and actions which, in a new unity, provide a transformed total experience of the world and of response and initiative within it. In just such a dramatic transformation do people respond to the impact of the Gospel.[27]

If faith is our way of being-in-relation to God, to our ultimate heart of reality, imagination then "is the principal human organ for knowing and responding to the disclosures of transcendent Truth."[28] Only through imagination can we come to know God as we interpret our God through powerful symbols. Only through imagination can we respond in love to a revealing Reality which first loves us. Only through imagination are we in faith able to envision new possibilities and future hopes in spite of the din of hostile or indifferent voices, the babbling whirl of advertising and media images.

Often we distort this necessary place of imagination in shaping our faith through anger, depression, violence. Our images of others and of God emerge as distorted and twisted shades of the "wholes" they might be. Or the numbing bureaucracy and reductionist technologies of the culture filter out of our images all references to a transcendent dimension. The vitality of bread and blood, death and resurrection no longer evoke meaning and provoke us to action and service.

And a more subtle danger to the imaginative capacity in faith, especially for those in ministry, lurks in the very call for professional development in our culture. As Urban Holmes has noted, the professional model focuses on the here and now, not the transcendent. It tends to equate ministerial function with one profession and one role. In this way the charismatic qualities, the "weirdness" involved in ministry, get weeded out. Too often we as church confuse genuine ministry with credentials, degrees, routines, and job descriptions. The imaginative power of the person and the mystery of his or her message loses to the routinized skill of the professional.

[Professionalism] is a model of interaction which comes out of the technological world, where control and prediction are highly valued. The effect is to reduce the kinds of behavior and values which effectively serve to open ourselves and others to transcendence. . . . The more we advocate the professional image, however, the greater seems the gap between our theology and our implied intentions in ministry. Theology talks about salvation by grace through faith, and professionalism talks about salvation by works. . . . The fundamental issue in ministry today is the recovery of a sense of enchantment and the ability to be enchanting.[29]

This is not to say that ministers should not be professional and competent. But their skills should emerge from their gifts and rest upon their imaginative capacities to interpret the kingdom reality for others, to envision new possibilities even in despair, and to empower others with a Spirit beyond their comprehensions. These qualities call for fostering and developing the rich resources of imagination as the "organ" of profound faith in Jesus Christ. In this way we can begin the task of recovering the enchantment and becoming enchanted in the ways in which Holmes speaks.

Imaginative Ministry in Faith

Throughout this discussion, the terms "ministry," "faith" and "imagination" have formed a whole essential to the task of this book. Ministry today finds its vision and power in the faith of each person and of the Christian community. Called by baptism the Christian minister responds out of an imaginative capacity for envisioning self and others as "more than" the surrounding culture and our own senses tell us. Through our faith in God and Jesus Christ we "see" and "hear" God's presence in the midst of despair, darkness, and death, affirming hope, light and life.

Yet the minister's response in faith takes unique shape depending upon the mature level of faith growth, what we will discuss soon as faith stage. And our times as well as our self-understanding as church today call for a maturity in ministry which reflects an equal maturity in faith. Does the minister see himself or herself as the one "in charge," carrying out a preconceived plan which suits the needs of the faithful? Or is the minister comfortable with sharing responsibilities on a team, acknowledging the full expression of others' gifts in their independent freedom? Perhaps the minister, aware of personal weaknesses and vulnerabilities, empowers others precisely by letting go of claims and precious plans in order to hear others' pains. And he or she sponsors those hesitant to explore their gifts, allowing for mistakes and failures. Each of these models of ministry reflects particular faith understandings and levels of faith maturity. Likewise each expresses a level of imaginative capacity to envision alternatives, take others' viewpoints, and symbolize anew.

Called in faith through our baptism into the Christian community to ministry, the minister in today's world and church faces a formidable task in establishing a sense of God's presence among us. This most fundamental work of ministry roots itself first in the imaginative capacity of each minister to envision, to shape a personal faith expression which captures God's self-revelation. The minister's own faith necessarily has to mature to the point of self-conscious expression before he or she can help others in ministry. This self-understanding in faith prevents the minister from inflicting his or her own concerns and interests on the very people being ministered to and allows the minister to imaginatively participate in the perspective of others in order to assist their journeys in faith.

In addition, imagination as the "organ" of faith serves as the basic tool for ministry in several other ways. For not only does the minister imaginatively understand God's presence in certain ways in our world, but he or she interprets God's living reality through symbols and images which must engage others in their personal and social selves. At what levels of faith growth or personal development are the persons whom the minister encounters? How do images from the past prevent them from hearing the "good news"? How can the minister enter into the worlds of other persons, groups, and traditions in ways that do not distort those worlds? Or what symbols can penetrate the numbing din of hostile or indifferent voices in our culture or reshape the myriad babbles of advertising and media images so that the gospel message can be heard?

The minister, then, becomes a cultural critic, engaging in a challenge to those patterns, images, and meanings which would filter out the signs of God's presence in the world. This role of "prophetic ministry" demands a continuous commitment in faith not just to action, but to transformative action which liberates oppressor as well as oppressed. The disruptive and creative powers of imagination burst forth in the minister's challenges and actions on behalf of a living gospel story of promise and redemption in which all peoples are brothers and sisters in Christ Jesus.

To love and understand others as they are in themselves, to envision just alternatives to oppressive situations, to interpret God's presence to a society soaked in images, to invite others to join in community and service—all these elements provide the context for ministry today, and each demands a faith steeped in a rich imagination. Ministry, then, is a personal response in faith to God's presence in the world in such a way that that presence becomes continuously more evident to all. In view of the central dimension of faith and imagination in ministry, then with Urban Holmes we can say that the primary agenda of ministry is to be in the world as one who images.[30]

Our next task involves the discussion of ways in which faith does image reality in the world around us. In the lives of believing Christians, what patterns of faith growth can we discern? Here the theory of faith development will provide us with important clues.

> If therefore we recognize that the quality of faith utterly depends upon the adequacy of the images it employs and how these images are held, then we will see that the composing of faith is, in essence, an act of imagination conditioned, in part, by structural development.[31]

The structured development of faith provides us with the framework necessary to discuss how we can more completely animate our particular ministries and ourselves as ministers. That is the hope of this discussion and of the following chapters. For if maturity in ministry demands maturity in faith, then our exploration of the structural development of faith will assist our pursuit of more responsive and creative ministry.

2. THE TRANSFORMATION OF FAITH

The ardent faces turned toward the flag, and with two fingers of the right hand touching the brims of their caps, the young boys solemnly pronounced the well-rehearsed words: "I promise to do my best to do my duty to God and my country, to help other people, and to obey the Law of the Pack." With the ritual over, bodies relaxed, smiles appeared, and a little horseplay emerged before the meeting's activities began.[1]

I see my values as being pretty transient, always changing. What keeps me going is a confidence in myself that I know who I am and that I will be able to come through crises. . . . I think everyone suffers equally; it is just part of the nature of the world. Suffering is part of the motivation to change what you are, where you are. Motivation to growth.[2]

I sometimes think that moving to a rock on the top of a mountain in Nepal might be the answer. To sit and meditate. . . . But to me that isn't possible, because to me what is important is what is alive and around me. I want to maintain a balance between that meditative, spiritual part and the real, the real—the suffering, the anger, the very heavy part of the world. It's like being a river going by a pyramid. A river: the pyramid is past, present, and future. And it's constantly going through and around and under; and the sky and the spirit and the earth, and the nurturing.[3]

In the previous chapter we examined the complex dynamics of faith as an imaginative, world-shaping and passionate dimension of the human person. This expression of faith saw faith as a whole, as a relationship between self and others, self and the world, self and the transcendent. Our final note in that chapter hinted at another aspect to faith. Not only is faith the transformation of the person through conversion and commitment, but each person's faith undergoes a transformation from within, faith's own "conversion" in patterned responses to human interaction, reflection, and the movements of God's gracings. This "composing of faith" as "an act of imagination conditioned, in part, by structural development"[4] assumes the structures of what we will now examine in the stages of faith.

17

The three vignettes mentioned above reflect not only three anecdotes of faith's expressions toward the world, but more basically reveal three different ways of imagining oneself in relation to the world, three "compositions" of faith. Each composition shows a more complex, more inclusive understanding of oneself and of the surrounding world. Each response indicates a "structure" or pattern which supports a whole set of beliefs, values, relationships, attitudes, and images.

That structure may reflect the ordered world of the young child, organized as in Cub Scouting through rituals of salutes and handshakes. Or the structure may reveal the clear self-consciousness and self-confidence of the young adult, toying with the relativity of ideas while expressing a need to impose concepts, in this case of suffering, upon all reality no matter what the complexity. Our third vignette shows yet another faith structure in which the ambiguities of life, such as the active and the contemplative, are held in creative tension rather than collapsed in one direction.

However, before we can describe each faith stage in any detail, we must reflect upon the meaning of a structure or stage of faith. And immediately, we run into a problem in the English language. For one of the key elements in our understanding of faith is that faith is an activity, a "doing" through which I invest myself in the reality to which I am "faithful." Yet we have no English equivalent for that "doing" of faith. Perhaps, as Fowler suggests, we should coin the verb "to faithe" to describe this essential characteristic of faith. Thus "I am faithing" or "I faithe" carries more of the dynamic activity of faith than does "I believe" or "I have faith."

Following our discussion of structures of faith, we will briefly examine each of the six stages in Fowler's scheme of faith development.[5] Then we will look at those factors which foster growth or transformation in faith in Fowler's theory. These factors in turn will serve as the main features of each of our discussions of faith development and particular ministries.

The Structuring of Faith

The very idea of "structures" of faith seems contradictory. On the one hand faith is a God-given gift beyond the ability of individuals and even groups such as the church to attain. On the other hand, faith is so particularized, so much a part of each person that it seems contrived to talk about a limited number of structures of faith. These important points need to be discussed.

We can acknowledge the giftedness of faith in God's free activity; however, we can also recognize that the person receiving the "gift" has been prepared for its reception in a variety of ways. Just as we expect different responses from the five year old who receives a gift and from the adult, so too the gift of faith takes root differently in the infinite variety of human persons.

The theory of faith development addresses itself to the human side of the faithing process, the side of the receiver. Through our imaginative capacities and through the communities which have fostered us and continue to support us we approach the giftedness of God's revelation and communication to us in patterns that can be described. The promise of faith development theory is that by understanding the dynamics of the human dimensions of faithing we can better discern the blocks to authentic faith and assist others to grow while refusing to impose our own limited faith understandings upon all faithful people.

When we speak of a "structure" to faith, or a faith stage, we are describing the set of abilities which support a person's believing, valuing, committing and acting. Structures are the sets of cognitive operations, or rules, which underlie kinds of knowing. For example, the child's insistence upon ending every past tense of a verb with "ed" as in "swimmed" or in putting the negative before the verb at all times as in "I no do that" is totally consistent with the rules for grammar. However, the child's cognitive operations are not only unconscious and so not subject to a repeated appeal to "say it right," but the "mistake" (only from an adult perspective) cannot be "unlearned" by repeating the correct "exception" to the general rule. The child's operations conform to general patterns or rules of thought. As the child grows and develops, generally his or her abilities to incorporate grammatical exceptions and different classes of objects develop. Structures, then, serve as an integrated set of operations which move from simple, global, undifferentiated capacities to more complex, comprehensive yet incisive and differentiated, distinguishing ones.[6]

In the area of faithing, a "picture" of a faith stage or structure can be glimpsed by thinking of all the characteristics we usually attribute to faith. In other words, what goes to make up "faith"? The answers would range from beliefs, to symbols, worship, relationships, values, truths or doctrines, prayer, and so on. But each of these is an inert noun which fails to point to the dynamics of faith as an activity. So on another level we can speak of faith as composed of activities such as believing, imagining, worshiping, relating, valuing, understanding, and praying, even resting. These are the activities which the individual "faithing" person is constantly "doing." These activities form a complex web of interrelationships guided by the "rules" of faithing. The "level" which underlies the activities of faithing, then, is the *structure* or *pattern of faith* to which Fowler ascribes the attributes of faith stage. Faith is not *identical* with the structure, but *faith* has a structure.

If this model of "levels" of faith proves helpful, two related corollaries follow. In the first place, the varied faithing activities are related in such a way that a change or shift in one can, slowly or quickly in the case of a "conversion" phenomenon, change other activities. For example, as many women have become more aware of their equal role with men in church and in society, their modes of believing, worshiping and relating have changed dramatically. Secondly, it could well be that people who are in times of transition between two stages may express seemingly conflicting patterns in expressing their faithing according to different settings and in different relationships. The times of transition can be quite prolonged. Faith growth is not a smooth process at all but has a number of bumps and grinds in which a particular pattern extends itself across the faith life. In this sense a faith stage can be thought of as the "resting place" where the various activities of faithing find greatest coherence and unity.

Precautions

Before we begin to describe the actual stages of faith which Fowler's theory and research articulate, we need to understand the limitations of the theory. In the first place a stage is not a box in which a person's being and value can be placed. Rather, faith stages are formal descriptions or models by which certain points of a person's valuing, thinking, and acting can be better understood, supported and challenged. (We cannot talk about a *person* at stage two or three but only a person's *faithing pattern* as stage two or three, etc.)

Secondly, the theory does not provide what has classically been understood as a "religious way," nor is a faith stage related to the intensity of an individual's faith. The stages do provide formal sets of criteria to examine whether a religious tradition provides and supports the development of faithing to include all the stages. Thus would the "religious tradition" (broadly conceived) which James Jones imposed upon his adherents allow for development beyond the early stages of faithing? Can faith development theory provide us with some illumination about the dynamics of the current wave of fundamentalism and cults?

Finally we have to distinguish between the structure of the individual or community's faith and the content of that faith. Thus two Christians may agree or disagree on particular truths of their faith, may worship together or refuse to acknowledge the validity of each other's worship. Similarly a Christian and a Buddhist will bring very different content to their faithing while the structure of that faithing may well be the same. Development in faith, then, does not take place by the *addition* of more content, but by the transformation of content of one's faith to new patterns of imaging, valuing, committing.

A final, difficult question remains. If faith stages do not determine or reflect a person's worth, then is one stage "better" than another? If "better" is used in the sense of "good" or "bad," the answer is clearly no. If "better" means that each successive stage deals with or responds more adequately to the increased complexities of reality which a person receives and then *conceives* or images, then it is possible to discuss the ways in which a particular stage is more "adequate" to enable persons or even groups to understand and respond to reality.

Thus for the Christian it is difficult to develop a sense of community if the capacities for empathy, relations, and valuing have not developed to a conventional mode. Or it is difficult to see how a response to *structural* injustice could be adequate unless the capacities to understand structural relationships or to develop perspectives beyond those of one's own group have grown considerably. In this limited sense at least we can talk of one stage as "better" than another. However, precisely this limitation coupled with a healthy understanding of our own faithing process should keep us from rushing to intervene in the faith life of others under the guise that all other Christians *should* be at a particular faith stage (or certainly at our own).

Faith Facets

If each stage provides a model by which we may glimpse the vitality of a person's faith life, that glimpse takes shape when we examine various interactive components or facets of faithing. When they are combined in a whole, the facets reveal the richness of faithing much as the facets of a diamond reveal its beauty while letting us know that much of the beauty remains beyond our limited vision.

The first facet, the "form of logic" or the "thinking" facet, is borrowed from the work of Jean Piaget and refers to the level of cognitive development of the individual.[7] Secondly, sensing order in the world, or "world coherence" as Fowler calls it, reflects the way in which each person sees the world "glued" together. This facet reveals the level of coherence imaged in the individual's relationships to others, the world, and the Transcendent. "Perspective-taking" or the ability to understand the perspective of others and ultimately of groups, classes and traditions different than one's own is the third facet.[8]

The fourth facet, the "God-boss," or "locus of authority," refers to the ways people construe the sources of authority for their faithing. Generally the movement is from authoritative voices "outside" the person to personal "authorship" for values, actions, and commitments. The "God-boss" is closely related to the next facet, the bounds of social awareness. In response to the question "*Whose* are you?" the individual responds to the extent of his or her ability to include others in his or her understanding of community.

The form of moral judgment or moral reasoning constitutes the sixth facet. Fowler has adopted the work of Lawrence Kohlberg of Harvard Univeristy for Kohlberg's insights into the moral development of people.[9] Finally the role of symbols or "symbolizing" facet is one of Fowler's most important and original contributions to the whole theory. Inasmuch as the very nature of faith life and religious reality involves the effort to relate to realities which can be mediated only by symbols, the capacity of symbolizing is a key to understanding faith as imaginal knowing. Only when we look at all these facets together are we able to tentatively understand and then appreciate the complexity of faith levels.

Factors of Growth

At this point we need to ask what are the factors which lead to growth in faith at all the stages. In reality we are involved in our own faith growth and in the faith growth of others in thousands of unknown ways. We are now asking whether we can put some deliberation into those many ways of living and working with others in their faith journeys so that we as ministers and educators do not become an obstacle to growth but actually cooperate intentionally with God's grace in developing more mature Christian "faithers." Although there are several ways to organize the development of factors of growth, I have focused upon symbol-making and breaking, perspective-taking and a sense of participation as crucial to growth in faith. These factors will serve as the organizing tools for each of our chapters on areas of ministry.

Symbols and Conflict

The first facet of faith growth, "symbol-making and breaking," denotes the complex ways in which our knowledge, values, and attitudes rest upon the kind of primal imagery and symbol-making we examined in the previous chapter. In theologian Urban Holmes' understanding, symbols are dynamic, physiological, social representations which embody many possible meanings and many possible feelings. Symbols are related to bodily feelings and needs. Symbols are ambiguous, and their full meaning is never exhausted in verbal expression.[10]

Growth in the faith development scheme will necessarily involve the eruptions and breakups of one image or set of symbols and their replacement with other symbols which more accurately reflect the new realities which we know and value. At times the changes in symbolic understandings, the "symbol-breaking and making," will take the form of largely unconscious, vague "senses" of change in attitudes and values: "I don't care that strongly about that anymore." This could find reflection in a "breach of faith" or "loss of confidence." At other times, the change will emerge in strong, cognitive conflict through dialogue, rejection of previous views or the pull of powerful ideas as in this expression:

> And now things are becoming a little more complex—it's an awful thing, but I don't care. . . . I should be more interested in learning. And, maybe, eventually I will be, because just in this past year I've noticed a change in me and I realize that it isn't stupid to ask questions that I can ask.[11]

For the minister, parent, or religious educator a question arises about the deliberate use of conflict and symbol-breaking as a method of promoting growth. Such conflict must take place in a full understanding of personal growth, not in some attempt to force growth artificially. One context for using symbol-breaking in a broad sense emerges in situations where people are invited to talk about their faith, about their beliefs, values and actions. Especially when more reflective abilities have developed in adolescence and young adulthood, such occasions often provide the first opportunity an individual has had to ever "hear" his or her own faith story in a trusting environment. This approach shares elements of the second factor of perspective-taking while involving the story-teller in the very process of hearing how the present faith life has challenged earlier forms of faith.

Perspective-Taking

While we have just discussed one possible form of perspective-taking as an element in symbol-breaking, we need to broaden the understanding of perspective-taking to mean any form of involvement in the ways of perceiving, feeling, and understanding of other persons and groups. The faith development approach sees such an ability to "walk in the skin of another" as not just a facet of a stage but also as an intentional approach to strengthening faith at any stage and developing a more mature understanding of the requirements of Christian faith for service and justice claims. This important capacity begins in childhood with growing understanding of the feelings of others, understandings of fairness, understanding the place of rules and guidance in games, work, school, family life and society. It later develops into more complex understandings of differences in relationships, traditions, cultures, social norms and rules, and so forth. And while we constantly have opportunities to "understand" others' points of view through media, education, travel, we are also limited by our personal, social, cultural backgrounds which, when unquestioned, filter what we allow ourselves to "see" and understand.

Certainly fairy tales and children's stories involving plants and animals acting as humans are attempts at perspective-taking, as are games, acquaintance with super-heroes and heroines, saints and pioneers. For many younger and older adults the life-stories of powerful models and the actions of contemporary charismatic leaders provide attractive motivation for adopting the more universal outlooks of those models. And work with people of other cultures provides a dynamic way of entering into the worlds of others which hopefully will broaden one's own perspective.

Sense of Participation

Finally, a third important factor centers around the possibility and the ability of people to participate in decisions which affect them. Participation is an outgrowth of our very understanding of the human person. As called by God to be a co-creator of the kingdom, all of us need to feel that we belong to others, to some definite group, and that we are valuable and necessary for the life of that group.

For young children, that may focus upon the family and the ways in which parents, brothers and sisters encourage one another to share not only the responsibilities of family life but the meaning of family and the ways of family celebrating together. With church life so centered upon adult needs, especially in worship, many children do not feel a part of the life of the church. Certainly for adolescents and young adults, the sense of involvement in the life of the church and of civic life becomes critical. Probably nothing brings a greater sense of alienation to young people than the anguished realization, or at least the perception, that "there's no place for us." The system seems closed, inflexible. By contrast the cult or counter-culture group offers some means of involvement and belonging which appear very attractive. And certainly throughout all the churches women, minorities, the sick and the aged have felt the painful exclusion from worship, governance, and other vital areas of church life.

Symbol-making and breaking, perspective-taking and a sense of participation—these factors can stimulate faith development during times of transition and can consolidate and strengthen faith in the total life of each person at any stage. Each of these factors involves an imaginative "entrance" into the "worlds" of others beyond our smaller, more comfortable world. And all of the factors are rooted in imaginings of some sort, expanding our self-centered boundaries outward in tentative thrusts which lead toward a more complete unfolding of the meaning of the kingdom proclaimed by the gospel message, a kingdom already at hand if we can only "see" with the eyes of faith. And now equipped with structures, precautions, facets and factors, we will examine the six stages of faith development.

Growth in Faith

The vast forest of childhood contains numerous episodes which both amuse and frustrate adults. Only as we learn to see those moments through the perspective of the child can we understand the importance of those real events for the development of a child's faith in self, the world, others and a God. From a developmental perspective the earliest years until about two to three and a half can be characterized best in terms of faith growth by the pattern of "basic trust vs. basic mistrust" toward reality described by psychologist Erik Erikson.[12] The child's sense of self only gradually becomes distinct from those who care for her or him, and faith has not yet taken enough form to be fully described. Nevertheless the infant and young child unconsciously form dispositions toward the world.

Imagine for a moment the plight of a six month old whose parent reorders the familiar environment of the infant's room daily, now calling the floor "a ceiling," the wall a "door," and so forth, renaming every object on a daily basis. The uncertain, changing world around the baby could not but leave a sense of distrust toward the "outer" world in addition to a great deal of uncertainty about the self. Faith in persons rests upon faith in a trusting environment shared by others in common language and rituals.

Important for our discussion is the way in which images from childhood shape the forms which faith later takes. Images supplant "reality" in many ways as they recede into childhood memories which become the very furniture of our adult lives. Writing on childhood in *The Mill on the Floss,* nineteenth century author George Eliot wrote:

> There is no sense of ease like the ease we felt in those scenes where we were born. . . . Where the outer world seemed only an extension of our own personality: we accepted and loved it as we accepted our own sense of existence and our own limbs. Very commonplace, even ugly, that furniture of our early home might look if it were put up to auction. . . . Heaven knows where [our] striving might lead us, if our affections had not a trick of twining round those old inferior things— if the loves and sanctities of our life had no deep immoveable roots in memory. . . . We could never have loved the earth so well if we had had no childhood in it. [13]

Stage One: The Intuitive

As the child moves from that early, "primal" sense of faith into the preschool and early school years, the capacities for faithing in a different way grow slowly but dramatically. This first faith stage begins about age three and a half to four and generally lasts until six or seven. The child's faith at this stage is one of magic, ritual actions, rules, moods and impressions formed by the parental authority figures in the child's life. Utilizing the stage facets described earlier, the "thinking" dimension is characterized by a concrete flux of perceptions in which events are not seen as interrelated. Thus while it may seem obvious to adults that the theme of the day on "Sesame Street" is the letter "A," for the child it just happens that way.

Reality is episodic rather than relational, put together in short sequences which have no beginning, middle, or end. A child's constant question "What's next?" at the end of a TV show or a book reveals the inability to conceive of causal relationships. Here continuity, ritual and routine are important in providing coherence and order to the world. There is only one perspective on reality, and that is the child's. Thus a parent who is angry or hurt by a child's action and exclaims "Can't you understand how daddy feels!'' is apt to bewilder the child. The child will sense the parent's anger by observing outside appearances but will not be able to see the situation as the parent does.

Authority, the ''God boss,'' at this period is based on qualities of size and power or position. Parents and parent substitutes tend to be the ground and source of faithing. It follows that the child's social identification, his or her answer to the question ''Whose are you?'' focuses upon family and family surrogates. Then because of the child's limited ability in perspective-taking and the need to have his or her own needs met, moral concerns tend to be dealt with in terms of physical consequences of reward and punishment. Or again, an action is wrong because ''somebody bigger said so.''

Finally, faith often has a magical quality in which the stuff of the imagination actually creates reality. Precisely to diffuse children's anxiety over possible effects of bad dreams or evil imaginings, Mr. Rogers of TV fame tells the story of the boy who felt responsible for his father's store burning. The boy was angry that his father went to the store instead of playing with him and dreamt that a dragon he created destroyed the store. If ''Dreams Are the Wish Your Heart Makes,'' then children must also be assured that ''Scary Bad Wishes Don't Make Dreams Come True.''[14]

Faithing at this stage involves so many central needs—the need for approval and support, for a sense of belonging and assurance, for involvement in family life, for exposure to a broader world—that the nurturance of a child's faith life can be done in a variety of ways which meet those needs. Certainly a key to faithing at this period and a primary preparation for adult faithing is rooted in the development of the imaginative capacities and the sense of a foundational order in reality which the child can trust.

Simple games, puzzles, building blocks and other forms of play which reveal links between seemingly separate parts are ''signs'' of security and stability in the world. These concrete, visible, physical manifestations of order ritually support the more symbolic sense of a ''nurturing,'' supportive order, which underlies the Christian religious experience of a loving God. Stories, fantasies, and fables which involve the real fears, anxieties, joys and sorrows of children played out in contexts where good triumphs over evil stimulate the children's imaginations and give meaning and direction to the rituals and order around them. The two dimensions of secure order and imaginative participation complement one another in rendering ultimate reality trustworthy and a mystery to be explored and loved.

Stage Two: Narratizing Faith

As the child's faith structure stretches into the second or Narratizing stage, the child is beginning to sort out the real from the unreal on the basis of practical experience (Santa Claus and the Easter bunny are only "pretendies"). A private world of speculative fantasy and wonder continues as the focus of image making. At about six or seven years, the child's thinking enters what Piaget calls "concrete operations," the ability to measure perceptions by appeal to concrete experience. Thus heaven is understood as "ice cream all day long, staying up past 9:00 o'clock, no school," and so on. In the new and expanding world of knowledge, brought on especially by formal schooling, the child begins to use classes and categories to order the world and perceives a certain lawfulness in surrounding actions.

Reality can best be understood in story form, and the child identifies with the great mythic heroes and heroines of the Bible or the super-heroes and heroines of the comics. Thus the legends of "our" religious group become important in establishing religious and personal identity as the child begins to order the religious world. Adults mistakenly impose adult meanings onto children's stories by asking the "moral" of the story instead of letting the story convey its mythic power to the child. One Sunday school teacher came to the end of the Prodigal Son story and was about to launch into its meaning when a small hand shot up. Thinking that the young girl was about to expound on the story's "moral" the teacher received the question, "Why didn't the son's father go with him to the far country?"

The ability to take other perspectives has developed to the point where the child is able to project himself or herself imaginatively into the position or situation of another. It now becomes possible to imagine how others feel. In *To Kill a Mockingbird,* southern lawyer Atticus Finch tells his young daughter that in order to understand someone she must be able to step into that person's skin and walk around inside.[15]

The role of "God boss" extends gradually to other trusted, or feared, adults, and the authoritative claims of those people are weighed in the balance of sensory experience. The rules of the group, parent, etc. become imbued with an inflexible power which the child can use for personal gain. Many a parent has heard "You promised" or a simple rule for the child turned against the parent as well.

The child has also emerged into a much wider social world of teachers, peers, community and even world leaders through experience in media. With the capacity to put objects and relationships into classes comes the wish for affiliation, as in the Cub Scout pack, the desire to learn about people and the differences between them. At this time prejudice can become a powerful force of narrow, group "faith." How parents, teachers, churches, and other social institutions deal with the questions surrounding "those like us" and "those different from us" is a central issue in the faithing process.

As the older child's world expands to include school, community, and even people and events from around the world through modern communications, care for others and a sense of justice can be powerfully promoted by a variety of sponsors at this faithing stage. Not only can the family encourage the child to assume more responsibility for family life, but other groups to which the child belongs can now involve the child in care for the aged, the handicapped, the poor in the neighborhood and around the world. Children can be involved in charitable collections, visitations, and community cleanups not only to gain a sense of responsibility but also to experience in a small way the life and struggles of other people.

The greater ability to take the perspective of others leads the child to take others' views into account in bargaining to meet his or her personal needs by cooperating with others. Thus, adopting the strategy of many politicians, the child applies the maxim, "You scratch my back, I'll scratch yours." Although it is a bit rudimentary, a genuine sense of fairness and equality has begun, often appearing in the form of a total equalitarianism with little flexibility for differences or exceptions.

Finally, at this stage a child's capacity for symbols is quite literalistic. While stories and myths have tremendous power over the child's imagination and indeed fashion the world for the child, the stories are taken in a literal fashion, limited to the concrete experiences of the child. Religious images of God and of sacred reality tend to be anthropomorphic, again as an extension of the concrete.

Participation and involvement, stories and service projects—these approaches strengthen the stage two faith perspective and help prepare the older child for the more complex world of reality in which the Christian is expected to take part and which he or she will help transform in light of the gospel. The narrative mode of understanding becomes the vehicle through which the child catches the tradition of the past, identifies the outstanding Christians of the present, and snatches a glimpse of how he or she can move into the future through the virtues and character of both the superhero and superheroine as well as the mature adult. The games and ordered play of late childhood with their sharp categories of good and bad, black and white, right and wrong provide the concrete induction into the more abstract categories of justice/injustice, right/wrong at later stages of faithing.

Stage Three: The Conventional

The key to understanding the person at a stage three faith level lies in the focus around personal relationships. "Social stories" or conventions of a social group now form the structure of the daily world in which the conventional way of understanding faith operates. The world is constructed in interpersonal terms, and the critical personal question becomes "Who am I?" Parents, peers, church leaders, political and cultural authorities all reflect back to the individual in these years the possibilities he or she can become, must reject, would dream about. While the conventional stage describes the period of adolescents most aptly, the dynamics of this stage also describe many adults whose faith is lived out at the conventional level, especially if the guiding theology of their church life, or its religious substitute such as party and state, calls for unquestioning or even begrudging acceptance of the dominant patterns of life.

In this highly charged interpersonal world not only is society held together by the people who fulfill the social roles, but the individual's self-understanding is constituted by the expectations of significant other people and of important groups. Thus a basic unrelenting question, whether conscious or unconscious, is what would "the gang" expect, what would grandmother expect, what would *they* say at church, school or the office. The task of faith and of the quest for personal identity is precisely to find the ways in which these various expectations can be held together.

In search of an answer to the questions of "Who am I?" and "What will I become?" the adolescent or conventional adult tries on different roles to see how well they fit, how comfortable they are, how much security they bring. These roles are worn by adults who both prove themselves trustworthy and lovable to the adolescent or conventional adult and at the same time confirm that he or she is a trustworthy and lovable person.[16] The search for identity focuses upon models who exemplify faith in the form of fidelity, a trusting commitment of one person for another. The model may be a realistic one of the local minister, group leader, or the highly charged, romantic pop idol, who sums up in his or her person the living out of the conventions and rules of the social, ethnic, or religious group.

At stage three the individual is able to undertake abstract thinking, examine hypotheses, and develop reflective skills to some degree. No longer limited to working with the concrete data of experience and its extensions, the individual can extend imaginatively possibilities of actions and interpretations of reality beyond his or her concrete experiences. Yet if the powers of thinking have expanded dramatically, the person's sense of world order is only a budding one. The "system" which holds the world together at this point is generally a tacit, unquestioned one. Questions are certainly asked. Yet either the questions can be answered by the "conventional understanding" which the system offers, or the questioner is willing to live with a shadow of mystery surrounding the central affirmations of the system.

The increased ability to take others' perspectives into account often leads to the dramatic character of this stage and to the predominance of feelings over thought. "I see you seeing me" reflects the overwhelming awareness of others which shapes the view the person has of self. The person comes to rely upon people who make the self feel most comfortable and accepted and who reflect the interpersonal virtues of sincerity, loyalty, authenticity and friendliness as criteria of truth and value. When these values can be discovered in one person who acts as model for a particular viewpoint, the faithing of the person or group at stage three can be conformed, challenged, or distorted in dramatic ways. Since authority for truth and value tends to rest in the trust-evoking personal qualities of representatives of particular perspectives, such as Ronald Reagan or John Paul II, the spokespersons had better look the part. If it is the trust-evoking, personal qualities which attract individuals to accept the system represented by the model, then signs of weakness, indeed of human mistakes, indiscretions, or misunderstandings can lead to a "breach of faith" with the model and thus with the system of thought, belief, value, and action which the model represents.

In the conventional stage the group serves as the source of the individual's identity and faith, and it can be called upon in time of crisis or celebration around important symbols, e.g., the patriotism surrounding the 4th of July or the invasion of Grenada, the visit of John Paul II to Poland, the deaths of the Challenger crew. For those reasons moral thinking at stage three centers around powerful expectations of significant others and of social roles. The central concern is to meet the expectations of those people in the group or in society who will then see the individual as "good" in the role he or she plays. For example, one of the most significant struggles in the lives of many men and women religious and clergy in the Roman Catholic Church was the movement away from the expectations of laypeople, religious superiors, or church authorities of the "good sister," "good brother," or "good priest." On another level, if the expectations are those of the *roles* individuals play within society and of society's *rules,* then the emphasis is upon maintaining the system of conventions. Challenges to that system, such as the attempt to gain an exception to a rule, are met with the response that the exceptions would violate the moral authority of the rules and of the rulers or that the exception would have to be extended to all members of the group and thus the system would collapse.

Finally symbols emerge as the mediating force between daily realities and the realm of ideals, values, and truths. Symbols achieve a pervasive, metaphorical quality with various meanings but are not turned into abstract ideas. To those for whom the American flag symbolizes a whole way of life it is indeed a profanation to see the flag worn on the seat of a pair of designer jeans or ripped from a pole. In the Christian context, God becomes real in terms of the affective and personal qualities of love, closeness, intimacy. God now becomes father while Jesus is seen as friend, companion, trusted confidant.

In terms of our discussion of the facets of faithing at stage three, central needs emerge for growth in faith. Among these are involvement in community, a participation in family and community life, realistic models of faithing, occasions to share faith stories, experiences of challenge and conflict, an exploration of the roots of the Christian life in scripture and theology, and particularly a method of understanding symbols which carries beyond the literal meaning. Literalism, the root of all fundamentalism, results from the confusion of the symbol with the reality symbolized, and the consequence is that God's mysterious, varied ways are reduced to "one way."

Because perspectives will also be shaped by the interpersonal view of the world and by the general acceptance of the social and cultural status quo, personal involvement with the aged, handicapped and the poor through volunteer agencies will be an important way to develop a critical perspective and sense of justice. Even the dynamic of friendship can be extended across racial, religious and national boundaries to include people in groups and countries different than one's own. This exposure to other people's cultures and values can expand the boundaries of social awareness and capacities for perspective-taking so important to a vision of social justice at stage four.

Finally, we might note a few of the limits of the conventional stage. The very willingness to live with mystery and accept a tacit world view reflects an inability to take account of the fact that persons are shaped and transformed by institutions. Morality emerges in interpersonal terms only.

The sufferings and injustices of daily life often are viewed as manifestations of God's will rather than seen as results of oppressive social systems. In addition the individual and even the community have not yet taken on the burden of personal and social responsibility for ideas, actions and life choices. Responsibility rests instead upon authorities outside the self.

This faithing view can be nudged into an individuating mode in several ways. The clash of images and symbols engendered by exploring different cultures, different social groups and religious traditions along with opportunities to articulate a personal faith history, to listen to those of trusted others, to ask serious questions and have them taken seriously by an admired representative of a faith tradition—all can lead to the self-conscious appropriation of a personal faith stance. Teachers, parents and mentors can also serve as models of faithful people who went through the same questioning and have developed powerful, life-giving world-views, ideal self-images, goals, and centers of ultimate loyalty. Perspectives can be broadened through education and travel. And finally the opportunities to take responsibility for others, whether in volunteer service or through a job, can develop the sense of personal worth and value which lead to an individuative faith stance.

Stage Four: The Individuative

The young man whose reflections on self-confidence opened this chapter is typical of faithing at stage four in his reliance upon conscious process and controls. The central characteristics of individuative faithing are a keen sense of owning one's personal beliefs and actions, a developing, strong self-identity, the powerful pull of the world of ideas and ideals, and the realization that the views and outlooks the individual takes demand some justifications. Strengths emerge from this meld of self-identity and an identifiable worldview such as greater self-reflection, a sense of system to thinking, a strengthened personal authority for beliefs, attitudes and values, firmer realization of the demands of peace, love and justice along with an articulate basis for the criticism of existing social structures and a delineation of the ways one's faithing is different from earlier times and from other people's faith views. "Make it your own" or "Don't buy a used system" might be the slogans of this stage.

But there are weaknesses too, such as the tendency to fit a complex reality into a "clear and distinct" set of ideas, the attraction to an ideological viewpoint which distorts other perspectives and the imposition of one's own perspective upon other people and groups. In the midst of this dynamic form of faithing, the central question which emerges for the

Christian churches is what ideal community do we have to offer and how is that ideal community made real in practice.

In general at this stage a person has developed the thinking capacities to utilize abstract thought in rather advanced ways. The ability to differentiate ideas clearly from others' perspectives leads to the acceptance of personal responsibility for beliefs, values and actions. Yet often the differences between viewpoints tend to be "dichotomized" into an "either/or" framework. This is especially true of some of the basic relationships between self and others, the individual and community, or truth and error. If the person at stage three tends to validate reality and meaning on the basis of feelings, the person at stage four tends to allow thought to dominate feeling.

Even more deeply concerned with persons, the person at stage four becomes aware of the ways in which complex social realities shape and control persons. The individual can often begin the task of understanding entire perspectives different than his or her own. The authority for one's faithing, then, lies in one's own outlook. This movement toward greater autonomy in faithing and in personal identity is essential to the development of the mature Christian. Thus, the sense of "calling and responding," of surrendering one's will to God in love, of becoming a disciple rather than an imitator of Christ—all depend upon the development of a sense of self which leads then to service with others.

The bounds of social awareness, too, have extended in dynamic relation to the capacity to take authority for one's own beliefs and actions. Thus the ability to step outside one's own perspective and the perspective of one's own group to understand the worlds of others is an essential characteristic in the ability to identify with the struggles of oppressed peoples. Such concepts as "kingdom of God," justice, freedom, equality, liberation, shalom become the goals of new understandings of what it means to be human. New possibilities of the social order are entertained, and new social identities are fostered. Action relates to the structures of society, the patterns which guide relationships. Sin includes sinful structures, and liberation of the self is entwined with liberation from oppresive social situations.

This ability, in turn, leads to more complex and varied moral thinking. The ability to use categories of equality, fairness, and care allows people to evaluate the rules and regulations of any particular society or group in terms of more universal norms. Yet precisely because of the distortions arising from their abilities in perspective-taking, the principles used often have a class or group bias. This leads to the danger of premature universalization, namely the belief that our perspective is the one true viewpoint which should be extended universally to all others. Yet while some may tend to absolutize their own perspective, others may adopt a principle of relativity in moral thinking, borrowing such phrases as the late Fritz Perls' ''You do your thing, and I'll do mine.''

Finally, the symbol-making capacity takes an interesting and ironic twist. In one sense symbols often lose their power to evoke the realities they symbolize. In the process of critical thinking the unconscious, affective dimension of symbols may be set aside from the concept or content which animates the symbol. As we have seen earlier in the chapter on imagination and faith, such a process robs symbols of their power to invoke imaginatively the reality beyond reason and reduces the evocative, emotional aspect of the symbol to a pale reflection of itself. Thus while the decline of uses of incense, large amounts of candles, Gregorian chant and the Latin language seems a step forward in making Roman Catholic congregations more participants in worship than observers of a spectacle, the power of those realities to evoke the divine has not been captured by what has replaced them.

Important concerns for the religious educator, parent and minister center around how well the traditional belief system can be reinterpreted in light of the new questions. How can the gospel be related to questions of justice and to the structural evil in institutions? How can we legitimate and foster models of community in parishes, religious communities, study groups? Can we recognize the need for a movement in prayer toward an awareness of God's personal presence and God's liberating action in the everyday world? Will we offer exposure to differing perspectives along with the developing awareness of the limitations of any particular perspective? Will we support these searchers' efforts with care, be with them through failure, and offer encouragement to try again? Churches in the recent past have been more relieved not to have such questioners around. And in some cases, even today, the most creative response we might have is to say with a great deal of grace, ''You might need to leave us for a while, but we'll always be open when you return.''

Certainly the exposure to people who incorporate more universal understandings of justice, love, and compassion will foster development toward stage five faithing where ''autobiography'' replaces the dynamic of ''biography.'' That is, the searcher is guided by his or her reflection on his or her own story with its strengths and weaknesses as well as by the autobiographical accounts of how others see themselves in the process of their own growth and development. Spiritually, the director or mentor is no longer a model but rather moves the searcher into areas of paradox, silence, and penetrating symbols. The searcher painstakingly becomes ever more ready to envision God's reality in the created world of sin *and* grace amidst the strong *and* the weak.

Stage Five: The Conjunctive

In the film "The Turning Point," Shirley McLaine and Anne Bancroft play two talented dancers who made critical career choices in their early years: McLaine for marriage and family life, Bancroft for her dance career and singleness. Reunited for a brief time, they each see in the other's choices a lost part of themselves with which they must come to terms. The film moves delicately in and out of their lives as they seek a new integration for themselves and a new level of friendship.

In much the same way, stage five or conjunctive faithing reflects a reworking of one's past, of both the personal and social unconscious and an insistence upon reclaiming what had been shut off, of rediscovering old abilities and working them into present life-patterns. That artistic interest of long ago is taken up again. A new readiness for intimacy with God begins to develop. Symbols re-emerge with powerful force to shape religious meaning reflected, for example, in the sense of balance claimed by the woman in one of the chapter's opening quotations. The sharp distinctions of viewpoints in stage four give way to the relativities of individual and social perspectives. "Either/or" is replaced by "both/and." Personal experiences with pain, loss, suffering and injustice have tempered the power of ideas.

As difficult as it is to describe faithing in all its complexity at this stage, a look at the facets of faithing will amplify the points mentioned above. Fowler calls the level of thinking exhibited at stage five "dialogical." By that he means that the complex structure of the world "is invited to disclose itself."[17] The usefulness of mental categories is replaced by the embrace of paradoxes and subjectivity becomes an important, critical and valued dimension of knowing. Truth is multi-dimensional. Reality is Christian pleroma and Buddhist emptiness.

The world holds together then precisely as a multi-verse. Or, in fact, the person may experience the ungluing of what had been so self-consciously put together. Yet, there is a willingness to live with the ambiguity and mystery which is revealed in our very failure to impose unity upon reality. When Lucy attempts to console Charlie Brown with the thought, "You get out of life exactly what you put into it! No more and no less," Snoopy reflects, "I'd kind of like to see a little more margin for error."[18]

Perspective-taking reveals a comprehensiveness and accuracy lacking at previous stages. The perceived threat to one's whole systematic perspective felt so strongly at stages three and four is gone, and it becomes possible to "step into" another group's perspective as a believer of that perspective might understand it. Likewise there is much greater internalization and deeper grounding of the criteria for faith. Those criteria are now more concerned with comprehensive perspective-taking, increased self-awareness, disciplined subjectivity, and multiple viewpoints than with strict definitions of truth and falsity, right and wrong. Although the authority for beliefs, values and actions is grounded in the self, there is a strong realization of the limitations and failings of that self.

Social identification is continually extended beyond the limitations of group, class, race and even religious tradition. In the ideological battles between perspectives, the person at stage five is often seen as vacillating, even uncommitted because he or she sees the value of alternative positions and attempts to minister to all members of various groups who are in need.

At stage five a clearer vision of justice gradually transcends the biases of economic, racial, class and even religious self-interestedness. Thus justice claims cut across neat lines of oppressor/oppressed, right/wrong, male/female, black/white. A sense of personal fallibility and the limits of solutions to human problems tempers justice with mercy, resulting in forgiveness and a developing sense of love as universal. Yet the very perceptions of justice and love may outreach one's ability and readiness to sacrifice personal goals, friendships and life-style in order to achieve a more just social order.

Community becomes a place in which one can explore vulnerability and openness with others. As the *sponsor* in community of the development of others, the individual becomes less judgmental and more tolerant of others' needs. And while a sense of aloneness may be more intense, the broader sense of community across boundaries sustains the tension between the universal and the particular. At this stage in moral thinking, individuals fulfill the capacity for principled thinking without the distortions of class or group seen at stage four. In addition, due to the understanding and experiences of suffering and ambiguity in life, the tendency to universalize any particular position, no matter how compelling, is overcome by the focus upon individual human persons as the goal of the moral life.

If symbol-making at stage four often meant the reduction of symbols to their cognitive meaning, this capacity at stage five leads to a new unity of the cognitive and the aesthetic, affective dimensions of symbols, the conscious and the unconscious. Symbols, myths and images play an important role in the descriptions of reality. There is place for the dark sides of personality and of the world. No longer is there an attempt to force the real world into the neat compartmentalization of a system of ideas, but there is a ''seeing'' of reality which can only be expressed through analogy and symbolic understanding. In the words of St. Paul the person ''sees through a glass darkly.'' For the Christian symbolic realities in the paschal mystery of death and resurrection become embodied in individual experiences of pain, suffering, and loss which deepen the spiritual dimension of life. The *seeker* of stage four becomes a *listener* to the silence of God through discernment of movements within the self and the world. God is present in the self and and is power in the world whose Spirit breathes life into all things.

The penetration of a stage five faithing mode into a whole life-pattern calls for visions to be constantly articulated and shared. Scripture must be heard and interpreted in light of daily life to provide meaning and to empower the visions which construct the religious understanding of reality. In this exploration old symbols and perspectives can be revived with new appreciation while new ones express the affective, cognitive dimensions of new insights and new revelations. In addition, the appropriation of the personal and social unconscious as well as a personal understanding of grief, loss, suffering and failure leads to an increasing commitment to others, particularly the oppressed, the poor, the disadvantaged in all classes.

In most ways people at stage five faithing tend to be ministering in their actions and caring in their responsibilities toward others. Yet they too have needs for support and encouragement in some form of community, expressed in the Creed as a true ''communion of saints.'' There is a sense of loneliness experienced in the distance one takes from the norms and values of the larger society. Thus sympathetic communities of support are needed where struggles are shared, where conflicts are encountered and can be kneaded carefully with a goal toward reconciliation, where one can find acceptance of limits and vulnerabilities.

Stage Six: The Universalizing

The final or universalizing stage of faith development is rare according to Fowler's research and certainly remains difficult to describe.[19] At best such a comprehensive form of faithing can merely be pointed to in the lives of those who live it. The very polarities experienced at stage four and the agonizing ambiguities of stage five are reflected in a simple but penetrating understanding of the unity of all reality. Whereas a person at stage five often acts out of conflicting loyalties or fails to act at all precisely because of the grasp of the multiversal nature of truth, a person at stage six overcomes those conflicts and loyalties through the actualization of his or her universal understandings. And in place of the symbols utilized at previous stages to grasp the transcendent, there is an immediacy of understanding which is not just a faint encounter of an ecstatic experience but describes a pervasive outlook upon reality.

At this point the transition to stage six faithing resembles less the voyage into the uncharted areas of faithing than some humbling experience of a graced "giveness." Whether expressed as a movement to the "unitive way," a sudden burst into "hyper-space" in Star Wars language, a new stage of consciousness, or a soft, gradual appreciation of the beauty and unity of all reality, the movement beyond stage five could be said more to happen than to be "promoted." Here the dynamic reality of God's empowering grace seems most graphically illustrated in the transition from autobiography to gospel story. In St. Paul's radical expression, "It is no longer I, but Christ, who lives within me." Or as Malcolm Muggeridge says of Mother Teresa:

> It is, of course, true that the wholly dedicated like Mother Teresa do not have biographies. Biographically speaking, nothing happens to them. To live for, and in, others . . . is to eliminate happenings. . . . She gave herself to Christ, and through him to her neighbor. This was the end of her biography and the beginning of her life; in abolishing herself she found herself.[20]

The various facets of faith we have previously used in our examinations of each stage form a dazzling unity at stage six which prevents us from fully describing the total beauty of this mode of faithing. However, we can comment at least briefly upon some of the most important features of this stage. An intuitive sense of oneness of being emerges which grasps the unity behind and beyond the polarities and ambiguities of daily living. If at earlier stages the world was held together by threads of permanent-bonding glue, at this stage the world is together because it is one. There never were threads or glue. Such a simplicity in seeing the world as one is perplexing to the rest of us who have inherited cultural or impose personal divisions of all kinds. Yet, those persons at stage six literally inspire or animate our lives with new goals and ideals.

This pervading sense of unity leads to a thorough extension of perspective-taking which includes a profound respect for all being, including inanimate objects. This capacity in turn involves a pervasive identification of the individual's interests with the needs and interests of all others.

Similarly while the locus of authority can be described as inhering most profoundly in the heart and mind purified of personal striving, the person at stage six would most likely identify the source of belief, value and action as rooted in the transcendent. This grounding in union with the transcendent and the intuitive grasp of the oneness of reality lead to an understanding of "right action" beyond distinctions of "right/wrong, good/bad." Rather the total love of being and a compassion for all reality become the foundational principle of moral reasoning and acting. Thought and action are now joined, not because one "does" what one "ought," but because the response is what "fits" the universal grasp of reality the person has. Precisely inasmuch as these people force us to examine our own lives, we often find we must put them outside of our ways of living. We may move out of their influence, diminish their reality by focusing upon their weakness, circumscribe them with a cult of devotion or in some cases kill them individually or collectively for the very visions to which they call us all.

Finally, in many ways these people of stage six faithing become living symbols themselves of the reality which they grasp and envision. In addition, they reimage and shape traditional symbols in new ways, whether a Jesus reshaping the meaning of Jewish law and the Passover meal or a Martin Luther King, Jr., reconstituting the Declaration of Independence and the Constitution to apply dramatically to black people. And yet the whole of their experience is rather in the nature of a gift, grace in a Christian sense, bestowed upon them in the very process of letting go of their own desires.

Words really fail to further describe faithing at stage six. Fowler has attempted to make this faith perspective more concrete by describing it in particularly Christian terms of the kingdom of God, and I would refer the reader to his careful discussion.[21]

Summary

Throughout this chapter on the structures of faith growth we have focused upon those dimensions which provide ways to examine specific areas of Christian ministry. In particular the factors of growth—symbol-making, perspective-taking and sense of participation—give us the necessary framework in understanding the applications of faith development theory. Although there remains much more to say about the theoretical foundations of faith development and about the stages themselves, our explorations now must turn to the ways in which Christian ministers and educators understand themselves, the people with whom they work, and the Christian faith which supports and sustains them.

Our next chapter finds us looking at the most basic shape that ministry takes in the Christian community, the understanding of the faith. From the infant to the elder, the Christian enterprise has erected manifold structures of religious education. First we will examine those early years through high school, when the church itself provides the primary outlet for Christian education. A later chapter then pursues education for the young adult through the maturing years. Successive chapters take up forms of ministry as the church extends its mission from its own community into the world at large. Thus we move from education to family and parish, to the hospital and aging, to prisons and justice work and finally to spirituality and worship, returning to the animating forces of all ministry. In each chapter we will use the three factors of faith growth as the organizing principles of our examination.

3. RELIGIOUS EDUCATION AND THE GROWTH OF FAITH

Education is a political activity with pilgrims in time that deliberately and intentionally attends with them to the activity of God in our present, to the Story of the Christian faith community, and to the vision of God's Kingdom, the seeds of which are already among us.[1]

Thomas Groome, *Christian Religious Education*

Religious Education is the ministry of a pilgrim church that respects the time and freedom its members need in order to make their own connections between the gospel and the transformation of the world.[2]

Mary Boys, "A Word About Teaching Justly"

All education purports to deal with justice; a religious education questions whether we know what justice means and whether we are certain of how to get there. . . . We do not know the full meaning of God's justice, and none of us knows how to make a just world. But we should be able to recognize injustice and to take steps that reduce the world's sorrows. Religious education is not a panacea, but it can be a significant help toward walking humbly and justly on God's earth.[3]

Gabriel Moran, *Interplay*

Last year neighbors who live in our parish sent their twin boys to the parish for Sunday religion lessons. The parents had been working with the boys at home in an informal way and now felt that their children needed a more formal introduction to the life of the Church. With some trepidation but willing to try, the boys set out with initial enthusiasm. The teacher was young and inexperienced, would often shift the lesson from the one stated on the plan which the parents had and finally resorted to M & M's and stickers to keep the kids coming and under some control. For one of my neighbor's boys the M & M's worked; the other soon complained that he wasn't learning anything and that the time was boring. Not only the teacher but also the materials were neither stimulating nor supportive of the particular needs and faith lives of those boys at their age.

By way of contrast, two young laywomen in the archdiocese prepared a week-long summer camp of clowning, liturgy, active involvement, dramatization and mime based on scriptural themes for forty children ranging in age from four to twelve. The week culminated in a moving liturgy expressing concern for one another, the wider church, and the global community. The camp was a glowing success.

Why did one program "work" and the other did not? We can list the usual factors of teacher experience, program coordination, dynamic presentation, community building and so forth. But I would also suggest that the first program did not take into account another factor, the developmental approach to faith and especially the pivotal incorporation of the imagination as the instrument for God's revelation to be "seen," felt and tasted in the children's lived experience.

In the next two chapters we will explore the different ways in which people are strengthened in their faith through the church's basic task of "teaching the faith." This chapter begins with the elementary school years and the classroom teacher, the parish religious instructor, or perhaps the director of religious education for the parish. During the adolescent years, we discover various educators again—the high school teacher, the parish religious education teacher, the DRE, and maybe a youth minister. In the next chapter we move into the young adult years, where the educators might include the campus minister, the college teacher, the religious education teacher, the youth and young adult minister, even a pastor or associate. And in the adult years, educators include parish ministers, parish religious educators, the DRE, and fellow adults. In many ways the context over the life-cycle is broad, but we will be looking particularly at those who are involved in religious education in a formal way.

Among religious educators today there is less concern in "preserving the deposit of the faith" with its emphasis upon rote memorization of dogma and prayers and much more energy, spirit and direction in nurturing the faith lives of individual Christians through a form of education which "leads people forth," as the Latin root of "education" implies, to more faith-filled living. Growth and development in faith have replaced preservation as root metaphors for Christian education.

Because religious education is the major area in which we examine ministry in relation to the life-cycle and the entire development of forms of faithing, many of the dymanics of faith growth mentioned in this chapter will serve as the basis for other forms of ministry in later chapters. Furthermore, as we examine the rich, diverse area of religious education, we will not be discussing the merits or defects of any particular program, technique or approach. But using faith development theory as background, we can suggest criteria, emphases, directions and values which ought to be incorporated into any meaningful program of religious education.

Background

In the past twenty years among both Protestant and Roman Catholic communities the changes in religious education have been momentous and dramatic but have also led to confusion and to a pluralism that seems to overlook basic "certainties" of faith. Questions about the nature of religious education, the prevailing theories and methodologies and their theological underpinnings are beyond the scope of this chapter. Yet we need to take a moment to reflect on the place and importance of religious education in the mission of the church.

In a practical sense the place and importance of religious education can be measured in operational terms, that is, how do church communities allocate resources, prepare teachers, develop curriculum for religious education? What is the priority of religious education with relation to other areas of church life? Or more broadly, what understanding of religious education is expressed in the liturgical life of the community, in evangelization efforts, the movement toward justice and peace or the church's decision-making procedures?

At another level religious education can be viewed as the means toward the full development of the church's mission to be open to God's kingdom among us. The authors cited at this chapter's opening mirror the new understandings of the mission toward which the church has groped its way since the Second Vatican Council in the mid-1960's. Increasingly the church, using the image of a pilgrim people, has grasped its mission as liberating service to the whole human community and not only to its own members. At the same time renewal in such areas as liturgy, the moral life, justice concerns and theology emphasizes the complete development of each person as gifted by grace to proclaim the full reality of God in his or her unique way. This new self-understanding of the church and its liberating mission in terms of the formation of persons and the transformation of the world has given rise to a dazzling and sometimes bewildering array of approaches to religious education.

In part this variety represents the decline of the common curriculum, objectives and even methods which characterized the previous dogmatic approach to catechetics in the Roman Catholic Church and the neo-orthodox approach of many Protestant congregations. At the same time, religious educators have begun to incorporate the insights of sociology, psychology and anthropology which focus upon the person, relationships, process and community as the core of a religious education or catechetical program. More and more religious "educators" envision themselves primarily as ministers. Critics of these movements bewail what they call "religious illiteracy" and the de-emphasis upon "solid," i.e., orthodox, content. In the midst of the battles over religious education and the avalanche of possible programs, religious educators themselves look for various theoretical models to assist them in grounding their approaches. The values clarification approach in moral education, Lawrence Kohlberg's moral development theory, John Westerhoff's intentional religious socialization, and even Fowler's faith development theory become new truths to replace the old dogmatisms.[4]

As we begin to look more closely at religious education, we need to note the limits of religious education. The nurturance of faith is not a direct result of education, although such education is crucially important. We are now much more aware of the formative influence of family life, social environment, psychological dispositions and so forth in their impact upon personal growth. But certainly faith growth does draw upon the language, meaning, and models which various communities provide, and in that effort education plays a critical part. If, for example, people interpret modern science to say that religious visions are merely the results of chemical stimulations to the brain, or if with Freud people argue that religion is an illusion, then religious people will no longer have visions! So what religious education does say about the promise and possibilities of relationship with God is critically important in our understandings of who and what we are.

In this discussion, however, I am limiting religious education to the formal "schooling" which church people develop to nurture the faith life of church members. As mentioned above we will look at this process from the elementary years through high school in this chapter and from young adulthood to adult religious education in the next chapter. Discussion of senior adults will be reserved for a later chapter on elders. The approach will include the private or parochial school and the "Sunday school" of elementary and high school years, the college and parish life for young adults and the renewed interest in adult religious education and adult spirituality. In each of these areas, we will use the factors of symbol-making, perspective-taking, and sense of participation to frame approaches to faith growth.

The Elementary Years

During these years of childhood, religious experience is still very much an integral part of the child's total experience of life. The differentiations which adults make between their "religious life" and their daily life are not that weighty in the child's world. In that sense, the particular roles of the elementary school teacher in the private/parochial school and the Sunday school teacher and director of religious education employed by the local parish overlap. And if possible, the two areas of school and parish can cooperate effectively in the religious education of children.

In earlier societies, children participated in the daily life of the community and in what we today would isolate as the society's "religious" expressions by watching adults participate in the sacred mysteries through seasonal rituals as well as the routines of birth, death, initiation and purification. In our day as a result of the diversification of modern, industrial society and the breakdown of a unified, Christian vision of life, religious education, like all education, has been viewed as a compartment, a segment of life, developed by an "expert" in the area, with little relation to the rest of the day, week, month or year. While a more holistic approach has emerged in religious education recently, we are still stuck with the institutional frameworks of Sunday school classes and private/parochial schools with religion classes at certain times of the day and week.

One response to these issues has been the rise of theories of religious socialization. It is true in one sense that "religious education for children is primarily a process of religious socialization and enculturation into the religious views of family, church, and community."[5] Thinkers like John Westerhoff and James Michael Lee stress the total environment of the child, and Westerhoff strongly challenges the dominant approach of isolated schooling in religion.[6] While these theorists call us to pay attention to the processes of enculturation and socialization taking place in the child's life, enculturation in the values and attitudes of adult believers is not all that is going on during these formative years. From the perspective of faith development theory, the eventual development of a mature adult faithing is rooted in the world-shaping realities formed by the young child, especially through the capacities of imaging and symbolizing.

Faith development theory shows us the ways in which children are unique in their understandings of reality.[7] And Jesus would have us dwell on those unique understandings as essential to understanding his Father, himself and the kingdom he preaches: "Unless you turn around and become like children you will never enter the kingdom of heaven" (Mt 18:3). As theologian Urban Holmes notes, Jesus is "talking about the capacity of the little child, aged three to seven, to think associatively . . . rather than reducing all meaning to a logical operation imposed by society's categories of reality."[8] As we discussed in earlier chapters on imagination and faith, such imaginings are essential dimensions of envisioning realities of the kingdom beyond our limited experience in the present.

Needs and Capacities

Although there are great variations during the years between six and thirteen, roughly the ages covering entry into school through junior high or eighth grade, we can make some general background remarks about the unfolding drama of childhood in relation to religion. During this period, early, concrete images of God emerge, and children interpret the events of daily life which impinge upon them in terms of the religious meanings that adults attach to those events. Through rituals, rules, morals, stories and religious activities children experience religious phenomena in a variety of ways. In addition, initial forms of prayer are nurtured. All of these are essential to a vigorous faith life in the adult years.[9] For psychologist Erik Erikson, these years support a sense of respect for law, human and divine, and the imaginative fantasy essential to myth and ritual participation. But in particular Erikson points to the importance of developing a sense of industry, "a sense of being able to make things and make them well and even perfectly."[10] Basically a child needs to know what he or she is good at, a prerequisite for the later issue of identity.

From our earlier study of faith development theory we have seen that the child also needs to understand and organize the bewildering world into categories which can "hold" all the information, facts and beliefs the child encounters. This organization of the world by "objects" such as geography, race, religion, nationality, clothes or whatever into related patterns grounds the later development of relationships among "subjects" which provides the basis for understanding a moral and religious universe based on love or justice. The physical building blocks of the infant become the building of concrete categories which later emerge as categories and relationships of spirit. And basically the imagination is fueling these developments. An organization of reality leads the child to develop a sense of belonging, first to family, then to community, nation and so on. This sense of participation grows through perspective-taking from an initial need to have the child's own needs met to a gradual feeling for cooperation and community endeavors.

Throughout the elementary years we must remember that faith is whole and cannot be divided among parents, school, parish, peer groups, and so on. In this sense too the entire school and parish are part of the "religious education" program. Thus the elementary teacher and the religious education instructor are not the only ones responsible for the formation of the children in faith. The challenge then is for all the members of the parochial/private elementary school or parish team to envision themselves as ministers to the children. In addition, events which occur in every area of the child's life are events in the process of faithing as well. As adolescents and adults we tend to separate "faith" and "the religious" from other parts of our lives and in so doing "neuter" our faith and domesticate its demands upon us. Fortunately the faith life in children is still commensurate with *their* life.

First and Second Grade

Somewhere during these early school years the first transition in the faith life is gradually made from the intuitive to the narrative mode of faithing. Although this development may follow a fairly natural process related to age development, the transition can be nurtured and deepened by a teacher sensitive to faith development theory. In the crucial area of the imagination, the teacher can encourage the child to explore worlds of possibilities through stories, especially fairy tales, folk tales and fables. Inasmuch as adult faithing involves the imaginative relationships between my personal story and the gospel story, with its power to convict, challenge and motivate me in my story, these early forms of story contain essential components for that later development. Borrowing from the work of Rosemary Haughton on fairy tales, Urban Holmes comments on "the sensitivity, awareness, and selflessness required of a Christian" in the wise animals; "in the real princess, a moral insight and willingness to suffer for the right; in witches and orgres, destructive evil and mindless greed; and in the quest, the Christian's pilgrimage." For children, these images "make concrete our experience of God, while not reducing that experience to the level of univocal tedium."[11]

For children who experience almost total boredom at adult worship services, the worlds of stories can provide both imaginative stimulation and elementary knowledge of human life upon which later faithing can build. For the young mind all life is religious. The importance of the biblical stories lies in giving the child a feel for language about the Christian community and the Christian story which enables the older child, adolescent and young adult to name in the language of faith the realities he or she encounters in later life.

Several authors have questioned the wisdom of using scripture with children. For Ron Goldman, the problem lies in the understanding that the Bible was written for an adult audience. Children will understand it in a literal fashion which only creates confusion.[12] Thus Jesus becomes the Master Magician. While much of this is true, our approach from faith development theory would argue that a careful use of the stories basic to our Christian heritage is very appropriate to young children. For when a child is "deprived of the opportunity of 'taking on' for himself or herself these stories, the child will find it difficult to develop a sense of belonging to his or her faith community." Since stages are sequential, then keeping children from scriptural stories "would seem to short-circuit the child's faith development."[13]

Perspective-taking emerges as a useful developmental tool at this age also. Through reading, acting or role-taking children can learn to discuss what was happening in the situation. For example, why did Robin Hood help Little John even though he was mad at Little John? Or by changing the story, the teacher can expose children to other ways of thinking about a problem and can expand children's sense of fairness as they learn to take others' perspectives into account. What would happen if Maid Marian led the troops instead of Robin Hood? Or again, the biblical account of Joseph's treatment by his brothers uncovers basic ideas of fairness and trust within the arena of family relationships. The sense of family can be extended to include the "human family" through accounts of other people in other cultures. This approach is crucial in curtailing the tendency toward stereotyping which emerges along with the child's attempts to organize the world into identifiable categories and classes for understanding. The idea of a "pen pal" is one way to bridge the worlds of different cultures.

Most importantly for a mature sense of justice in adult life, the teacher must try to acquaint the young child with the needs and perspectives of the poor, the elderly, the handicapped, the underdog. Whether through stories or actions such as mission collections, canned food drives, and the like, the teacher needs to be aware of the ways in which those stories and actions are related to developmental levels.

Another perspective which can be developed during this period rests upon the child's earlier interest in animals and plants as central characters in life's dramas and of equal value with humans Where we as adults once labeled such thinking as "primitive," our growing consciousness of our fragile environment reveals the wisdom of such "holistic" thinking about nature. The teacher can nurture the child's sense of nature by showing respect for animals, plants and the non-organic elements of nature as parts of God's creation and as revelatory "traces" of God's presence in the world. In this way recycling, conservation, and repairing of worn-out items become ways of fostering God's creativity among us rather than purely economic necessities.

Another critical factor in perspective-taking is the child's opportunities for faith sharing and listening to the faith stories of others. While this will not be the developed narratives of older children and adults, the young child will express his or her "story" primarily through anecdotes, a process all too many adults see as a waste of time. In expressing and sharing anecdotes children are experiencing the reactions of others to their own personal worlds and learning about the worlds of significant others in their lives. As Urban Holmes remarks, the story in anecdotal form constitutes "the subjective intentionality, and hence the character, of a given individual."[14] Thus the teacher should pay attention to the anecdotes children tell of their own accounts and should encourage "anecdote" sharing as a prelude to more developed faith sharing in adult years.

As a final element in perspective-taking, we can look at the important place that rules play in the lives of young children. Whether in games, through play, or the "laws" of God, home, and school, the young child feels the imprint of society and of the divine in rules. Toddlers play games with a seeming anarchic disregard for the "rules" which totally frustrates the child of seven or eight for whom rules constitute the nature of reality. Rules represent order, which is a key need of the stage two faither. Charges of "cheater" abound among the young child as the rules of the game or playground or home and school are hammered out, often through trial and error, with final appeals to authority such as teachers, parents, and rulebooks.

While children emerging into stage two will take the rules in a literal way, the teacher's role is to provide for the exceptions, for equity in applying the rules, and for flexibility in interpretation. In this role it becomes critical for teachers to explain the reasons for the rule and the exceptions. For example, such statements as "We ask others to play" or "Everybody needs a turn" need to be accompanied with an explanation that appeals to stage two thinking, such as "Then others will ask you" or "Then you'll get your turn." The danger in stating rules with no explanation is that we fail to prepare for a broader understanding of rules as the development of community concerns. For in another sense, rules establish a sense of limits and subordination of selfish interests for a broader concern. While development in imagination and symbols helps envision possibilities, the limits of rules can provide a realistic sense of the possible as well. The absence of a good, balanced sense of rules leads to illusions of grandeur and the self-centered desire to control the world around us.

If rules develop a sense of order and a concern for the perspectives of the broader society and its just regulation, they also allow the children opportunities to participate in social life through games, play and daily rituals. In the classroom or religious education setting, participation must be fostered both as a way for young children to feel trusted and "faithed in" as well as a process for developing an early sense of community which answers the questions of belonging, "Whose am I?" Certainly role sharing and play acting serve as methods of participation, but more particular methods can involve some form of shared decision-making and class meetings where the problems and needs of the students can emerge. These approaches help construct an environment of respect for other students which initially builds upon the sense that if all are mutually respected, then each individual will receive respect.

Young children can also assume responsibility for clearly defined tasks in the classroom and for the production of items needed for class. Having children make things for class or home not only serves to develop a sense of responsibility and participation but also helps resolve what Erikson sees as the "crisis" for this age, namely, the sense of industry, of "what I am good at." Another approach to participation involves opportunities for service to the elderly, the needy, or the handicapped.

Finally it may be too hopeful to ask that young children participate in the development of their own liturgies and prayers. The children at this young age can become involved through their own design of the worship and through the creative use of tales and biblical stories. Prayer life, too, can be nurtured by having students share their needs and "anecdotal" stories as prayer forms. Yet the importance of formal, structured prayers such as the "Our Father," etc. should not be overlooked as ways of ordering prayer for children who for one reason or another cannot vocalize their own experiences. Such formal prayers also serve as methods of ritualistic repetition to establish an attitude of reverence which helps in later life to create a receptive environment for hearing God's word.

Third Through Sixth Grades

For the child during those years of approximately eight through eleven, the imaginative world of fantasy still exists but it is coupled with a growing sense of concrete reality as well. Thus the narrative mode now must involve stories of heroes and heroines, super-people who show an exaggerated sense of accomplishment, of "industry" in Erikson's terms. Saturday morning TV literally explodes with stories of the "super-heroes/heroines" and comic books become vehicles for articulating values of truth, justice, and all too often an uncritical glow of the American way.

But the child also needs some acquaintance with the heroes and heroines of the faith, past and present. In this way, not only does he or she encounter definite believers who exhibit the same concrete, good qualities as the super-people of TV and comics, but heroes and heroines of the faith become embodiments of real possibilities for living a vibrant faith. In addition they keep alive the language and context of the Christian story with which the students can identify in terms of their own stories.

More generally, secular legends and sagas, say of George Washington and the cherry tree, or the travels of Odysseus, can also serve as ways of identifying the human values at the heart of the gospel message. Stories provide avenues for children to find expression for concerns which they are unable to voice—fears, anxieties, joys. Throughout this period, then, stories of super-heroes and heroines, of real people, saints or cultural figures, fantasies and legends all serve to continue the development of the imaginative capacity and to provide models for individual achievement and development of community which will emerge more strongly at stage three.

The perspective-taking element during these years becomes increasingly important as older children learn more about their city, country and the entire world. Teachers can build upon the child's sense of an expanding universe of people through films, books, guests from other countries, faith traditions and ethnic groups which expose them to views different than their own. A system of "pen pals" can bring about new understandings of people from other cultures and traditions. Newspaper stories, TV shows and books about real "heroes" and "heroines" enable students to grasp the sense of service these people incorporate in their daily lives. Or through role-playing, acting and other techniques the students can continue to take on others' perspectives.

Such programs as the annual UNICEF collection at Halloween or the Multiple Sclerosis Read-a-Thon become ways in which students can learn about children in other cultures or about the handicapped and needy while performing a service to the community. Through these services or through visits to the aged and those in need the students also begin to develop a sense of the community's response as well as personal obligations for the welfare of others. The introduction of such programs at this age can encourage a more expansive sense of justice, service and community care.

Continued concern for the environment builds upon the older child's sense of reciprocity. The teacher can begin to explore the difficult concept of the interrelationship among all the elements of nature through which the child senses the responsibility which humans have for the nurturance of the earth. Although this will be interpreted primarily in terms of "we take care of the earth so the earth takes care of us," the way is prepared for a more inclusive sense of oneness with nature and of reverence for the reality of nature in its own right.

Certainly opportunities for faith-sharing emerge among these students. They are ready for more developed forms of telling their own stories and their anecdotes, but the teacher must construct a responsive and trusting environment in which such sharing can take place beyond the "show and tell" approach. More self-conscious about themselves, these students will more likely use stories about others as a means of telling about their own struggles. And at this age the teacher must nudge students to take the perspectives of others rather than to resort to physical violence or harsh recrimination.

Finally the teacher becomes instrumental in assisting the older child to understand the place of rules and rule-making in establishing community and in developing notions of fairness. As the child begins to sense the flexibility of rules, he or she will also test the rules all the more strongly. Thus the teacher must begin preparing for a broader understanding that rules are for the good of the community and hold relationships together. Games and play, the concrete expressions of rules, become more subtle but also lay the basis for greater cooperation among the players once the power and authority of the rules themselves give way to mutual benefit in following the rules for everyone's welfare.

While imaginative ability and perspective-taking have extended throughout the life of the older child, the quality of participation and the need for it have increased dramatically. As we just noted, an ability for cooperation emerges along with the ability to take the perspective of others even if initially just to make sure personal goals are met. But children develop budding friendships now, and these become the foundations of community.

Within their own community children at this age can begin to share responsibilities for the resources of their own group. Thus they can buy the supplies for group activities, can raise money for projects or contribute their allowances. Teachers can encourage students to continue to reuse materials both to gain a greater sense of the earth's resources as well as to develop their own sense of accomplishment and responsibility in avoiding consumptive habits.

As with the younger children students in this period are able to take greater responsibility in the development of the class and can be encouraged to establish their own rules with the desire to move them toward a sense of shared responsibility required at stage three. Community service projects also enhance their sense of responsibility and being "entrusted." And in particular the students can take greater responsibility for worship and prayer events, possibly designing the liturgical celebration for the adult worship service so that their contribution could be acknowledged by the whole community. This reintegration into the adult worshiping community would become increasingly important in the upper elementary years.

Seventh and Eighth Grades

While the teachers and religious educators working with the third through the sixth graders can nurture and enhance the gradual development of narrative faithing, the junior high years present a different set of problems. This period reflects the emergence of more conventional modes of faithing as these pre-adolescents move into the beginnings of more critical thinking and the development of strong feelings. In addition the capacity for real friendship is growing while the junior high person begins to feel the pressures of many different individuals competing for his or her allegiance.

Once again stories play a prominent role in the faith life of these older children. Yet now the stories involve the real person who can articulate the developmental needs of the student in an increasingly complex world. The arrival of puberty or its increased intensity for those who experienced its arrival earlier means that the readiness for friendship in which the needs of another can be subordinated to personal needs is coupled with a growing and confusing sexual self-awareness. The models whom the student encounters as teacher, minister, community leader need to become sensitive to the questions which seventh and eighth graders may not even vocalize to adults but which plague their feelings and thoughts. Most of these questions center around how "I" appear to others who are significant to me— too tall, too short, too thin, too fat, too intelligent? And the list goes on.

In faith development terms, the basic question around imagination and symbols concerns the literalism which has served to ground the appreciation of concrete reality for the stage two faither. This focus upon language would seem academic were it not for our understanding that the language we use forms and shapes the realities we understand, and the ability to envision different meanings to words and concepts is related to our ability to pass beyond literalism to symbolic understandings.

For the religious educator one approach to the problem of literalism is a view of scripture which moves from the discussion of events to the stories of Joseph and his brothers, of Esau and Jacob, of Saul and David, of Ruth and Esther, the multiple relationships of Jesus to his disciples, to Mary Magdalene. All serve to raise questions of friendship, sexuality, personal identity and family patterns. These stories can begin the discussion for junior high school students whose boredom with scripture is easily read in glazed eyes and tortured expressions because they are so familiar with the "exploits" of biblical characters. They have emerged from the stage of narrative heroes and heroines and need to look at the lives of real models who exhibit some of the same concerns arising in their own lives. Utilizing the relational patterns found in scripture would be one way to capitalize on the rich texture of scripture in light of the students' needs.

Similarly perspective-taking takes on a new dimension during these transition years. The burst of self-awareness among early teens often coincides with an ability to take multiple perspectives into account. Initially this becomes an agonizing realization as the young person struggles with the knowledge that so many different people are looking at him or her in so many different ways *and* expecting so many different things. Parents, teachers, ministers, the peer group, trusted friends, "the opposite sex"— all these individuals and groups confront the seventh and eighth grader's conflicting images of the self. As these struggles emerge more completely into stage three faithing, the "conventions" and rules of those groups become both guides for acceptable behavior and restraints upon a growing self-awareness.

The feeling for friends offers an opportunity to extend students' concerns to others outside their own group across ethnic, religious and even class lines. There are many stories and films which are excellent for this purpose. Again letters and exchanges through international agencies to "pen pals" or school peers in other lands can become ways to overcome stereotypes and the ethnocentrism which each culture develops. Since friendship is emerging for these young people as the most dynamic manifestation of God's love, then speaking of friendship relations even among nations can become a way in which seventh and eighth graders can appreciate the idea of uniqueness and self-development of all peoples.

On the level of personal awareness an increased ability at perspective-taking allows students to share faith stories with greater empathy. And it is equally important for the teacher and minister to share at least part of their own stories, both as models of developing Christian lives and as evidence of trust in these young people. In addition reading about the faith journeys of people of other faiths reinforces the sense of God's universal love and of the legitimate differences among peoples in being "faithful" to the transcendent dimension in life.

At the same time the teacher and minister can help students grasp injustice through sharing stories of the pain and suffering of peoples in the United States and the world over. Those presentations can challenge the students to ask the questions of why those sufferings happen and continue. A careful reading of biblical material with emphasis upon the prophets' and Jesus' concern for the poor and oppressed will help students forge the link between their Christian faith and the doing of justice so essential to the full gospel vision.

Working to enlarge the perspective of the students also impinges upon their sense of participation. Not only must they be encouraged to take the perspectives of other members of their immediate and global communities, but opportunities for active participation must emerge if faith is to become a lived reality. Under the guidance of the teacher, students can be led to develop their own rules about cheating, stealing, cleaning up, helping, and so forth in ways which build up community. Shared decision-making and greater responsibility for carrying out decisions not only enhance the sense of being trusted but help the students establish themselves in their own eyes and in the perspective of their fellow students. In an environment of trust and respect students can support one another in times of trial and can openly confront conflict with each other in ways which lead toward resolutions based on love and justice.

Within the strictly "religious" context, these students can take a much larger share of responsibility for planning and carrying out worship services. Once again, their involvement in worship becomes a way of developing their imaginative understandings of symbols as well as providing direct participation in the central events of the worshiping community. In view of their growing self-awareness of their own needs, they can begin to replace patterns of formal prayer with personal prayers, both as part of the worship service as well as in their own times for prayer. This corresponds to the development of a sense of Jesus as friend beyond his wonder-working which was so powerful at earlier stages.

Certainly some service component will be an effective factor in the movement toward a well-developed stage three faithing. Their service can take the form of helping younger students or serving as big sister or big brother for the younger children on an outing, a service project or other event. While the opportunities for community service are endless, teachers should spend time with the students in discussing what the service meant to them, how it reflects what Jesus asked them to do, how those helped respond to the service, and a host of other questions. In addition, students can begin to make the connections in some cases between the social ills they see in their service—poverty, hunger, malnutrition and so forth—and the causes of those conditions.

And now at last we come to the end of our discussion of the early years of religious education. There are probably other applications and dimensions which we have overlooked. Yet hopefully the discussions around categories of imagination and symbols, perspective-taking, and participation have provided some guidelines with which programs can be developed and critically examined. In the next section we move to the more difficult and more challenging years of adolescence where the complex patterns of conventional faithing merge with searching questions of personal and social identity.

The Adolescent Years

Beset by peer pressures, conflict with parental and societal values, the highs and lows of emotional life, the discovery of sexual attraction and romance, encounters with prejudice and stereotype, new ideas and ideals, sudden conversions and loss of faith, the adolescent struggling with new questions about identity and loyalty enters a region of unchartered and tormenting conflicts. The faith development theory indicates that within this swirling vortex of questions and conflicts adolescents are involved in the difficult transitions from the literalism of stage two through dependence upon conventional understanding of faith on to at least the beginnings of independent faithing. Now that the adolescent is pulling away from the home environment and developing strong peer relationships, the supports for faithing shift dramatically. Within this mobile world of interpersonal relationships and intense feelings, the private/parochial school or the church teen center can provide a ''nurturing environment,'' continuity and challenge for negotiating some of the difficult transitions of teen years. In this sense the school or parish setting offers much more than a series of classes.

Needs and Capacities

In addition to the conflicts mentioned above, the adolescent experiences new physical development, increased intellectual understandings in early abstract thought, and heightened emotional life. In the area of faith these developments often mean conflicts with the religious understandings of childhood as well as distrust of the structured and seemingly cold patterns of adult beliefs and practices. Furthermore, as Erikson notes, "the adolescent fears a foolish, all too trusting commitment, and will, paradoxically, express his or her need for faith in loud and cynical mistrust."[15]

At the same time, researchers note that adolescence is a time of deep religious awakening and strong response to the evocative power of symbols, images and myths. In addition, often during the high school years "young people make a decision for or against the religious faith in which they have been socialized."[16] The task for the teacher and minister serving the adolescent is to shape an adult faith to fit the needs and developments of adolescents.

In her provocative study of high school students Dr. Margaret Gorman found that a functional literalism served as a hindrance to later stages of faith development.[17] In particular such literalism centered around the perceived opposition between religion and science and the literal understanding of biblical materials. What seemed to help in this transition were activities and courses involving an understanding of myth, symbolism, science, evolution and religion. The strictly cognitive dimensions of these courses could be supplemented by retreat experiences, exposure to older people whose faithing has developed to stage three and beyond, and powerful experiences of liturgy in which such symbols as light, water, bread, wine, incense are explored. Without such challenges and experiences the symbolic realities of word and sacrament may be locked in a confining literalism.

In addition, the "faithing" person must develop the ability to step outside his or her own perspective and work to understand the world as others understand it. Certainly one of the most important tools which enables students to take other perspectives is cognitive conflict. Exploring other perspectives within a student's own tradition or looking at other religious traditions through classes, visits and speakers can serve as ways of helping students articulate their own faith concerns as well as experience different understandings of faith questions from other traditions. Raising critical questions about the ways in which our social structures are arranged or who profits from existing arrangements can challenge students to examine social issues in a broader context and in light of gospel values.[18] In Dr. Gorman's study teenagers felt that their teachers and ministers did not address their own faith concerns. In response to questions on death, suffering, injustice and values, students stated: "Nobody ever asked me about these before."[19] Certainly a fundamental dimension of faith growth from adolescence on is the opportunity and *encouragement* to articulate a personal faith understanding without being judged and the chance to hear the "faithing" of others without imposing judgment.

In this context the "faithing" community should offer all participants the opportunity to articulate their faith journeys while listening to those of other community members. Biographies of committed individuals who demonstrate their faith in their own lives can be utilized. And students could be encouraged to write statements of faith which in senior year they could share with one another in a seminar, in liturgies, or on retreats as testimony and witness to their own growth and faith.

Another aspect of perspective-taking involves the creation of a trusting environment in which such sharing and conflict as described above can take place. In particular that involves the legitimation of conflict and disagreement and the exploration of skills to articulate those disagreements as well as to resolve them. The entire context demands a growing sense of responsibility for one's own ideas and feelings and a care for the ideas and feelings of others.

Certainly students should be involved in the planning and administration of school and other programs as much as possible. Adolescents will feel "faithed" in, trusted and thus trusting, when they *experience* being trusted with responsibilities. Besides the obvious example of liturgy in which they choose the readings, prepare the music and carry out much of the service, adolescents should be encouraged to assume responsibilities in governing the school, preparing classes, teaching fellow students, leading retreats and so forth. This kind of community recognition and support strengthens the emerging self-identity and fidelity necessary to the independent faith stance of the mature, committed believer.

A second dimension of participation involves the growing practice of involving teenagers in programs of community service. From the point of view of faith development such programs are particularly important inasmuch as they expose adolescents to perspectives and life-styles different from their own and provide confirmation for personal faith. Furthermore such programs involve the teenagers in a sense of justice on a level at which they can understand the meaning of justice best, that is, in terms of fairness in interpersonal relations. Adolescents also gain a strong sense of responsibility for and with others from these experiences. The teenager's overriding concern with self expands to include the problems of others and the problems of the world at large.

To further serve growth in faith, the program must also incorporate some reflection upon service experiences. Through discussion, adolescents can support one another, analyze their successes and failures, see the relationship of their work to the larger framework of the church's mission and begin to develop a more critical understanding of the ways in which those whom they serve are not being served by the larger society and why.

If faith in the early high school years is emerging from the narrative, literal form of stage two and searching for an embodiment in real adult models, then every adult in the high school or church setting becomes a faith model, of "bad faith" as well as "good faith." Placing the total responsibility for religious education upon the "religion teacher" or "youth minister" misses the complex ways in which teenagers perceive the reality of church. Further if the adults in those settings are models of faith, then those models must be seen as worthy of the trust and loyalty of the adolescent and must show in their lives that they trust in and are loyal to the God of the Christian tradition.

Just as importantly, the religious educator and youth minister as models of faith are carriers of faith histories and visions which can be shared with one another and with young people. If we accept the findings of a recent study of faith development that biographies served as an important element in the development of faith, especially in the movement toward stage four,[20] then we can understand how the examples of people who have a sense of their own identity and who are faithful to their visions provide powerful faith models for others. In addition, younger teenagers could benefit from hearing the faith stories of the older teenagers who are themselves models. Such sharings would provide confirmation of faithfulness in a variety of ways and would stimulate the challenge to an individual's faith perspective which is necessary for any development.

A note of cautious realism creeps in at this point. For a fundamental question concerns the operative concepts of church and of a faithing person which inform the educational program. If the primary image is that of church as embodiment of rules and regulations which foster loyalty to the institution, then the faithful person is one who conforms to those rules. Violation of the rules and disloyalty to the institution constitute "unfaithfulness." The painful and difficult transition from stage three to stage four will not find nourishment in such a conforming environment. In this regard a faith "rebellion" or lapse into "a-theism" may be a response of independent faithing against the constrictions of a very conventional, dogmatic faith.

If we turn to the model of church as community, a different process for "faithing" emerges. Church in this sense would mean the web of relationships which confirm and challenge the adolescent yet nourish a movement from a stage two mode of "faithing" to stage three. Here the community provides for the older adolescent a support for the kind of individual challenging of the conventional "faith" world which leads to an independent "faithing" in young adulthood. Further this concept of the church as community also implies that students must be trusted to make decisions governing their own relationships. Most student governments are only advisory, and the students in realizing their lack of real power over their lives feel the lack of trust in them as persons. Using a model of moral development with high school students, Dr. Lawrence Kohlberg of Harvard University's Center for Moral Education has demonstrated the possibilities and promise in allowing students to develop their own governing patterns and concepts of justice.[21] The faith development model demands an even greater context of trust and "faithing" on the part of religious educators and school faculty members and administrators and calls for a faith-sharing dimension which could permeate the classroom, retreats, liturgies and decision-making processes.

In relation to the private or parochial high school, these reflections require that the school examine the faith atmosphere on campus. The understanding of faith as interpersonal and communal at stage three, the operative stage of most adolescents, calls into question the structure and functions of the high school. Clearly some structures and functions are more suitable for developing and nourishing faith than others. And the question is whether a bureaucratic, rule-dominated, hierarchical organization in which "ministry" is relegated to the functions of one person or department promotes development as well as a participatory, organic, interpersonal structure based upon a sharing community and a shared sense of ministering.[22]

Summary

I have argued that the Christian parochial/private school or to a lesser extent the parish youth ministry program provides a unique setting in which the richness of the content of the Christian faith (the cumulative tradition) can interact with the stages of "faithing" appropriate to children and adolescents. For too long, growth in faith has been identified with religion classes, and those students were considered to be "faithful" Christians who *knew* well the doctrinal, moral and historical dimensions of Christianity. How they acted was a different question.

Instead I have stressed that only when the child or adolescent is viewed within an environment of the school or the entire parish youth program which informs, supports and challenges faith will the content of the Christian tradition provide nourishment and growth for the individual Christian. As a corollary, I have emphasized the roles of all adults in the educational setting as models of "faithing." At the very least the faith development model has given us some important understandings of what not to do in terms of faithing. More positively the theory has provided a way of looking at every dimension of the religious education program in the continuing development of "faithing" people and in the task of building a community which incorporates a vision of the coming kingdom. In the next chapter we will take up faith development in the religious education of the young and the mature adult years.

4. RELIGIOUS EDUCATION FOR MATURING FAITH

The original and authentic meaning of the word "professor" is "one who professes a faith." The true professor is not one who controls facts and theories and techniques. The true professor is one who affirms a transcendent center of truth, a center that lies beyond our contriving, that enters history through the lives of those who profess it and brings us into community with each other and the world.[1]

> Parker Palmer, *To Know As We Are Known*

Adult religious learning can be broadly conceived as part of each person's daily life and experience.[2]

> John Elias, *The Foundations and Practices of Adult Religious Learning*

Picture a student who is manufacturing his or her own world view. . . . One could call such a person a philosopher capable of picking and choosing a world view from a wide variety of sources. . . . To have a world view still a little simpler than the world is the mark of a hard-won battle for wisdom.[3]

> Frank Gross, on stage four in *Passages in Teaching*

The Young Adult Years

In this section we move from the relatively homogeneous world of the adolescent to the complex span of life called "young adulthood," roughly corresponding to the years from eighteen to thirty-five. The complexity is compounded when we incorporate the diverse setting of college life, work situation and, for many, family responsibilities. In today's world many people are co-existing in all three situations while striving to develop themselves as faithful people. And the responses of religious educators, parish and campus ministers can no longer rely on the formulas of the past.

Needs and Capacities

As we look at the diverse range of people, needs and potentials in the young adult group, we must keep in mind that we are covering the transitions from the conventional through the individuative and even into the beginning of the conjunctive stages of faith development. The difficult task for the educator and minister is to recognize the different stages and transitions and adapt approaches to the active faith lives of individuals. For the sake of our discussion here, we will look upon the dynamics of this life period as centered around stage four, including the early transitions to or the initial emergence from that stage.

Certainly people in this age group are dealing with central issues of identity and intimacy which have enormous repercussions for their faith life. A recent study of young adults in the Toronto area suggests that the affective experiences of young adults in relationships provide the incentives for involvement in more inclusive communities and in turn lead to involvement and commitment to service activities. As young people become actively involved in issues and concerns outside of their normal milieu, the integration of their knowledge gained from involvement with their personal perspectives became a prerequisite to their development in faith at higher stages.[4] This result was confirmed by the author's own study of ten young adults over a period of two years in St. Louis, Missouri. As these young people finished their college work, entered careers, married and had children, their intentional community developed stronger bonds of interpersonal relationships (intensified their affective experiences) and deepened their commitment toward community service as they reflected more and more the self-understandings of stage four.[5]

The task then is to understand the needs of young adults to search for and maintain a strong sense of their own identity and to begin sharing their lives and visions with others, while responding to the young adult through approaches which meet the criteria of the appropriate stage. Young people emerge from the teen years into the early twenties with an idealism and sense of omnipotence which meet a challenging world, and they need to discover limits in a way which will not overwhelm their own sense of who they are and what they can do. In the later years of young adulthood, during the thirties, needs center more around settling into the routines and patterns of life in order to build a stable environment.[6]

The movement through these years of faith growth can be fostered in a number of ways. For many young people, whether students or in the work force, the consolidation of conventional faithing must first be furthered by support groups, study groups and small community settings in which the examples of powerful models challenge them to live up to the ideals of their faith community. Faith-sharing experiences, participation and responsibility in the college or parish community, exposure to theological developments and other religious traditions all can be used to support conventional faithers while expanding their search toward a more individuative and authentic faith stance. Searching questions require reinterpretations of the "traditional" understandings of the faith which good theology can provide. Scriptural discussion must relate to the personal issues of young people as well as incorporate the basis for justice claims. The cries of suffering peoples can complement social and theological analyses of structural evil and social sin, the causes of poverty, unemployment, war. Basically then religious education and ministry at this point center around providing place and space for strengthening identity, fostering relationships, exploring meaning questions and offering service opportunities.

In relation to the need for a supportive community, new understandings of the church's mission, the person of Jesus, the nature of God's revelation and other basic theological issues need to be harmonized with the lived experience of the community young people actually experience. In our highly technical, bureaucratic society, it is difficult for young people to see around them the manifestation of a community which integrates their life questions with a commitment to the gospel. Somehow those kinds of communities need legitimation, not in the sense that all are called to join them but rather as witness to one way of developing an integrated Christian life. In addition, within any form of community on the campus or in the parish, individuals need help in learning ways through communication skills to be present to one another in times of joy, sorrow, anger, passion.

In one way or another, these facets of community are reflected in group worship as well as personal prayer. In ritual celebrations the campus or parish can foster more challenging understandings of God's revelation of the call to service and of the broad reach of the church's mission. In developing new forms of prayer, the campus or parish minister can support a more intimate relationship with God as indwelling presence. The more reflective abilities of young people can become the basis for meditative and contemplative prayer styles which explore issues of personal integrity and community service. At this point the minister needs to have some experience of spiritual guidance to nurture this new exploration in the style of a master-disciple relationship.

Young Adults and Campus Life

As we focus on the college setting, we need to note the changing population of people attending colleges and universities today. On many campuses, a larger and larger segment of the student body is over twenty-one. Not only does this mean that the needs are different but that many students will occupy jobs, some even full-time, and have families. In addition, more and more students, older and younger, are commuting. For many of these people, then, their educational needs in the area of religion may be better served by their local parish than by campus efforts.

Nevertheless, if the challenges are stronger than ever, so are the needs. Many young people come to the campus as alienated, dissatisfied with their local church, or unchurched in any sense. Certainly, many young people come to the campus with some formal identity in a church tradition but do not accept many aspects of the church's official teachings.[7]

One of the elements of college life which has surprised and confounded church officials is the rise or emergence of fundamentalist groups, charismatics, and cults in and around the campus. In the midst of an environment which cultivates the elements of critical reason, many ask how it is possible for students to become involved with seemingly irrational, mid-controlling efforts. Such a "rational" approach to the issue misses the mark in several ways, for it is precisely those groups which meet affiliative and symbolic needs that more formal campus ministry efforts have neglected. On many Catholic campuses, for example, the attraction of benediction, rosaries, and charismatic meetings may rest in the needs of a generation of young people who did not have the symbolic experiences of stage three faithing such as stations of the cross, rosaries, and processions, through which earlier generations could express their religious feelings.

An uncritical fundamentalism needs to be challenged through questioning, symbolic understanding and reasoned criticism, but the appeal of such groups as Campus Crusade for Christ or religious cults is a reminder that the strictly cognitive approach to the faith life upon which much campus effort has relied does not do justice to the needs of young people to *experience* and not just *understand* their faith. Certainly courses in literature, biblical works, symbols and the unconscious are helpful. More particularly, however, we are driven back to the development of rich

opportunities for worship which on the one hand call them to a more reflective, meditative experience of the divine dimension within them. Recall the highly symbolic and structured rituals of cults with chanting, loud
music, incense and candles to develop a group spirit in which the individual is submerged. We are talking instead of worship which may incorporate those elements to express the affective dimensions of people but
which leads to more critical and reflective understandings of church, society, and the transcendent.

For many students prayer groups and scripture study groups foster a
deeper sense of the symbolic in relation to the more rational approaches
of critical, theological inquiry. These approaches will further faith growth
when the method allows the young person to relate his or her personal
story to the biblical story in a reflective manner and when students can
appropriate for themselves a faith perspective which answers the challenging questions they raise. In all this process, the minister can serve as
a model and witness to adult faithing by sharing his or her own story and
by showing how he or she wrestled with some of the same questions while
maintaining a supportive environment.

Another important resource for faith growth lies in the retreat experience. Again through faith sharing, prayer or scripture, theological reflection and liturgical expression, a retreat environment can root the
developing bud of individuative faithing. Since students who elect retreats
are self-selective about their readiness for faith growth and challenges, the
retreat experience can build upon a willingness to engage in critical examination of personal faith. The retreat can also open the students to the
social nature of their faith commitment and to the necessity to working for
justice in the world.

If liturgy, Bible study and retreats are important methods of developing a sense of the symbolic among college students, they are also key
factors in perspective-taking and a sense of participation. Beyond exposure to points of view different from one's own, an individuative faithing
demands that young people critically reflect on their own faith view in
light of other people's challenging perspectives and in relation to complete
systems of thought which might challenge, support or modify their worldview. Due to the plurality of viewpoints expressed on campuses today the
student needs the supportive guidance of the campus ministry team to put
his or her ''world'' back together again.

Up to this point our focus has been upon the needs and abilities which
the student brings to the faith development enterprise. The campus or parish minister has been envisioned as the responder. However, for the ben-

efit of students, as well as other members of the campus community, the campus minister must go beyond the priestly, pastoral role to a prophetic role in the college or university. In the first place, he or she can keep questions of value constantly in the view of the academic community through guest lecturers, classes, colloquia or other expressions of intellectual support for faith perspectives. Through retreats, spiritual guidance and special liturgical expressions campus ministry can also nurture the faith life of the non-student members of the community. And finally, he or she can challenge the practices, policies and at times the philosophy of the university when those threaten the full growth of people in the university or the broader community. We have seen memorable instances of this prophetic role of campus ministers who challenge campus communities in the areas of sexism, racism, alliance with war policies or bureaucratic callousness in dealing with issues which reflect a campus' value system.

Stage four faithing rests upon the assumption of responsibility for oneself and for one's actions and ideas in the development of a somewhat systematic understanding of the world. Thus exposure to models and charismatic people who are able to live out a committed Christian life serves as another way to foster growth toward and through individuative faith. As mentioned earlier, biographical and autobiographical material can support young persons struggling amidst the complexities of modern life and in the seeming betrayals of fidelity and loyalty seen in film, media, government and perhaps in their own family environments.

In a way, this is an updated approach to the "lives of the saints" which nurtured earlier generations. However, the emphasis in these portraits is less on the ways in which these people serve the conventions of the institutional religious organization than on the strong, personal faith of the "modern saint" forging his or her own person in the surrounding world. The lives of Gandhi, Martin Luther King, Jr., Thomas Merton, and Mother Teresa are only a few of the examples which could be used to help young adults "construe" more adequate understandings of the world.

And finally, some form of community service provides another means of perspective-taking as well as a very personal sense of participation. In the research of Lawrence Kohlberg in moral development, the development of concern for the welfare of others was found to be a key factor in the movement toward a principled mode of thinking associated with individuative faithing.[8] In reflecting upon such service the campus minister or the classroom teacher can explore the relationships between the concrete needs of the people the students are helping and the more systematic issues of poverty, racism, sexism, militarism and so forth.

Clubs and student organizations which look at social issues also help students relate their faith to questions of peace and justice and thus promote the extension of the students' social perspectives at the same time as their intellectual worlds are expanding through the classroom. On many campuses courses in theology, philosophy, public service and other disciplines are integrating a service dimension with the theoretical elements of the class.

Broad participation in the community of faith and in the larger campus community through real responsibilities fosters a sense of "ownership" among the students for their ideas and actions. Through involvement in clubs, student government activities, and course design and execution, these campus young adults can gain the confidence of being "faithed in" by others as well as confirm their own abilities. In addition, such participation and involvement enhance the sense of responsibility for the welfare of others which broadens perspective-taking and stimulates the imaginative capacity to understand individual and group needs other than one's own, a key development in the extension of a sense of social justice. Yet the young adult at this point is an explorer in the unchartered area of the interior life and needs the guidance, support, and interpretation of the minister in the role of spiritual guide or director.

In sum the young adult on campus experiences a much more complex "universe" than the high school adolescent. As in the elementary and secondary school setting growth in faith must be seen in terms of the total environment of the campus and not just the campus ministry office. The faith life of young adults is a seamless fabric, affected as much by what occurs in the classroom or through rules, regulations or the "atmosphere" of the school and the presence of faculty and administrators as in the efforts of the people in campus ministry. To foster such a perspective on today's campus is as difficult at the Christian institution going through its "identity crisis" in a pluralistic society as at state colleges and universities. Nevertheless the place of the institution as a whole in the socialization of young people on campus must be seen as an essential element in shaping the environment in which growth in faith takes place during the college years.

Teachers play a central role in the critical interpretation of reality which accompanies individuative forms of faithing. Through presentation of a variety of viewpoints the teacher challenges the conventional world view of the student. Faculty can focus explicity on subject matter which stretches students' perspectives, such as global studies, cultural interface, the handicapped, hunger, poverty and so forth. Through example the teacher can provide a powerful model of one who constantly questions yet roots self-understanding in firm convictions and the lived expression of those beliefs and values in actions of fairness, integrity and compassion. Although to some extent every teacher becomes a "sponsor" for better or for worse of students' faith growth, the teacher who intentionally views students with some understanding of faith development can discern more adequately the needs and interests of the students.[9]

Leadership roles, class presentations, and group discussion can encourage students to share their "stories," to listen attentively to those of other students, to perceive differences of opinion without personal threat and to take responsibility for the development of their own world view and their own actions. And finally, in her or his role as the "sympathetic ear," the teacher becomes a personal sponsor of growth in faith. How many of us know well the student who comes to our offices with a "question" about class materials, only then to say, "Well, the real reason I came to talk to you is. . . . " The person of the teacher as model and sponsor has revealed an openness to the student's needs for clarification and sense of fidelity to the quest for truth and faith.

The administrator and staff member also shape the campus environment through fairness in decision-making, consistency of viewpoints and the ways in which their actions reflect a broader sense of mission and commitment to truth, human service or other explicitly Christian values. Students are quick to perceive the discrepancies between broad, general statements about value on campus and the actual decisions that administrators, staff and faculty make about student welfare. Here a stronger participation by students in the life of the university can enable students to understand more completely the ambiguities of some decisions as well as keep those involved in the decisions more aware of those whom the university services. Not only is this a question of strong and "enlightened" leadership struggling to prevent the cynical erosion of support, but more importantly greater participation in decision-making by all parties promotes a livelier community life and a sense of shared responsibility for the life of the campus.

In our discussion of ministry to young adults, we have taken individuative faithing or the movement toward it as the dominant mode of the young adult on campus and indeed, as the next section will reveal, of the young adult in general. Yet faith development is not necessrily linked to age. So there are young adults whose faith life reflects a conventional mode which is vibrant, vital and life-giving to the individual. The task of the minister or teacher dealing with that young person is to nurture, support and also continuously challenge that mode of understanding. The minister and teacher must check his or her own attitudes to prevent a kind of ''faith development'' dogmatism or imperialism in which the minister/teacher *assumes* that all young people *should* be at a particular developmental stage and, even worse, *needs* to make sure that they are. This is certainly to ascribe to oneself God's role for grace in the broader life of faith. At the same time, the minister/teacher must support the growth of the ''older'' young adult who is ready to move out of the individuative faith perspective toward a more conjunctive understanding of faith. We will discuss that transition in the section on the mature adult years.

Young Adults and Work

The extensive treatment of young adults on campus may give the impression that we are short-changing the much larger population of young adults. Yet our study of campus young adults has provided us with a microcosm of many of the needs and crises of young adults generally. When we talk now about the young adult *not* in a college or university setting, we are still talking about the development toward and through an individuative faithing. However, the setting and the factors for such growth have become much more diffuse and challenging. In addition, the focus for ministry shifts from the campus minister and college teacher to the youth and young adult minister, the parish pastor and director of religious education.

In essence the tasks remain the same as for the campus minister: (1) focusing upon continued identity and intimacy needs; (2) presenting a clear and compelling understanding of faith which incorporates freedom, responsibility, justice, peace, love; (3) challenging young people to take responsibility for their own lives; (4) providing expressions for worship and prayer which nurture the growing awareness of inner presence; (5) stimulating challenging discussions and the sharing of faith stories which express growing responsibility for faithing; (6) providing opportunities for involvement and participation in various communities; (7) exhibiting models of individuative and conjunctive faithing personally and in films, books and speakers. No doubt this is a tall order for the young adult minister, pastor or the DRE, and a realistic approach will assume that ministers to young adults touch only a small segment of the lives of the young adults with whom they come in contact.

Because of work schedules and the age range of the young adult groups, the young adult minister, pastor or DRE has to select those times and places which can best promote some of the factors we have just highlighted. Since the ministry is so diffuse and development can range from the conventional to something approaching the conjunctive, the settings and approaches need to be geared to specific audiences as much as possible.

Yet most if not all of the factors which we outlined in the section on campus life can be transferred to these young adults as well. In one critical area, however, the campus setting offers an opportunity difficult to duplicate, that is, the time of what Erik Erikson calls a "moratorium." In Erikson's words:

> A moratorium is a period of delay granted to somebody who is not ready to meet an obligation or forced on somebody who should give himself time. It is a period that is characterized by a selective permissiveness on the part of society and of provocative playfulness on the part of youth, and yet it also often leads to deep, if often transitory, commitment on the part of the youth, and ends in a more or less ceremonial confirmation on the part of society.[10]

While Erikson emphasized the variations in the ways society provides its youth with moratoria, through apprenticeships, adventures, travel and so forth, the campus allows for the moratorium in unique ways. The setting provides an atmosphere in which new ideas, values and behaviors can be "tried on" for size, for feel, for fit with the young person's emerging sense of identity. The student can "lay aside" conventional attitudes and values momentarily, or even permanently. For the non-college youth the minister and educator must provide opportunities for such examinations of faith and religious belief, and they must be sensitive to much of the "posturing" that goes along with the "trying out" of new ideas, values and beliefs to see how well they fit.

Finally as the young adult approaches the time of "mid-life" with its attendant crises surrounding career, marriage and family life, the correspondences with factors of mature adult life which we will describe in the next section overlap. On the one hand these people become models for the younger adults with whom they may have associated in work, play, prayer and discussion. At the same time their experiences with suffering, loss, grief and injustice reveal a greater willingness to tolerate ambiguity and explore their own and others' vulnerability with understanding and compassion.

The Years of Maturing Adulthood ———————

In the movement from young adult to maturing adult there is no boundary line, no critical year or cultural rite of passage such as marked entrance into the other life periods. In this range of maturing adulthood we experience people who manifest all the stages of faith development from the conventional to the universalizing. While the religious educator and minister need to be very sensitive to that diversity in program and planning, the diversity itself makes it difficult to deliniate specific applications of theory to practice.[11] However by utilizing the categories of imagination and symbol, perspective-taking and participation, we can make some general observations for adult religious education.

First let us examine a number of reasons for the growing importance of adult religious education in the life of the believing community. In both Protestant and Roman Catholic church bodies, changes in structural organization from a hierarchical model to one of greater shared authority require a more educated adult population. More participatory forms of worship demand greater understanding and responsibility by adults. Divergent developments in theology and the moral understandings of human behavior present people with a bewildering array of opinions requiring study and thought. Movements such as the charismatic or neo-pentecostal expressions have given rise to strong interest in spirituality, and the renewed relationship between religion and social justice fuels a need for further education on all levels within the church and even outside the institutional church setting. In the midst of these changes and upheavals, more and more adults are experiencing personal crises of faith as the traditional patterns of church attendance, clerical preaching, and personal piety fail to deal with the issues in the larger society which touch people most.[12]

Recent documents of the Roman Catholic Church emphasize the importance of adult religious education as well. Thus the General Catechetical Directory states that "catechesis for adults, since it deals with persons who are capable of an adherence that is fully responsible, must be considered the chief form of catechesis." The National Catechetical Directory for the United States re-emphasizes the point: "Because of its importance and because all other forms of catechesis are oriented in some way to it, the catechesis of adults must have high priority at all levels of the Church."[13] In terms of faith development theory, the "fully responsible" adherence mentioned in the General Catechetical Directory coincides with the development of the higher stages of faith, that is, of those ways of faithing in which individuals can grasp the full meaning of the gospel call for establishing a kingdom of love and justice not restricted by particular views of nation, ethnic group, or even religious tradition. Thus holistic adult religious education is a prime necessity in the nurture of faith-filled people.

Needs and Capacities

Although the developmental levels of adults range from the conventional to the conjunctive, the needs of adults vary at different times in their lives. While the young adult is initially concerned with establishment of self through marriage, work, college and career, the older adult with whom we are now concerned moves through other moments which call for different assessments and different strengths. The raising of children and their subsequent departure from the household, job transition, divorce and remarriage, marriage renewal, death of a spouse or family member, increasing involvement in the community, eventual retirement, the prospect of pain, suffering and physical deterioration as aging takes its toll and finally eventual death—each of these transition points, minor rites of passage through which adults pass, can become a graced moment of reflection on one's lived faith life.

In Erik Erikson's developmental scheme the key crisis which adults in the mid-life period must resolve centers around generativity or ways in which adults sense that they are passing on something of themselves to the next generation.[14] They watch as others take their places, younger people who seem to have greater vigor, enthusiasm, energy and are appropriately rewarded more substantially. Yet through their care for others, the mature adult can become a sponsor or promoter of others' growth without threat to his or her own.

In addition, as mentioned in one of our opening quotations, the term "religious" in "adult religious education" moves beyond church-related events to embrace all the factors of adult living inasmuch as they are open to a transcendent dimension. Furthermore, the whole life of the church involves religious education for the adult, that is, the forms of worship and preaching, pastoral counseling, service, the architecture and uses of the buildings and even the development of the parish budget. In this sense just as we indicated for the elementary, secondary and to some extent the college situation, the world of the adult provides a basis for learning which either supports or countermands the efforts of formal teaching/learning situations. However, adult religious education today also demands the development and programming of structured learning environments in which the specific goals of adult religious education can be carried out.

Regardless of how these goals are developed, and different theorists develop different goals, they will concern (1) the enhancement of the giftedness of adults as responders to the gospel, (2) the interpretation of the meaning of the gospel and adult responses in human freedom, (3) the evaluation of the life of the church and adult contributions to it in view of the gospel, (4) the commitment to the transformation of society from the perspective of the gospel and the Christian tradition, and (5) an understanding of other Christian and religious traditions. Within that broad framework, the thrust of an adult religious education program ought to encourage adults to talk about their needs while listening to others and to sensitize people to issues and concerns of other groups around the world.[15] And all the while a developed religious education program for adults will, when it can, target specific groups with specific needs—the widowed, separated, retired, divorced, parents, single, married, minorities, handicapped, homosexual, the imprisoned and others. Large tasks in times of dwindling resources!

In looking at the complex interrelationship between the field of adult religious education and faith development theory, I would first enumerate five areas which every adult program can incorporate in the total educational effort: (1) the exploration of faith roots in scripture, particularly the New Testament, (2) the support for adult faith in a solid theological framework with emphasis upon moral growth and Christian social teaching, (3) a lived spirituality which emerges from scripture and theology, (4) the development of communities in which faith stories are shared, and (5) opportunities for service, participation and decisive action. We will examine these five factors in the framework of images and symbols, perspective-taking and participation.

Certainly one of the most important developments within the Roman Catholic Church and many Protestant churches is the "rediscovery" of scripture. Lay people and clergy alike are using scripture and the resources of scripture scholars for the renewal of their personal lives, church organizations, ethical considerations and even budgets. When complemented with theological reflection in small groups of people willing to share their personal stories, scripture study becomes a powerful means to interpret our personal stories, provide meaning to our lives and develop visions which shape new possibilities and new realities. Around the metaphors and myths of personal story-telling in the framework of The Story such a study invites adults at the conventional mode to articulate their own faith and hear their story apart from the "conventional" patterns, while it allows those in the individuative stage to critically reflect upon the relationships between their stories and scripture. And finally it enables "synthesizing" adults to incorporate new, symbolic understandings of their lives. Certainly, for example, the exploration of some of Paul's later writings with their ambiguities and paradoxes will empower a conjunctive understanding while it may only confuse a conventional thinker. So the teacher needs to have an understanding of the patterns of thinking of the adult group as well as the different understandings within the body of scriptural writings.

Classes or discussions around spirituality provide another fruitful area for adult faith growth. Once again we find a renewed interest in spirituality among Roman Catholics and an enthusiasm for forms of spirituality from Protestants whose traditions have not previously articulated a formal spirituality. The causes for such renewal range from the increasingly depersonalized, technological and bureaucratic nature of contemporary society to the decline of popular forms of piety after the Second Vatican Council and the emphasis upon social action for churches without a corresponding development of the roots of such action in the life of the Spirit. In the move to the more verbal, cognitive dimensions of the faith life which followed the Council we are only now beginning to develop more adequate forms of spiritual renewal. The demise of conventional formulas and practices demands more individual responsibility along with greater understanding of oneself and recent theological developments.

In the case of spirituality, classes and discussions must be combined with practice in prayer and worship, both elements of adult education. For the person in transition from the conventional to a more owned, individuative faithing mode, the minister or educator might suggest some type of spiritual direction and readings in spirituality which examine styles of prayer and exercises in line with needs for strengthening personal identity, initiating relationships and assuming responsibilities for a larger world. For the individual moving toward a more conjunctive mode of faithing, prayer and meditation allow room for paradox and ambiguity as the person incorporates the dark dimensions of self and the world into a more complex worldview. The mystery of Jesus' words, ''Whoever loses his life for my sake shall find it,'' or of Paul's phrase, ''I live, now not I, but Christ lives in me,'' takes on new meaning as the spiritual path demands a letting go of set ideas and control. The pattern here is that of the paschal event, the death and resurrection in people's lives, dying to self, letting go so that transformation can take place.

When joined with an understanding of the particular needs of individuals and groups, the faith development scheme can provide new understandings of the areas of scripture, symbols and spirituality which hopefully will result in programs promoting faith growth. Likewise, the faith development model provides some clues to programmatic developments around the factor of perspective-taking. As with adolescents and younger adults, the most important dimensions of perspective-taking are the articulation of one's own understanding of the world and the self, listening with care to the views of others, being exposed to differing world views and religious traditions and enlarging one's commitments to increasing sectors of the global family.

Certainly one of the most productive, initial undertakings here is the development of small groups who share faith stories. These groups might well assemble around particular needs, such as divorce, single parenthood, sexual assault and so forth. For adults, these small groups serve as communities within the larger, more remote church and society. As such, they can become the challengers to conventional faithing, the critical reflectors to individuative faithing and the supportive community to the conjunctive faithers whose actions for justice or whose theological explorations and spiritual journeys may not always be understood by the other members of the community. However, very few adults can afford the time for such a commitment to a continuous group, and thus other forms need to be developed also, from retreats and conferences to personal visits.

Another area of perspective-taking basic to an adult education program involves a continually developing theological updating. Hopefully this theological discussion can be structured around the involvement of all the participants in reading and articulating their own understandings, with only an occasional need for the expert's lecture. In this way the learning environment enables those adults to take responsibility for their own learning. Admittedly, this environment reflects at least a move toward an individuative mode of faithing. Nevertheless it can easily become comfortable to adults who prefer lectures and listening.

For the person of conventional faith, the theological ferment of the day is heady stuff and perhaps threatening; good guidance and leadership is required here. For the individuative faither, theological updating provides a necessary and important intellectual foundation for the developing world view and sense of personal responsibility for thought and action characteristic of stage four. Perhaps that will emerge in dogmatic and ideological form, maybe in a belligerent manner. Yet such "posturing" reveals the articulation and ownership for new ideas which allow the intellectual grounding of faith to develop.

And finally for the synthesizers in the faith community, theological developments will prove most beneficial when they promote the dimensions of mystery, paradox and depth which are at the heart of the Christian "mysteries" of trinity, incarnation, sin, redemption/liberation, creation, and resurrection. Most often for these people theological exploration allows them the opportunity to discover other ways to express their understandings and provides them with "dialogue partners" in the authors or speakers presented. At the same time, in the small group these adults become the interpreters of the tradition for others in both what they say and how they live.

Finally adults must be invited to share in the many dimensions of church life. While such participation is important in the development of a sense of community, involvement can enhance the adult's sense of worth and value while acknowledging the "giftedness" of these mature adults. As distinct from particular jobs and roles they might have in society, a recognition of the talents and gifts they have developed during their lifetime reflects the actual needs of the Christian community for contributions from its members. Too often in the past this has amounted to a policy of "free labor" from the laypeople or low wages from priests, brothers, sisters and ministers who are employed regardless of their own gifts in order to perpetuate the particular needs of the institution. A "theology of gifted participation" seeks to enhance the gifts of its members in their ministry to one another while making sure the needs of the people in the church, civic, and global communities are met.

A further dimension of such participation would be involvement in service activities promoted through the church, on the job or in public service. Such service will take on different expressions according to the level of faith growth. Thus a one-to-one direct service program might be appropriate for the conventional faither with some theological reflection in discussion groups to begin probing the questions of structural injustice. For the individuative and synthesizing faither social analysis and movements for change consistent with a gospel vision of peace and justice are more appropriate.

This differentiation may help in planning for classes and discussions centering around the church's teachings on justice and peace. For people whose faith follows conventional patterns, topics like "social justice" are not attractive in themselves because the causal and structural analysis implied in such a phrase are not well understood. In addition, most Christians have not understood that their faith demands more of them than occasional outpourings of charity at given times of the year. Thus while a topic might still cover social justice, the language of "neighbor to neighbor" or "helping those in need" might be much more attractive. Here too a scriptural discussion on the demands of the gospel as seen in the life of Jesus can provide people with new imaginings of Christian faith in action as they re-examine Jesus' encounters with those people in his day who represent oppressive structures. In this respect Christians will be called to greater involvement on behalf of justice precisely inasmuch as they envision Jesus involved in such activity.[16]

A final dimension of participation concerns the ways in which service to others involves the "generative" dimension of development which Erikson mentions. At each stage of faith growth, this dimension will be incorporated in different forms. For the conventional faither, service allows that person to take some responsibility for the welfare of others, to take the perspective of others and so enlarge his or her own. The individuative faither finds in service a contribution to the improvement of conditions for others and a way to express the ideals of strongly held beliefs. For the conjunctive mode of faithing, service as an expression of generativity incorporates both of the previous aspects and adds the dimension of model, mentor or sponsor for the growth and development of others. Each of these three modes utilizes service as generativity but with a different intentionality and faith perspective. Yet every mode is an embodiment of the gospel call to serve others.

Scripture, theology, spirituality, communities of faith sharing and service—five components for an adult religious education program which can support, challenge and foster faith growth in adults. We have looked at those components in terms of the ways in which they can express factors of faith development theory such as images and symbols, perspective-taking and participation. While the diversity of needs, interests and even developmental understandings makes any religious education program for adults difficult to carry out, the faith development scheme can provide useful ways to evaluate existing programs and develop programs more suited to particular peoples. But beyond programs, the use of faith development theory demands a religious educator not only sensitive to the resting places of people in their faith journeys but also willing to explore her or his own growth in faith and to continually challenge the institutional church to promote the faith of its "faith-filled" people through its policies and practices as well as its theology and spirituality.

Intergenerational Education

Throughout this chapter we have examined the different settings of religious education as they are found in most churches, Roman Catholic and Protestant. Each age group is treated in isolation from others—children, adolescents, young adults, maturing adults and senior adults whose concerns we will take up in a later chapter. While these divisions express a realistic and legitimate care for the particular needs and interests of each time of life, important elements are missed in this approach, especially the sense in which faith is a lifelong process and takes place within the broader church and society. As a counter to these divisions, some church groups are experimenting with lifelong, cross-generational or intergenerational education. Faith development theory itself provides a basis for such an approach since its roots lie in the understanding that prior faith perspectives are transformed through exposure to later, more developed faith patterns. Certainly the family context in which faith is first nurtured is intergenerational, and many of the aspects of faith growth we have talked about utilize the notion that older students, for example, are models to younger students.

While it requires a different orientation in planning, educational philosophy, resources and professional expertise, the development of models of intergenerational religious education promises to raise important issues. For one, such models can incorporate the socialization aspect of religious education essential in understanding the dynamics of the holistic growth of faith. For another, adult religious learning would become the central focus of Christian religious education, and the education of children and adolescents would be viewed as preparatory, developmental stages to adult faithing.

In addition, the adult learners, equipped with some understanding of faith development patterns, would be able to listen more attentively to the concerns and questions of children, adolescents and young adults without relegating those concerns to "passing phases." Adults would grow from the challenges of responding to seemingly simple but disarming questions of children, while children, adolescents and young adults could visualize the ways in which faith continually grows by being party to the concerns and questions of adult faithers. The nine year old who asks why she should go to church services since she doesn't understand them raises more than a question of parental authority.

Finally, adults within the church could take greater responsibility for the religious education of all concerned as they became both teachers and learners. Not only would this allow the trained religious educator to utilize his or her own time and resources more productively, but such an approach would build community around themes of common scripture readings with multiple understandings, common worship with a variety of developmental expressions, a formative spirituality even in the early years and programs of service which involve multiple levels of sponsorship and modeling. This approach would not eliminate the need for more age-related divisions around particular needs, times of worship and prayer, theological understandings, community events and so forth. But it would shift the focus from those factors which separate the community to those which unite all age groups, namely the sharing of faith stories in light of the gospel story.

Summary

Throughout this chapter we have been concerned with the ways in which faith development theory relates to the concerns and problems of religious education for adults. Certainly other approaches to religious education provide equally adequate ways to plan and implement a sound religious education program. However, faith development theory does offer some formal criteria by which any faith perspective or program can be critically evaluated, renewed and revised and can provide a useful tool to assist professional educators and ministers in their programs, even in their own lives and understandings.

While it may seem from the past two chapters that the tasks of the religious educator are overwhelming, it is encouraging to note that as lay people assume greater responsibilities in the church, these adults look upon themselves as educators to one another and to the larger membership of the church and their fellow citizens in society. In this way religious educators can do the best they can and can truly entrust their concerns to the graced giftedness of others in the community.

5. FAMILY AND PARISH: FAITH NURTURERS

The Christian family constitutes a specific revelation and realization of ecclesial communion, and for this reason too it can and should be called "the domestic church."[1]

> John Paul II, "On the Family"

The significance of the Church community will depend on its ability to relate to the broader society and the new institutions and circles within which people live their lives.[2]

> Philip Murnion, "The Parish as Source of Community and Identity"

The minister must be able both to hear the religious dimensions of the human story when it is articulated in secular language and to handle explicitly theological questions. . . . He should be able to relate the Christian story to the concrete, everyday activity of the parish.[3]

> John Shea, "The Religious Mission of the Parish"

The previous chapters focused upon the centrality of religious education as a major form of ministry in the Christian churches. In this chapter we look at two equally important areas of ministry in church life, the family and the parish. Certainly the family forms the primary environment in which the dynamics of faith are shaped, while the parish remains the place where the people of God experience church and its formative influence in their daily lives. By looking at the two areas together, we are emphasizing their interrelationship as well as their central importance in the renewal of the church and the faith lives of Christian peoples. As recent church documents and episcopal statements have noted, the basic emphasis upon evangelization in the world is carried out through the renewal of the local parish and the development of family life ministry.[4]

In the past the family has served as the basis for parish life, providing children for education, adolescents and young adults for vocations, and adults, mainly women, for volunteer work under the watchful eye of the pastor. In this sense the family has served as "minister" to the parish. From another perspective, sociologists have pointed to the parish as complementing the absence of family life for people such as the widowed, childless couples, single parents and others for whom the parish serves as surrogate family.[5] While that important function of church as comforter cannot be overlooked, we question whether in its role as surrogate family the parish ministers in order to help people grow in their faithing roles in the world or in order to keep itself alive. An additional concern focuses upon the very activities which seem to reveal the vitality of parish life. Do such activities as educational programs, parish outreach, teen forums, senior citizen evenings and so forth *substitute* for the family and so take family members away from one another? Or is there a way in which parts of parish life can be restructured around the support and continuity of the family, from religious education efforts to community service?[6] While the responses to these concerns are beyond the scope of our discussion, these issues impinge upon our analysis of faith development and parish and family ministry.

Another relationship between family and parish revolves around the language with which the church describes itself and its members—the language of the family. Thus the use of words such as "father," "sister," "brother," "mother" to describe church personnel and the constant reference to church as family reinforce a symbolic relationship between family and parish. In more recent years, the linguistic references have reversed, and the family has been referred to as "the domestic church." While these analogies have created unreal expectations of both family and church life and have contributed to authoritarian modes of governing in both areas, perhaps we could argue that changes in our understandings of the family *and* the church have led to greater equality and sensitivity to the human person in both of these settings.

A final relationship between family and parish exists in the growing need for community roots in our highly mobile, technological society. As Most Rev. Howard J. Hubbard, Bishop of Albany, noted at the National Pastoral Planning Conference, March 10, 1983, "Americans today are searching for a sense of community. Theoretically the parish is the place where this sense of community ought to be found; but as we all know from sad experience, many parishes . . . are not the caring communities they ought to be."[7] Inasmuch as the family too is deeply involved in the foundational formation of the Christian faith, family joins with parish in the development of a sense of community life.

The Family and Ministry ─────────────

On May 3, 1978, the National Conference of Catholic Bishops voted to approve a holistic approach to the life of the Christian family. The response of the bishops and the United States Catholic Conference is known as "The Plan of Pastoral Action for Family Ministry." In addition, the bishops designated the 1980's as the "decade of the family." On December 15, 1981, Pope John Paul II took up the theme of the family when he indicated that "the family has a mission to become more and more what it is, that is to say, a community of life and love in an effort that will find fulfillment . . . in the kingdom of God."[8]

The bishops' plan of action and the Pope's document reflect an increasing awareness that the family, certainly in the United States as well as around the world, faces great problems today. Yet their concerns also reveal a new theological understanding of the central place of family in relation to the mission and role of the church. Before we can discuss the relationship of faith development to family ministry, we must explore both of these dimensions affecting family life.

Social Setting

To many people the family appears threatened, indeed overwhelmed, by changes and forces over which it has no control. Divorce, drug abuse, child abuse, abortion, child pornography, single-parenting, financial instability, latch-key children—everywhere the family seems caught in a vortex of social wreckage. And certainly the statistics are grim. Between 1970 and 1982, the number of single-parent families headed by unmarried women rose by thirty-six percent. The divorce rate doubled between 1965 and 1985, and the average size of the American household has dwindled in size.[9]

The White House Conferences on Family, conducted from 1979 to 1980, reveal that families themselves say that their situations have deteriorated over the past fifteen years. Fully forty-five percent checked "worse" while only thirty-seven percent said "better" and twelve percent stated "the same" when asked about their family prospects. The Gallup survey which accompanied the final Conference report indicated that respondents felt that alcohol abuse, drug abuse and a decline of religious and moral values were the three factors most harmful to family life.[10]

All these considerations certainly lead to a firm conviction that the church in these times must spend time and money in ministering *to* these hurting families. But what must also be acknowledged is that in general family life is still strong and that before church professionals institute yet another ministry they must also assess the changing meaning of family itself. If we limit our understanding of family to mean a nuclear family of both parents present with family intact, then any deviation from that norm will indicate a "deterioration" of family life, a broken family and so forth. And family ministry will then mean efforts by the churches to restore "balance," heal the break and in other ways restore the family to the imagined order of an earlier time. Thus depending upon the definition of "broken family," the phrase could become a self-fulfilling prophecy if, for example, churches, schools and professionals treat the single-parent family as "broken" without recognizing the patterns of wholeness that exist in such a situation.

In addition to our perceptions of the role of the family in American society, our views of the family and family ministry in relation to the church will also shape the responses of family ministry. Keeping in mind the emerging sense of renewal and concern for family life in the church and society, we can discuss "family ministry" in terms of three important dimensions: (1) the continuing ministry of the parish and church to families in need, (2) a new understanding of the ways in which family members can be empowered and trained to minister to one another, and (3) the ministry of families to neighbors and the larger human family.

Underlying these dimensions is a broad view of family as nuclear *and* extended, headed by one parent or both parents, with children present or without. Correspondingly, the theological expression of family is that of people called through baptism to ministry in general but channeled through their unique constellation as family into a covenant of loving, challenging and inviting relationships open to others in time, energy and service. Just as each person uniquely expresses the reality of God in his or her own giftedness, so each unique form the family takes manifests a gifted set of qualities expressive of God's love. The family is no longer seen as the source of parish volunteers and the basis of ministry to the parish, but as an environment of God's activity which must be supported by the parish and the church as part of the church's mission in extending God's rule into the world.

Certainly there are blocks to these manifestations of ministry within the family and to ministry by families. The older clerical model is still practiced in many parishes; only "Father" knows best. In addition, Dolores Curran names obstacles such as a failure of pastoral vision, a failure of the church to transmit a sense of shared ministry and a failure to share the vision of the parish (and, I would add, of the family) as a faith community.[11] In addition an undue emphasis upon the parish religious education program and objective content about Christianity has left most parents with great feelings of inadequacy about nurturing the faith life of their children. In spite of these formidable barriers to family ministry new directions are emerging, and we will now turn to the relationship between those promising directions and faith development.

Family as Faith Community

The family as the domestic church "has within itself the essential aspects of church and can be an authentic ecclesial experience for family members." Among those essential aspects are (1) the ways in which family love and care for one another express the very presence of Jesus, (2) the experience of sacramental community whether in baptism, Eucharist and reconciliation which can take place in the family environment or through the God-revealing dimensions of family joys and celebrations, sorrows and conflicts, and (3) the care and service which the family can give to neighbors and the community.[12]

That theological dimension of family builds upon the sociological and psychological patterns of enculturation into society which the family provides. From the earliest moments of birthing, throughout childhood, adolescence and into young adulthood, the constancy, affection, values, attitudes and beliefs of parents provide the primal context in which children's interpretations of their experiences are shaped. While there are negative as well as positive types of family environments, the family can provide a Christian faith understanding to daily experiences which enables the Christian family to have the most unique opportunity of catechesis of any subsequent school, church or "religious education" experience. Likewise children and adolescents support and challenge the faith life of their parents in myriad ways, from asking those unanswerable questions of "Why did God make the grass green?" to their exposure of our adult hypocrisy in not acting out in our lives what we tell our children to do. Thus if the family setting involves "announcing the good news to those within the immediate family circle first of all,"[13] then the living, daily activity of family life becomes a constitutive dimension of the experienced faith of young and old alike.

The Dimensions of Faith Development

In this section we will focus upon the symbolic dimensions of faithing in family life through the people, language, routines, rituals, play life and even the places and spaces of family living. Thus while parents provide the initial atmosphere of trust so basic to children's further development, other family members add important aspects to the nurture of children's faith life. Grandparents, aunts, uncles and cousins enlarge the bases of family celebrations. They also bring a continuity with a living family tradition and provide children, especially in the elementary school years, with "others" who might listen to their problems and concerns where the children think their parents would not. "Indulgent" grandparents release children from the routine burdens of the everyday for "trips" of imagination and fancy. They provide children with images and understandings of the past which challenge "the way things are done nowadays." And through sharing their memories of times and places past, the grandparents recall the ways in which they were also nurtured, challenged or even hurt. In this way the children provide these older adults with the opportunity to reflect on their faith and even to examine parts of the past too painful to face in earlier years.

Language becomes an important means of shaping faith life. By the intonation of words and through the names ascribed to objects and relationships, parents and other family members connote the affective dimensions of the worlds which the child encounters. For example, for the child passing through stage two faithing, initial attitudes of prejudice can find legitimation or can be challenged through more inclusive language. On a positive note, naming and discussing the world of the mysterious in ways which the child can understand shape the child's apprehension of mystery through the symbolic power of the words used. God as provider-creator, Jesus as friend-brother, Spirit as comforter-enabler, church as people of God, sin as broken relationship, good, bad—all these and other foundational words uncover the religious dimension of reality and establish the basis for adolescents and adults to interpret their ordinary experiences as religious and open to Mystery.

Not only through words but also through the careful use of other symbolic elements the family lays the basis for a richer faithing pattern. Earth, fire, water, bread, meal, cross, mountains, seas, body, birth, death, forgiveness—all become avenues for the "sight" and "sound" of God's creativity when filtered to the child through the family. In revealing this sacramentality of God's presence, parents open their children to the children's own participation in the divine.

While grandparents may allow children an occasional escape from the crushing weights of ordinary living, parents must provide the routines which form the very basis of constancy, fidelity and trust essential to faith growth. In these routines and rituals of family life, children find the security necessary for ventures and adventures as well as the limits to what they might attempt in their imaginative forays into the unknown. If a parent is not immediately available, the "routine" provides comfort for the moment.

Among the various rituals which families develop, reading times and celebrations deserve special mention. Reading to and with children not only provides a special time of sharing when parents and children "hold" one another close through the imagined world of the book, but even more importantly the reading time stimulates the imaginative capacity of children so important in the faith developmental pattern of adult faithing. And celebrations become the active way for family members to share common experiences, joys and healings. Special commemorations provide the times for, in theologian Bernard Cooke's words, "the realization that one's self, one's life, is a good and precious thing given by a loving God."[14]

In games and family play, the faith life is nurtured in myriad ways. From the young child who "names" and manipulates relationships in the form of dolls, tinker toys or action figures to the adolescent who works in crafts or sports, playing becomes the arena for imaginative participation in other realities and the reality of others, for perspective taking and cooperative endeavors, for the development of a sense of self through participation. Certainly the creativity of children making their own toys and of all family members developing their own forms of recreation and sports provides more adequate opportunities for the kind of imaginative stimulation and participation important to the faith development scheme than the over-abundance of manufactured toys and "organized" sports found today.

The invocation of "Let's pretend" for children or "Charades" for adults calls us into an arena of exploration in which we can suspend cares and expectations of the everyday and enter into a broader community. Children's games involve adults in a world perhaps too long forgotten and on occasion allow parents to share rich moments of their own childhood with children and even grandparents. At the same time parents and grandparents can challenge the children by asking why the game is played in such and such a way, what other possibilities exist for developing the game and so provoke a push for more comprehensive understandings. In short, family members who play together not only relate to one another in supportive and challenging ways but also evoke imaginative fantasies and recall evocative memories that nurture the faith life of all.

In day-dreaming we also encounter the world of the imaginative possibilities not realized in the everyday. As parents we often tend to look upon day-dreaming as idle time, and when we hear the reply "Nothing" to our question "What are you doing?" we all too quickly round up some task or project for the grumbling child or adolescent. But day-dreaming is as rich a resource of imaginative capabilities as reading, playing and celebrating, and although not to be encouraged when moments of concentration and attention are needed, day-dreaming can be a time of conscious contact with symbols and meaning stored away during "work" times. Explicit prayer together serves as another enrichment opportunity for family members to minister to one another. Whether around the dinner table to share the concerns of the day, through morning greeting or in weekly prayer times, the modeling of parents who pray reveals chances for expressing gratitude, asking forgiveness, fostering reconciliation and naming family experiences in the context of the transcendent, religious environment. Prayer serves as the most fundamental way that the family as a unit can create a receptivity to God's presence in their lives.

And that brings us to a final consideration in the area of the symbolic and imaginative, namely time, spaces and places. Are there times of quiet in family life, time for prayer, daydreaming, musing, for talking together, probably around the dinner table, and for play *at the time when the players* (usually the children) *are ready?* As for places and spaces, are there places where each family member can find an occasional refuge? The "favorite chair," "quiet nook," and "special window" become symbols for that environment. All the various physical factors become important components of the constellation of family living around respect for one another, integration of private and community moments of the family, possibilities for perspective-taking and a sense of participation in family life.

Certainly the family provides the basis for multiple occasions of perspective-taking. From the earliest age on children are invited and encouraged to take the perspective of their parents and other parental figures. These important patterns become *stimulators* of moral and faith growth when parents take the time and patience to explain their behavior, attitudes and values to their children and when they encourage the children to express their own views and provide reasons for their own behavior in an open, non-judgmental fashion. Even when punishing errant behavior, parents have the grand opportunity to challenge children and enlarge their perspective by detailing consequences, providing alternatives and meting out "just" punishments which match the offense. Likewise parents also have a responsibility to their children and to themselves to explain the reasons for their own acts and thoughts.

Another dimension of perspective-taking involves family members in forms of story telling, the sharing of life experiences of the past and present. Although the child may tire of the constant phrases "When I was a kid . . . " and "Back in my day . . . " these evoked memories also provide children with a sense of the family story. The incidents provide a context from which the children can discern *whose* they are. For many parents hearing *their* parents recall what they were like as children not only provides the current generation some comic relief and perspective on their own parenting but also binds the two parental generations in continuing ways.

But if children listen to parents and grandparents recall the "good old days," story telling also means that the children get the opportunities to share their anecdotes of the day. "Guess what happened at school today?" and "Do you know what I saw today?" may become stock clues to a mounting avalanche of words, but the sharing lets the child feel valued and trusted while encouraging the child to give meaning to his or her experience in the telling.

For many families in today's society these opportunities seem to converge around the meals taken together. As each member has the chance to share his or her day, questions arise, explanations emerge, concerns burst forth which allow parents to take children's perspectives as much as the children understand the parents' views. But faith growth would require that family members try to explain viewpoints different than their own and that parents talk about the problems of the larger society and the global community. In turn children, and especially adolescents, need opportunities to voice their ideas in a supportive and even challenging atmosphere. From his theory of moral development, Lawrence Kohlberg sees these family opportunities as key to moral growth: "With regard to the family, the disposition of parents to allow or encourage dialogue on value issues is one of the clearest determinants of moral stage advance in children."[15] Certainly some knowledge of the faith development scheme can assist parents and others ministering to children to understand the needs and patterns of faith growth for particular ages.

Finally the family can foster broader perspective-taking through various forms of "service," whether visiting a sick neighbor, contacting others through community service projects or working for volunteer organizations which serve the poor and deprived. The family can utilize collections for the poor and needy as a way of enlarging understandings of poverty, hunger and so forth. Pictures of hunger situations or political prisoners and calendars with listings of historical events and people associated with peace and justice issues serve as reminders of heroic people and difficult times in the past years. In addition, the family's service activities provide the occasion to address not only the justice issues of the larger society but justice within the family as well. For children have a sharp sense of justice done to them by those upon whom they are dependent and can hardly develop the capacity to empathize with those treated unjustly unless they themselves experience just treatment in their own lives.

Now we come to our final component of faith growth in family life, a sense of participation. Participation in the family is played out in the growing relationship between assuming greater responsibilities and duties on the one hand and giving oneself to others, here family members, on the other. "Family responsibility" should mean not just the drudgery tasks of taking out the garbage and doing the dishes but also purposeful work in which children and adolescents perceive a sense of their own worth and develop their unique gifts. This may involve meal preparation or rotating the leadership of the family meeting. And while there is certainly a real concern about participating equally, parents must attend to *unique* participation. Negatively this means not comparing children or spouses to others who carry out the same tasks. Positively, parents must imaginatively call for the the unique aspects of each child through the child's participation in discussions and activities.

As the children grow older, parents can encourage their children's active participation in the community around them through sports, community organizations, a job. These outside activities are an important way for the child to discover which particular gifts and skills he or she has. While the hectic pace of transporting kids to practices, games, lessons, jobs and service may be a bit much, these opportunities provide the children with evaluations from other adults and peers which are essential in arriving at a sense of self-worth, of identity and purpose and of ministry to the larger world.

The Family Minister

Thus far we have looked at family ministry from the perspective of family members ministering to one another. At this point we can turn to the role of the family minister. In a new and growing area of ministry, the family minister continues many "services" of the parish to families but also has the chance to provide new understandings of the role of families in their own ministry. In this sense, the first requirement of anyone in family ministry would be that the minister know his or her own faith history as a family member. Such a "meditation" on the part of the minister may call for some reconciliation and healing with family members before the minister can effectively help other families in their own discernment.

Beyond this awareness of personal history, the family minister serves as liason with the local parish. In a basic sense, then, the family minister provides the services or supports which families have always needed, especially in moments of crisis. A part of this role involves the parish as "family surrogate" to the childless, the widowed, the divorced, the single and the aged. But beyond this continuing role, the new excitement around family ministry comes from a more expansive sense of family ministry as an opportunity to empower families to minister to themselves and to help family members envision their own giftedness for the service of the community.

The family minister can provide opportunities for families coming together to listen to their own needs, can furnish the resources or lead people to the resources they need and can serve as the channel between church as family and church as parish. Precisely in this role, the family minister may well need to challenge the parish's traditional approaches to the development of the faith community. Thus in taking seriously the role of the family as catechist, the family minister may see the necessity to support the family as formal teacher of the faith rather than the school. Or if the family is a worshiping community, elements of the eucharistic celebration may well be incorporated into family life rather than just parish Sunday liturgy.

However, one last reflection challenges the place of family ministry in the life of the church. There is a tension between family values and gospel values with their call to a larger community of all peoples. When this tension has not been recognized, as so often in the past, "there is a real danger of domesticating religious values—or removing religious concerns from the broader community and restricting them to family concerns."[16] Keeping this tension in mind, the minister to families can constantly challenge families to view themselves in relation to the larger human family which is the proper mission of the church in the world.

In addition to understanding the faith development scheme as it applies to individuals, the family minister can approach the family unit as a whole environment of faith. Thus the description of family at a "modal" stage three faith level may well explain the family's tendency to focus upon its own concerns to the exclusion or minimalization of issues in the larger world as Elias noted above. In this family faith stance, "greater emphasis is placed upon sincerity and genuine feeling in one's faith commitments than upon intellectual or critical clarity about the contents, meanings, or warrants for them." Such a faith position relies upon a strong sense of parental and conventional authority and views the "neighbor" primarily in terms of those whom we meet in face to face encounters. "The modal level, found in a majority of Christian families," concludes Fowler, "can be best characterized in terms of the Synthetic-Conventional stage of faith development."[17]

However, if an adult Christian faith calls for acceptance of critical reflection and individuated commitment, then the task of the family minister in faith developmental terms may be to support a modal family movement to a stage four faithing. Fowler describes those families thus:

> Where parents and other nurturing adults have struggled to critical and self-reflective decisions about their own faith commitments, they are likely to encourage their children to discuss, question, clarify and evaluate with regard to beliefs and values from an early age.[18]

Other components of such a perspective on the part of parents include an equalitarian approach to authority, the encouragement of authenticity and clarity in the children's commitments and an extension of love to include social justice. Then utilizing the theory even further, Fowler sees the emergence of a stage five modal level of parents as helpful in "sponsoring" their adolescent teenagers through that difficult period of teen faithing.[19]

Utilizing a faith development approach, the family minister would encourage the development of a rich symbolic and imaginative life within families. This could involve approaches as various as family liturgies, scripture lessons, prayer times or even family plays. The minister could develop perspective-taking by challenging family members to read about social issues, other countries, other religions and by encouraging the family in service endeavors. He or she could introduce the concept of the family meeting and encourage parents to spend time daily listening to the concerns of their children and of one another. And certainly the minister, while ministering to the particular needs families might have, can show families how they might encourage a stronger sense of participation.

Finally while the faith development approach has shown some complementary enhancements to the work of family ministry, the real growth of such a ministry depends upon a larger context of developments within the church and society. The discussion of the role of a family minister within a parish and of the enablement of families to minister to themselves and to the larger society brings us to an examination of the parish as the context within which the Christian family gains its sense of ministry and as the source of those professionals and volunteers who engage in ministry to, for and with families today.

Parish and Ministry

If the family has been called "the domestic church" in recent understandings, the parish has become the center for the larger systems of support for families and other members of the Christian community. In some areas of the country parishes undoubtedly still retain images of the closed, hierarchically structured Catholic ghetto where priests minister for the "salvation" of the souls of the faithful. But whether such parishes can actually be found or are lingering fantasies from the days of "Going My Way," today's parish is much more than a collection of families under priestly guidance. Whether rural, suburban, inner-city or "floating," the parish has become a place of renewal not only for families but for groups as diverse as youth, young adults, seniors, singles, divorced, and the poor and most recently a sanctuary for political refugees from Central American dictatorships. In terms of its internal life and external relationships with the larger society, the local parish has shed its narrow focus upon the salvation of its own members' souls, the neighborhood's "barque of Peter" floating in a sea of cultural hostility, to become a sign to the larger society, although all too imperfect at times, of God's saving presence in a troubled world.

The very meaning of the word "parish" may reveal this new understanding of parish as "sign" of God's presence. Originally "parish" meant "sojourn," and that sense of parish has led William Bausch to view the parish as the place where the "travelers" come together to tell their stories.[20] More precisely, says theologian John Shea, "The religious mission of the parish might be characterized as providing the resources and structures for the ongoing interrelating of personal and communal stories with the larger Christian story, for the purposes of redemption."[21] In examining parishes from these aspects of "sign" and "place for sojourning story-tellers" the faith development approach becomes especially helpful in providing criteria to discern the particular meaning of the sign and to interpret the faithing dimension of personal, cultural and Christian stories.

Social Setting

In many ways the current structures and new understandings of parish stem from complex changes in society and in the church's response to the world around it. In the past the church, as one of the stable institutions in society, provided an anchor for individual and cultural identity. Not only did the church through the parish provide theological meaning and clear regulation to Christian living, but through its feast days, special observances such as meatless Fridays, signs such as medals, sacramental life, social services, special language and even names the parish gave everyday life a sacred place and provided an intimate, if somewhat narrow, community. But in recent years the parish has been beset by the same "breakup" of "community" identity as has the family through divorce or the nation through Vietnam, Watergate and other faith-breaching issues. Such factors as greater economic and geographic mobility, broad social movements such as the women's movement, more services offered by public agencies, the decline of authority and tradition in the formation of values and greater demand for participation in decision-making all make church people feel "less dependent on Church services and less loyal to the communities of the past."[22]

Practically this has meant a drastic decline in membership and participation from the highs of the 1950's and early 1960's. Parish schools have been closed and plants consolidated. In some areas of the country, parishes are without priests, while in others, priests are stretched thin in carrying out ordinary parish duties, let alone taking time for the reading and reflection necessary for good ministry.

Yet these very challenges have created a new understanding of parish life and promising opportunities for ministry within the parish. In the first place a Catholic revival has been emerging slowly but at times dramatically since the Second Vatican Council. The cursillo movement, the early liturgical reforms, Bible study groups, marriage encounters, prayer and retreat groups and most recently the growing thrust toward peace and social justice have all given new life to what seemed an inert church.

As these movements developed, clergy declined and new leadership emerged. Religious women and men along with lay people took prominent parts in the new revivals and reforms, especially in the parish. In many rural areas, brothers, sisters and lay people carry out "pastorly" duties, recognized in all but official title as "pastors" of the local church. In turn, training programs for clergy, religious and lay people have sprung up rapidly around the country, first at the university level, then in the form of diocesan training centers. At the parish itself, experiments with parish councils, the parish ministry "team" and broad community participation in parish life continue. In sum, at the 18,600 or so parishes around the country, parish life seems more vital and more concerned with the issues of the larger society than ever before.

At least in the outlines of a broad sketch, the parish has gone through the same "modal" transitions in faith development terms as Fowler described in speaking of the family. Particular parishes will still exhibit the hierarchical patterns of authority, the passivity and lack of participation of lay people, the smothered symbolism of liturgies, the defensiveness of protecting "us the faithful" against "their" attacks upon the true faith and other characteristics of stage three faithing. But in general the changes we have just described have led to the kind of communal appropriations, personal responsibility for faith life, understandings of social justice, development of symbols, theological world-view and sense of participation characteristic of stage four faithing. In this way the faith development scheme can become a criterion for charting the faith life of the parish in its renewal.

Ministry in the Parish

The description of a "modal shift" in parish life has already provided some initial clues to a discussion of parish ministry in particular. For the stage four characteristics just mentioned cover the new sense of ministry which has emerged in recent years. The immediate needs of the church determine some forms of ministry, but in general ministry today arises from the interaction between the needs of the parish and the gifts of its members. While we unnecessarily restrict such an understanding to those "new" ministries formally recognized by the church such as deacon, eucharistic ministers and so forth, an additional aspect of parish ministry includes those whom the people themselves acknowledge as ministering to parish needs and performing community services.

In exploring this new understanding of ministry as the development of a parish community enabled by officially designated ministers, the parish "staff," to minister to one another, we can divide our discussion according to the faith growth of the staff and the faith development of the parish which the staff assists. And once again, the scheme of symbols and imagination, perspective-taking and sense of participation can provide the framework for our approach.

The Staff

Whatever form the staff takes in ministering to the parish, it becomes a community unto itself; and ultimately this core staff sets the tone for the quality of ministry in the parish and serves as a model of ministry to the parish in terms of its own inner life. Ideally every staff member would have received some form of training which integrates the professional approach required for the tasks of community building with personal skills, vision and empowerment of the Christian life. Scripture study and prayer must nurture the staff members, but the occasions and process of sharing together can be structured to develop faithing modes reflecting stage four and five understandings of the gospel message and of forms of prayer life. Team members can challenge one another to a more personally appropriated vision of scripture and more interior forms of prayer and meditation.

Liturgy, language, play times and celebrations also become means of consolidating and promoting faith growth. Involving all staff members in planning and executing the liturgy and discussing the meaning of the readings chosen enable the symbolic dimensions of the liturgy to support faith growth. The language used not only during liturgy and prayer times but also in meetings and work together can challenge members to become more inclusive in their understandings of, for example, the role of women in the church and the place and problems of minorities and the poor. Finally play times allow staff members to experience dimensions of themselves and one another which break through routine and expectations and reveal untapped gifts and talents.

Into every staff's life there must enter a little conflict. And the ways in which the staff models conflict for the parish rests upon a certain amount of perspective-taking. A stage three model of team may well suppress conflict in the name of "staff unity" and defer all decisions to the central authority figure. Or conflict might be acknowledged but not discussed lest "the faithful be disturbed." With some skill training and a level of genuine participation and responsible acknowledgement of feelings, conflict can promote a more caring environment as well as challenge individual members to broaden their perspectives of themselves and one another.

Regular theological reflection, opportunities for sharing faith stories and retreat experiences can all provide the support and challenge needed to develop a more individuative faith stance for staff members. Certainly staff members must shape together a common vision of the parish through challenging discussion of their various theologies of parish and ministry, their multiple understandings of the church and their analyses of the problems facing the parish.[23] In addition, members can provoke greater perspective-taking by sharing readings, ideas and feelings from classes, lectures and films about other groups, other religious and cultural traditions, histories of persecuted and oppressed peoples.

For truly effective ministry the parish team needs some tools in social analysis, organizational behavior and change patterns. The individual problems of parishioners, such as the aged or the abused child, reveal structural dimensions of which the team must be aware so that a response in ministry can address not only the immediate problem but also the underlying causes.

Yet "effective" ministry may be misleading in this discussion because an "effective" team which delivers services to the church community may not be an open, participative team. Only through the mode of participation are the gifts of the individual team members acknowledged and supported. In every area of life participation becomes a key criterion for assessing the ways in which any group promotes the full worth and dignity of each individual. For a parish team under the leadership, most often, of priest-pastor, then, as model, sign and prime story-tellers of the Christian experience, participation is foundational.

In part, participation means creation of a trusting and supportive environment in which people can challenge one another in the knowledge that each cares for the other. A stage three approach may reflect that care in a paternalistic manner which nevertheless shows genuine concern. In a stage four approach each team member recognizes his or her responsibility for the development of the team community and participates to the full extent of abilities and gifts. This will involve some form of shared responsibility, which should not be equated with equal responsibility and equal authority.

When each member has the necessary information, has had the chance to express his or her views, has listened carefully (with great perspective-taking skill!) to others and feels that he or she has been "entrusted" by the community as "people of God" in this decision, then full participation in all decisions seems to reflect most completely the many gifts needed to build community in ministry. In that case, consensus decision-making practices seem much more appropriate than parliamentarian processes of majority rule. For the consensus model demands that members confront not only the issues but listen with care to the concerns of each member and incorporate the unique insight of all into any final decision.

And finally a stage four team model demands accountability from each team member for actions and ideas. One advantage of a more authoritarian model lies precisely in the ability to hold only the person in authority accountable. In earlier days that was the pastor, the priest, and his accountability ran upward to bishops rather than to the people he served. Now the members of the parish team are accountable to one another not only for what they do, functional accountability, but in what they *are* in ministry, accountability as person. This approach demands a much more critical evaluation of personal behavior and life-style which utilizes gospel values of simplicity, love, justice and peace.

In this discussion of the team, I have not looked at a stage five model since the current understanding of ministry and the requirements of a Christian parish can be well met through a parish team whose modal level is stage four. However, a stage five "team" would express the characteristics of community described in earlier chapters, especially the dimensions of sponsorship, incorporation of weakness and vulnerability, acceptance of limitations, exploration of the mystical and transcendent in prayer and reflection, a more inclusive extension of social justice concerns and a greater tolerance of ambiguity.

The Parish

When we move from the core staff to the life of the parish itself, we embrace multiple levels of involvement, responsibility and accountability which are difficult to describe in terms of any particular model. For these levels involve everyone from the "pastoral staff" and "persons-in-charge" of the parish's programs to the Sunday-only parishioner. The difficult challenge from a faith development perspective is precisely how to form and promote the faith life of such a divergent assembly. Here we are dealing not only with different understandings of the content of the Christian faith but with differing personalities and variations in commitment, age and experiences. The faith development scheme can help provide criteria with which to evaluate the strategies and goals the staff develops and can provide some image of what a parish growing in faith might look like.

In the area of language the core staff must examine how the people of the parish utilize the language of faith to describe God's activity in their daily lives, in the life of the parish and in the larger society. On one level the language in liturgies, parish meetings, socials, educational settings and parish activities describes the parish people's vision of themselves, their inclusive or restrictive outreach to others, their understandings of justice and of ministry, their appreciation of one another, the place of women in ministry and so on. On another level, the language discloses the understanding of God's revelatory activity in the experiences of people's daily lives.

An earlier, modal stage three level of faithing used language through which God acted "supernaturally" in some extra way or in a two-layered approach to human experience. Our language accustomed us to speak of "mystery," to hand over all difficult events to "the will of God," and utilized formal, dogmatic statements which "covered" the human experiences of suffering, evil, injustice.

To promote stage four faithing the core staff can promote faith growth in the very ways in which they assist people to describe their experiences of loss, suffering, joy, happiness and celebration as moments of grace, sin, kingdom, Eucharist, redemption or gospel. This discernment necessarily involves the staff in gathering the people of the parish together on all levels to interpret such experiences, to become a community of interpretation. In this function John Shea describes the most important skill of the parish minister as "the theological ability."

> The minister must be able both to hear the religious dimensions of the human story when it is articulated in secular language and to handle explicitly theological questions. He should be able to surface the religious, theological, and ecclesiological assumptions which dictate people's perceptions and the direction of programs. Finally, he should be able to relate the Christian story to the concrete, everyday activity of the parish. [24]

Liturgy becomes a vehicle for storytelling, for revealing the divine dimension of ordinary experiences or for prophetically calling people to action on behalf of the gospel message. Through its symbolic power liturgy can form a sense of the "new reality" of the Christian vision.

Yet the faith development analysis shows just how carefully the liturgy, especially the Sunday liturgical celebration, must be prepared in order for the people of various ages and faithing experiences to emerge from the liturgy with renewing and even challenging growth. In the first place, such an approach calls for a liturgy of active involvement, not just on the part of ministers, ushers, and musicians, but of as many of the people present as possible. Merely utilizing congregational singing instead of a choir does not necessarily mean greater participation. But vicarious participation can be invited through the symbolic power of the liturgy itself, through mime, dance or most powerfully through story-telling as the Word is read and proclaimed.

Examples of the different ways in which liturgical celebrations can be geared to differing faith levels include a celebration of children's play life at stage one, with body movement and the description of the liturgical materials as "a few of my favorite things." A celebration for older children of stage two faithing may involve narrative, readings or acting out the Bible stories. While at stage three, the lives of real people, modern saints, who exemplify the gospel readings along with a balance of songs and symbols might be meaningful. A liturgy aimed to promote stage four faithing would focus on theological interests, the freedom in Christ, justice themes, responsibility for the earth, all reflected in a variety of scripture readings. And at stage five, the patterns of death and resurrection, explorations of ambiguity and mystery would characterize the particular approach. Perhaps only with children and teens would any particular liturgy be developed for just those audiences. In the larger parish liturgies, the different levels of faithing of the people could be reflected at different times in different ways.

In the area of spirituality, renewal and prayer the parish staff can provide opportunities for retreats, faith-sharing sessions, small scripture groups or classes in which people can articulate their visions of themselves and church, are empowered to recognize their gifts, and are given opportuntities to express those gifts. Again experiences of telling personal stories, sharing faith experiences and challenges, exploring the meaning of scripture in shaping our daily lives and learning new ways of prayer can all promote vigorous faith growth toward more individuative forms if appropriate.

In some way or other, all the symbolic activities we have just discussed, but especially the liturgical celebrations, serve as perspective-taking activities. For they invite us to examine our ordinary experiences with an awareness of God's place in our lives. In addition, the staff can promote faith growth through perspective-taking in its teaching, healing and outreach activities and in the development among people of a range of skills:

> Communication skills are needed—the ability to listen with accuracy and empathy to others; the ability to disclose information about oneself, one's needs, expectations, definitions of community—neither apologetically nor aggressively, but assertively. Skills of conflict resolution, negotiation, problem solving are essential to the effective incorporation of diversity within community. Skills of empathy and imagination enable us to dream beyond the problem that seems to separate us, to a new solution in which we can stand together. And special

skills are necessary for the celebration of both our diversity and our community.[25]

All these skills are essential in challenging people toward a stage four mode of faithing in which they take responsibility for their ideas, actions, feelings and visions.

Inasmuch as the tools of basic communication skills and an atmosphere which promotes personal responsibility are integrated into the various aspects of parish structure, the healing ministry of the parish takes on a new dimension in the transition from a modal stage three level to stage four. The staff must ensure that the personal and social frictions which develop within the parish are aired and confronted so that some form of lasting reconciliation can take place. The open acknowledgement of conflict and differences within a supporting environment provides the only basis for eventual reconcilation within the parish. This will involve the staff in assisting people to take others' perspectives on issues and in developing opportunities, even liturgies, where healing can take place.

Finally, the Christian faith of the parish manifests itself most completely in the service it offers others. Through reach-out programs the staff has another opportunity to promote and challenge the faith growth of parishioners. First, in scripture sessions and discussions of the churches' social teachings parishioners need to explore the dimensions of Christian service seen in the Hebrew scriptures and especially in the life and ministry of Jesus and in the history of the church. Finally, the staff can provide parishioners with opportunities for direct service in the parish itself or can refer people to various social agencies. In whatever form the reach-out ministry takes, however, the staff must take care to emphasize that these efforts are not mere matters of the charity of individuals or the parish but are necessary expressions of the faith of every Christian.

The faith development scheme again provides guidance in approaching the social justice question for the parish. In whatever way it can the staff should devise programs which reflect different levels of faithing in terms of justice programs. Thus children and adults alike might become involved in a form of outreach which reflected an interpersonal understanding of justice by helping the needy directly. Through visits to the sick, elderly, the imprisoned, the poor, and work with food banks, parishioners can provide necessary services. However, a developmental justice program would also challenge parishioners to inquire about the structural causes of the problems they see around them. The important point here is to emphasize the developmental nature of a parish reach-out program so that it includes a progression from concern for the needy of the parish itself to the larger neighborhood and indeed around the world and then provides the kind of social analysis which challenges people to enlarge their understanding of structural evil and social justice.

If parishioners are to see themselves as valued, as responsible for their own faith growth and for the faith life of the community of which they are a part, then their basic understanding of themselves as ministers of the Christian faith must be nourished through forms of ministry to one another. Whether formed into "ministry teams" or dispersed throughout the neighborhoods of society in other ways, parishioners must be provided with opportunities and challenges to take responsibility for their mutual ministering to one another.

Already our discussion of ministry has involved us in some analysis of structures to ensure participation in parish life. Probably most of us once looked to the parish council as the primary vehicle for participation in the parish. Composed of a small group somewhat democratically elected, the parish council was to oversee the development of the parish's vision and mission, always in conjunction with the pastor and staff.

However, from a faith development perspective the parish council was often a concession by a stage three structural mode to people exhibiting stage four or five faithing desires: "The concept of the parish council was an attempt to make way for more effective lay participation without any essential modernization, renewal or reorganization of parish structures."[26]

An adequate stage four structural model demands a form of participation and responsibility which does away with hierarchical structures and provides open communication, the delegation of authority, shared responsibility and accountability among the differing levels of authority. Whatever forms these structures take, the staff cannot ignore the fact that structures "establish norms which hinder or promote differing organization climates . . . and should be evaluated on the basis of the organization climate [they] encourage."[27] From our perspective such structures should be evaluated from the "climate" they create for the faith development of staff and people of the parish.

Hence does the structural model promote the qualities of stage four faithing? Does it acknowledge the value and unique gifts of each member of the staff and each person in the parish? Does it allow each person to hear his or her own story, to share with others personal journeys? Does the structure enable people to minister to one another and thus take responsibility for their own actions? Does it recognize the validity of conflict and deal with the conflict in an open, trustworthy manner, or does it avoid conflict lest the ''faithful be disturbed''? Does it allow for alternative visions to be nurtured and for challenges to be expressed? Only when the parish has developed to some extent the kind of ministry and structural form we have just described will it be able to minister as a parish to the growing needs of the parish and society at large. From concern for family and school, the modern parish's ministry has evolved to include singles, seniors, the divorced, separated, remarried, alienated and countless others who yearn for spiritual nourishment, liberation from oppressive situations and a caring community.

Now that we have examined some of the ways in which faith development theory provides formal criteria and practical guidance for the growth of the parish faith community, we must also recognize that there are limitations to such an approach. The very complexity of a modern parish, the mobility of its population and the pluralism in theological understandings and life-styles make it difficult to talk about the ''faith growth'' of a parish as a whole. Not every parish can attend to every area of parish life we have examined. The proposals we have made in this section, then, should be viewed as helpful tools to be used inasmuch as they challenge some approaches to parish ministry and support others.

Yet ultimately the goals, strategies and efforts of the parish minister must emanate from the Christian vision, commitment and care the minister brings to the parish. In describing the needs of today's parish practitioners, Msgr. Jack Egan underscores well the ultimate purposes of the minister's vocation:

> They need a great and noble vision of Church as a sign of the Lord working in the world through them and demanding that they give of their lives to the building of a new and finer world which will move all of us into the fullness of life in the Lord. . . . They also need skills in human development and systems management which will enable them to build those relationships with others which will, in the present day and in the future, fashion a people who will form communities committed to justice, to love, to growth and freedom, to holiness.[28]

''Building a new and finer world,'' ''the fullness of life in the Lord,'' ''fashion a people who will form communities committed to justice, to love''—these are the visions which nurture the parish minister's goals. In its way the faith development scheme can support those goals and provide ministers with realistic evaluations of their efforts. In this way faith development is not *the* only model possible but complements other approaches ministers can use in living out their ministry more effectively while nurturing their own growth in the Lord.

Summary

In this chapter we have concentrated upon two basic forms of Christian ministry. Indeed within the past eight or nine years the church has devoted great attention to family and parish as, along with evangelization, the keys to church renewal in the United States. These ministries should not be viewed as competing nor discussed in terms of what each can do for the other, but rather should become what David Thomas calls "one basic form of Church interrelating and *respecting* another form: the local church serving the family, and the domestic church building up the parish.[29] In addition, along with religious education as broadly described in the last chapters, family and parish continue to serve as the foundational ministries of the Christian community, and their vitality, renewal, support and restructuring will profoundly affect the faith life of Christians in the United States.

To the extent that the faith development model can enhance the ministries of education, family and parish, the theory serves as an important tool for ministry. Although we have treated each ministry separately as a help to those individuals who minister in each area, the complexity of everyday life as well as the integral unity of each individual served requires that our approaches to ministry become more imaginative. With the automobile and access to modern communications systems, the geographical parish unit may not be the best place to locate what are now "parish" ministries. Through better education and maturity families in all their forms are ready for a greater share in the church's sense of ministry.

All those developments require discussion beyond the scope of this book. Hopefully, however, in looking at these ministries in a narrower framework, we have contributed to the exploration of possibilities yet to come. For now, our next discussion leads to those areas of ministry which derive from the extension of ministry beyond family and parish, to the sick, aged and imprisoned and to aspects of peace and justice issues, contemporary spirituality and worship.

6. MINISTRY WITH THE SICK

In the previous two chapters we have concentrated upon ministry of the church to its own members. As major social institutions school, parish and family play an active role in community and social life, and ministry in those areas reflects the church's concern for its own active, healthy, somewhat prosperous Christian people attempting to live faith-filled lives. In the next four chapters we will probe areas of human existence which reveal other, darker dimensions of life—suffering, death, diminishment, injustice, oppression. In the plight of the ill, the elderly, the imprisoned and the oppressed, we encounter not only the usual blocks to growth in faith, but institutional and structural obstacles which trap both the weak, aged and imprisoned as well as the strong, young and free peoples of society.

In these situations, people have experienced severe losses of meaning and power in society, and other people or alien forces determine their fate, even their every move. The sick, aged, imprisoned and oppressed are indeed "strangers in a strange land" of institutions, marginal to the concerns of the larger society. In its ministry here, the church carries the message of God's healing presence and transformative power beyond its own immediate members and structures to the world at large.

Beyond our immediate concern for the welfare of these "marginalized" people, we can also see how factors of physical, psychological, social and economic survival screen out larger concerns and relationships which are essential to a strong, developing faith life. And so, as we look at these various areas of ministry, we will be concerned with such questions as the extent to which hospitals, nursing homes, extended care facilities, hospices, retirement homes, prisons, hospitality houses and other structures support the faithing process in terms of images and symbols, perspective-taking abilities and sense of participation and active involvement in social life. Do these institutions provide such a hierarchical and authoritative pattern of response that communal and individuative patterns of faithing cannot emerge in personal and community life? What are the ways in which ministers in these areas can promote personal relationships and institutional changes which offer greater possibilities for active and lively faithing? And what understandings of the Christian faith are appropriate for people at various levels of faithing in relation to the issues and institutions of sickness, aging, imprisonment and oppression?

These questions center our approach in the following chapters. In this and the next chapter we will explore two elements of existence which affect us all at various times—sickness and aging. These "afflictions," as we call them, come upon us through the course of natural events, although we are learning more and more of the human, avoidable factors of our ill health and aging. In their commonality around physical suffering, deterioration and death, the church's forms of ministry in these areas take somewhat similar shape, especially through the sacrament of anointing and its prophetic call to the sick and elderly to live out a "vocation" in their situation. And they present a different set of factors than do imprisonment, unjust treatment and human oppression which we will examine in subsequent chapters.

The Hospital and the Pastoral Team ———

I walked into the ultrasound room clothed in two white gowns and prepared to climb onto the examining table. Since I would have my stomach examined, I started to lie on my back. Just then the technician, fully clothed in white, said "Lie on your back." Immediately I started to lie on my stomach. The technician laughed and commented that most people make the same mistake. But why, since I intended to lie on my back, did his command leave me with the idea that I was wrong? What was the disorientation I was feeling?[1]

After suffering an acute heart attack, the middle-aged physician continued with his rigorous work schedule in spite of the ministrations of his family and colleagues to take immediate bed rest and remain quiet. Twenty hours later he died in his office. Why did this man who knew so well the effects of such an attack deny his own vulnerability? What images of health and service had brought him to neglect his own body?[2]

When we look at health care and hospital ministry, a complex environment confronts us which appears too vast to analyze in terms of our faith development scheme. Yet in spite of the variety of peoples, the limited scope of the hospital pastoral team, and even the brief nature of pastoral encounters with patients, the use of a faith development perspective can assist the care giver in better understanding ministry in a hospital setting and can provide a context for examining the quality of care within the health system.

For example, a faith development perspective might provoke the following questions. What are the controlling symbols of health care? What images do doctors and nurses have of patients and patients of themselves? How are hospital personnel enabled to take the perspectives of the patient, the patient's family or one another? How well does the hospital take into account the needs of the poor who are ill? How much information does the patient get? How is the patient empowered to participate in his or her healing or even dying?

We will begin the following discussions with a brief look at the trends in health care and then will examine the various components of the hospital system, from the patient to the family, the staff, the hospital environment and finally the minister in light of the faith development scheme. In each of these areas we will use the framework of (1) symbols and imagination, (2) perspective-taking and (3) sense of participation.

Changes in Health Care Ministry

> The apostolate to the sick proposes four specific goals toward whose fulfillment the chaplain should strive. They are: (1) daily visitation of every Catholic patient; (2) daily Holy Communion for as many as desire to receive our Lord; (3) a daily special visit with the critically ill . . . (4) arranging Masses on Sundays and holy days.[3]

These comments from a 1967 guide for Catholic chaplains seem to view hospital ministry as a gas station which "fills" patients with the appropriate words and ministrations. The main minister is the chaplain, in this case a priest who alone administers the sacraments. My point in using this text is not to deny the importance of those functions nor to challenge the place of the priest as minister. Rather the quote illustrates the rapid changes that have taken place in hospital ministry.

As hospitals have centralized, grown in size and technology and cost, more Americans are likely to utilize a hospital setting than ever before. Over thirty million Americans rely on the Catholic health care system alone in any given year. Fully seventy-one percent of all deaths take place in hospitals.[4] In view of their place in interpreting the meaning of suffering and death, then, the hospital ministry team becomes the vehicle for God's saving action for thousands of Americans.

Certainly as our quotation revealed, the structure and composition of the "ministry team" has changed. The priest-chaplain, who may have visited several hospitals in one day, has been replaced in most settings by a pastoral care team, often ecumenical. Volunteer lay ministers augment the professional ministers, and their roles have continually expanded. Workers in ministry view the hospital as a setting for faith growth and not just faith maintenance, especially in the case of the dying. "We can dare to include death in our life of faith: we can support one another in this final stage of our journey."[5]

The holistic health movement coincides with a renewed emphasis upon the integration of the spiritual and the bodily in the healing process. In addition to "curing" there is a renewed emphasis upon "caring." This perspective has produced a revolution on the care of the dying through the incorporation of Dr. Kübler-Ross' insights on the dying process and the hospice movement pioneered by Dr. Cicely Saunders. Many hospitals regularly provide training on "hospital-ity" for their doctors, nurses, and other personnel. Although this development is partly an economic response to greater competition, it also reflects greater concern for the patient's welfare.

Theologically, the notion of "extreme unction" has given way to new understandings of the meaning of suffering and of anointing as a vocation of the sick, a community response to their marginalization in society and a sign of inner healing. "Christian healing is a Gospel sign that points to the reality beyond the present suffering of a creation groaning to be set free."[6] Furthermore, inasmuch as the hospital can be viewed as a "sacrament" of the entire saving mission of Christ, the hospital can be seen as a "eucharistic community" and as a parish in terms of its organization.[7]

While the faith development scheme will not resolve the many issues facing hospital ministers, there are several areas in which the scheme can assist ministers in carrying out their tasks.

> First, the theory provides important diagnostic and treatment information. As a diagnostic tool, the therapist [minister] can utilize an understanding of the stages in order to more fully appreciate the nature of the client's [patient's] internal world. As a treatment tool, stage development theory can enable the therapist [minister] to more ade-

quately plan interventions. . . . (T)he therapist [minister] would best
encourage the client's [patient's] growth through a sensitive application of knowledge about how the client [patient] is structuring meaning. Second, Fowler's theory provides a framework within which the
therapist [minister] can listen to and interpret the client's [patient's]
deepest story. Here is a tool which is inherently religious and pastoral
in nature.[8]

We will now look at the various components of the hospital setting in relation to growth in faith.

The Patient

Whether we are concerned about the overnight patient, the chronic
patient or the dying patient, we can identify a number of common concerns
in relation to entering and staying at a hospital. The experience of disorientation in the hospital setting described earlier is a small example of
the problems confronting anyone entering the hospital environment. The
hospital and its uniformed personnel convey powerful symbols of a new
organization of reality in which the patient's place is sharply defined and
limited. When the patient enters the hospital, he or she receives an identification badge wrapped around the wrist, a new set of clothes and a new
place to live apart from loved ones. In subtle ways patients hand over their
autonomy to others, hopefully for their own good. The patient's very images of self and of the hospital, the language used in the hospital environment, and even the clothes of the hospital personnel effect growth in faith
during the healing or dying process. Symbolic transformations have taken
place in a short period of time with little place for the patient's wishes and
often outside the patient's control.

Does the patient see the hospital as a place of "rewards and punishments" in terms of cure or pain, a mechanical setting in which bodily ailments are separated from the spirit? Or is the hospital a community of
people working at a common enterprise? Does the authority of doctors,
nurses and staff along with the sophisticated technology of modern medicine overwhelm the patient's personal concerns? And do the almost
"magical" powers of the doctors and nurses with their miraculous med-
icines further reinforce a "faithing" mode along the lines of stages one or
two even for adults?

The hospital serves as a symbol and maker of images of persons in
another way. Doctors and personnel in their records often refer to patients

as parts rather than wholes, as ''the diabetic in 2A'' or ''the heart problem in 3G.''

> When physicians and staff view persons only as patients, the sick individual suffers from both a diminished state of health and a diminished sense of autonomy. The individuals find themselves in an imbalanced relationship of almost childlike dependency on the healing, profession.[9]

In summary a new self-image as patient, depersonalized language, doctors, nurses and others clothed in garments of authority and the hospital setting are all factors on the level of symbols which can thwart faith growth in a hospital setting. And there are other factors to include.

Within the hospital setting most patients, understandably worried about the upcoming operation or fearful of dying in a hospital bed, are unable to adopt others' perspectives. All too often the ''perspective'' of the hospital as a place for the sick and dying and the perspectives of the authoritative doctor or nurse reinforce patients' preoccupation with self. Patients do not always participate in important decisions about their health care. The hospital staff may not have time or may not be oriented toward creating a supportive environment. Fears of loneliness, the inability to control one's life and the lack of the familiar comforts of human interaction assault the patient.

In relation to the patient, then, the minister who utilizes the faith development scheme will not only see an operative faith stage which the patient brings to the hospital but will also acknowledge the obstacles to growth in faith which arise from the very process of hospitalization. With the help of the faith development approach the minister can intervene in the interaction between the patient and the hospital in important ways.

Thus the minister can approach the patient as a whole person, countering the depersonalized image of self as ''patient.'' Through visualization of past health, present healing processes or a future life, the minister can employ the patient's imaginative powers for treatment and for meaning in the present situation. In addition the minister can help the patient respond to the symbolic ''authority'' of the medical people, especially in the cases of patients with a narrative or conventional approach to faithing.

When looking at the explicitly religious meanings given to pain, suffering and death, the minister's role as interpreter of the faith tradition is crucial. Questions such as ''Why me?'' ''Why now?'' ''Am I a good patient?'' ''Will I fully recover?'' ''Am I dying?'' often reflect patients' particular faith levels. For example, patients with a stage two faithing may well see their suffering as a punishment from God the demanding Father for their own sins. Or some who passively resign themselves to dying or a debilitating disease may be responding to the conventional acceptance of events as "God's will." The Christian truths of death and resurrection may have only a literal meaning or may become the key metaphor for interpreting a current illness in the hands of a faith-filled minister. Regardless of whether the patient curses the suffering in a stage one or two fashion or wrestles with its ambiguity in a stage four or five manner, the faith development approach amplifies the minister's key role as faith interpreter.

Finally, in the area of the symbolic and imaginative the sacraments of anointing and Eucharist provide the ministry team with powerful modes of fostering faith growth. Many patients still surround anointing with many of the magical features of bodily healing common to a stage two faithing. Yet precisely at this moment the minister can introduce a more extensive faith understanding of anointing as a ritual of wholeness in the face of seeming bodily disintegration, "the articulation of the community's recognition of the paschal mystery as concretized in sickness."[10] In addition anointing addresses the "marginalization" of the sick person by "the restoration of the significance of life through invitation back into community"[11] as a communal faith dimension of stage three and beyond.

This movement in understanding from a magical stage two mode to a more reflective stage four or even five mode has a counterpart in helping the patient understand his or her vocation and witness to the whole church. Not only can the sick provide us all with a deeper meaning to illness and death, but they also "proclaim that sickness need not be a threat to their fellow Christians whose lives need not be characterized by fragmentation." The sick person announces that the "fragmented and alienated life can recover its significance."[12] This vocational dimension of anointing offers the minister the opportunity to broaden the perspective of both the patient and the Christian community from an individual concern to the broader mission of the church.

Even while a patient experiences his or her pain and loss so intensely, the minister can help enlarge the patient's narrow perspective which immediate pain and a hospital setting almost necessarily bring about. Thus the minister can encourage the patient to incorporate the redemptive meaning of his or her suffering in relation to the immediate needs of friends and relatives in a stage three faith perspective or to more global needs of suffering peoples in a stage four and five fashion. I do not want to give a mechanical interpretation to the faith stages approach but rather to underscore their use in interpreting the patient's concerns as well as enlarging the patient's community of fellow sufferers. This requires a delicate balance of comforting the patient while fostering the patient's own faith growth.

And finally the minister should support the patient's need for a sense of participation in the decisions surrounding his or her life and in the hospital community. The minister can sustain the patient's right to information about the pain, suffering and hospitalization process. Even more importantly, the minister can encourage the patient's struggle to re-establish a sense of authority over one's life and the hospitalization routine and thus gain or regain the sense of independence so essential to mature faithing.

The dying patient has particular needs and offers a special challenge to the minister. All the fears and anxieties of loneliness, abandonment, loss of control and loss of meaning to life which the ordinary patient may have felt the dying person feels deeply and constantly. And certainly all the areas we mentioned above concerning self-image and images of the hospital, focused perspective upon the self and lack of participation in community and life come to play here even more dramatically.

In working with the dying the minister will encounter the patient responding not only in terms of a faith stage but also in relation to the phases of the dying process outlined by Dr. Elisabeth Kübler-Ross: denial, anger, bargaining, depression, and acceptance.[13] Yet the minister must be aware that not everyone goes through all the phases in the same way, nor is progression through the stages always in a neat, orderly fashion. The phases are a tool, then, and never "a norm to judge the rightness or wrongness of an individual's responses."[14]

In this area the actual phase of the person's dying process may not be a good clue to a faith stage. Thus the bargaining phase, so central to the whole dying process, seems to reflect a stage two faith response. However, the minister must explore the whole bargaining posture of the patient. At the same time the minister can utilize knowledge of the faith stages to help the dying patient interpret the meaning of his or her dying. Thus the different approaches to praying with the patient, celebrating the sacraments, interpreting the meaning of death and resurrection and sharing faith stories should be undertaken with some understanding of the faith stages.

The types of prayers used with patients will also reflect their faith growth. Many will be able to treat of death only in terms of the familiar prayers of the church. Some can be challenged to express their needs in their own words in a more individuative form, while still others may be drawn to express their inner life in terms of the ambiguities of living and dying. If it is true that "No one has reached maturity until he has learned to face the fact of his own death and shaped his way of living accordingly,"[15] then the minister has a unique opportunity to help patients interpret the meaning of death according to their measure of faithing. At stage three the dying patient may be comforted by the simple words of scripture and the prayers of the church for the dying, while someone who is challenging the meaning of his or her own death can be drawn into more individuative or synthetic modes.

In addition the minister can support the patient's faith growth by reflecting an integrated sense of body and spirit in the very face of the body's decline. Again that may be in a simple acceptance of the idea of bodily resurrection, even in the most literal sense, or the minister can share a more dynamic sense of the interpenetration of body and spirit as in Teilhard de Chardin's notion that as the body literally breaks apart the spirit gains entrance to a deeper core of meaning.[16] Above all the minister must discern the faith stage behind such open questions as "What is after life?" or "What is the meaning of death and resurrection?"

Certainly the meaning of suffering will reflect the various stages of faithing, from punishment for one's sins to participation in Christ's redeeming power. But the dying obviously face a more profound question of meaning, the ultimate meaning of death itself. In working through a final acceptance of death's inevitability, hopefully the minister will enable the dying person to "let go" of the elements of self-identity which have sustained life up to this point—family, friends, a job, position in the community, even future plans. All these "losses" are part of the final loss of life, and the minister's understanding of the faith stages can be helpful in guiding the dying person through these earlier grievings. This may be particularly difficult for a stage four faithing mode with its emphasis upon the sense of control and strong self-identity. Yet for that mode as well as others, such a "letting go" may be the important step for an opening to deeper understanding of God's love, wisdom and justice as well as a broader extension of the patient's compassion to others in their suffering and dying.

In this primary role as interpreter of the faith tradition and guide into the unknown, the minister has a further opportunity to express the "witness" power of the dying process. That is, the mode of dying itself becomes a sign of Christian hope and vision to the community surrounding the patient. While such hope and vision cannot overlook the grim reality of death, the last moments of living can provide a testament to the reality of God's gracing presence in every aspect of life itself.

In areas of perspective-taking and participation the minister is in a unique position to foster the dying patient's faith growth. By inviting the patient to acknowledge the real losses in the dying process and to share the feelings surrounding those losses, the minister may be able to shift the patient's perspective on his or her own grieving. In particular, through a life review process the minister can generate the kind of faith sharing which allows the patient to see his or her life with its moments of wholeness and integrity and assist the patient in reinvesting time, energy and resources in those areas most enriching for the remainder of life.[17]

At the same time encouraging the patient to adopt as independent a posture as possible in caring for immediate needs, drawing up a living will or just arranging the atmosphere of one's room can help the dying patient gain or regain a greater sense of independence and dignity. If the patient is in a hospice setting, then the minister along with family, friends and staff has an even better opportunity to provide the patient with some semblance of independence, self-respect and dignity through control over the living environment.

Yet realistically all too often the patient may not be open to discussions about faith or personal matters. Certainly the minister must respect the patient's wishes in this respect. Yet the minister should also view his or her efforts at basic human encounter as fruitful in themselves. The needs of the patient are common to all, and in ministry to every patient the minister "will seek to meet these needs in a faithful way, even though faith in God does not appear to be an explicit part of that care."[18]

The Minister

In many hospital settings today, pastoral care units work together across denominational lines to care for the sick and dying. In that respect much of what we said in the previous chapter about parish teams will apply here also. Yet precisely because of the unique context of the hospital setting, illness and dying, we do need to look at those aspects of the faithing paradigm which shape the role of the hospital minister.

In the first place, the minister's knowledge of the faith stages provides a reflective basis for examining his or her personal journey in faith. In one way or another the minister's own faith stage will influence the ability to interpret the faithing of others.

Certainly in the area of symbols the minister's own image of self as care-giver and witness come into play here. Especially in the hospital setting with the extensive use of medical technology, the patient faces the danger of almost total separation of the physical and the spiritual. In his or her own person and through the vision of bodily and spiritual wholeness in the service of God as Creator, the minister becomes a testament to the process of integrating one's life and not just restructuring or repairing body parts. And the hospital minister is the instrument through which the patient is reminded that he or she is remembered and cared for by a community of people united in faith in a reality beyond present suffering or the onset of death.

Beyond the minister's own person and vision, the minister utilizes prayers, stories and rituals, especially the powerfully symbolic sacraments of penance, anointing and eucharist to root the images of suffering, death and resurrection in the patient's own experiences. Knowing whether the patient sees illness and death as magical punishments for personal misdeeds, as manifestations of God's mysterious will, as personal experiences which cry out for explanation in a systematic way or as ambiguous and paradoxical expressions of a universal, redemptive love may enable the minister to develop those prayers, rituals, stories in ways which reach each particular patient.

In a fundamental way, the minister involved in illness and dying is an interpreter of reality who proposes to the patient a dynamic shift in perspective from the physically-oriented hospital environment. While this effort demands a real capacity for perspective-taking on the part of the minister, it also requires a reflective perspective *upon* the very person of the minister. That is, the minister must have a realistic assessment of his or her own limitations in ministry but especially of personal finiteness and fears of suffering and death. These awarenesses are essential to the empathy needed to minister to others.[19]

And precisely inasmuch as the minister involves himself or herself in the lives of the patients and their families, there is all the greater need for the minister to share with others in order to gain perspective, relieve personal grief and share personal and faith challenges occasioned by the work. The minister needs support, a sense of personal worth and companionship whether provided by the pastoral team or some other group utilizing the processes of team building discussed in earlier chapters.

The Family

Just as was the case with the patient, the family sees its identity changing, finds itself dislocated, feels intimidated by the authoritarian nature of the hospital system and senses a tremendous loss of control over its own life. Disengaged from their normal routines, family members require information about their loved one, and at the same time they need some way to interpret the illness or dying process for themselves and to their personal communities of friends, relatives and acquaintances.

In many ways the role of the minister with the family follows what we have said earlier about the minister's role with the patient. Beyond serving as the bearer of good or bad news, the minister will become the interpreter of meaning in the areas of suffering, sickness and death. Yet family members may well challenge the minister's interpretative scheme more than the patient does. Thus only by understanding the family's differing perspectives, their faithing capabilities and even the content of their faith tradition will the minister discover a chance to respond to the family's deepest concerns and anxieties. The minister must find times for talking, for sharing, for praying, even for celebrating rituals with the family during the illness or dying process.

The family needs to share in the patient's worldview in some way. Through opportunities for the family to share feelings and anxieties or to explore fond memories and hopes for the future, the minister can provide a context in which the family ministers to the patient and to one another. This setting will challenge the minister to assist the family in taking the patient's perspective and will demand that the family grapple with the same understanding of suffering, sickness and death that the patient has. Here too the minister recognizes the communal nature of the healing process, all the way from physically holding one another to sacramental rituals, and enlists the family in ministry to the patient.

For the family faced with the loss of their loved one rather than a welcome return home, the task of the caring minister continues after the patient dies. The minister needs to integrate the various phases which the grieving family passes through in the face of such a loss with knowledge of the family's particular faithing patterns. Initial shock and numbness will be replaced by a certain amount of disorganization. Contact with the minister who knew the patient in the dying process may be pivotal in moving to the reorganization of life patterns which signal a return to normal living.[20]

Depending upon the family's faithing mode, celebrating rituals of the dead person's meaning to the family and simply praying, talking and reminiscing with the family can provide the basis for developing new images of family life and new reconstructions of the family social system. Especially does the family need to talk about its grief with a sympathetic listener and to tell the many stories about the loved one. Since the death of a loved one is often a traumatic shock to family members' outlooks on life, the minister as faith interpreter needs to pay attention to apparent "regressions" in the faithing process. The bargaining, anger, depression which the family experiences will seem like aspects of stage two faithing but may well indicate a deep probing of God's providence on a stage four or five level. The faith development scheme may well assist the minister in interpreting these differing modalities.

Children often blame themselves for a parent's death or feel guilt from unkind comments or actions left unresolved. In this case the minister can interpret the meanings of death and loss according to the child's understanding and can assist adults to discern the child's expressions and respond in a helpful manner. Here it would be important for adult members to understand that at different faithing periods of the child's life, the meaning of the parent's death may have to be reinterpreted.

The Staff

The patient, the minister and pastoral care team and the family interact with a multitude of people in the hospital setting. In various ways these staff members can help or hinder ministry to patients and their families. Thus the minister and pastoral care team must recognize the importance of viewing all hospital personnel as "ministers" to the faithing process. In much the same way as we saw in the school, family and parish setting, the staff members provide the ordinary context within which the patient and even the ministry team function and find meaning for their experiences of pain, suffering, loss, joy and death.

Through a combination of workshops, in-service programs, and one-to-one relationships with staff, the pastoral care team can develop important perspectives for staff members in relationship to patients, families, one another and the hospital environment. Inasmuch as the team acquaints the staff with the faith development scheme, staff can reflect more intentionally upon their patient's needs and their own style of intervention. First, then, the pastoral team can assist the staff with development of their own image as care-givers and challenge them to move from the authoritarian role they inevitably play to treatment of the patient based upon respect for the total person. In light of the depersonalization of the institutional setting, the patient's initial sense of loss and the almost exclusive emphasis upon the body and its parts, the staff must be challenged "to recognize the autonomy of persons . . . to protect persons whose autonomy is impaired . . . to promote the well-being of persons . . . (and) to treat each person fairly.''[21] One of the most crucial factors involved in this perspective is helping to restore the imbalance created in the hospital-patient relationship by the patient's dependence upon staff, lack of information needed for personal decisions and loss of control over personal relationships.[22]

Within the Christian hospital, these factors take on a distinctively religious dimension. This involves acquainting the staff with Christian interpretations of suffering, pain, loss, death. In addition, the religious understanding of each person as a ''created presence''[23] of God means that as sacramental signs of Christ's healing presence staff members must treat each patient with compassionate love. Finally to further assist the staff in understanding their role as ministers of healing, the pastoral team could train staff in such areas as pastoral skills, an understanding of the faith development scheme and an acquaintance with the Kübler-Ross phases or other patterns of dying. Not only is such development and training important because of a broadened understanding of ministry and Christian mission, but through such an approach the pastoral team can better utilize their own time and resources knowing that they have enabled staff members with the skills and understandings to carry out hospital ministry.

And yet beset with the constant demands of needy patients, the heavy workloads of hospital work and the emergencies and crises in their units, hospital personnel also need to support one another as they learn to provide more supportive environments for patients. Through small groups, retreat settings, regular staff meetings or other times, the pastoral team can provide an atmosphere in which staff members share faith perspectives, challenge and support one another and explore their concerns surrounding patient care and hospital procedures. In addition, through classes, liturgies, social celebrations and other occasions staff members can develop a stronger sense of themselves as a healing, just community of care-givers. In all these efforts, the team can support, consolidate and challenge the staff members' own faith growth with careful attention to the modes of conventional, individuative and synthetic faithing perspectives expressed by the staff.

On one level, then, the pastoral team can help staff members in orienting patients, providing information and establishing an environment which shows care and concern for the patient. On yet another level, the team can empower staff with a sense of their own abilities and gifts as ministers and can assist them in their own faith journeys. Hopefully in both these areas the hospital as a setting can become an institution supportive of faith growth.

The Hospital

Although our hopes for such a development as just described are high, the pastoral care team itself must constantly assess the hospital setting as an environment for the growth of patients and staff. Since the perceived level of the institution is a key factor in moral and faith development, the team must constantly ask how the staff, patients and families view the hospital. In part the occasional necessity for strong intervention by the pastoral team centers around the "regression" which the hospital as institution may engender because of its own bureaucracy, the nature of authority and dependency of health care delivery and the awesome complexity of hospital technology. Is the hospital a magical center of bodily manipulation? A hierarchical structure of competent, even caring, authority figures in which conformity to expected patterns is the only accepted mode of operation? Or is it a community of people attentive to the dignity of each person and equipped with a sensitivity to the hospital-patient imbalance and the need for participation at all levels? From a religious perspective, is the Christian hospital viewed as an extension of Christ's healing mission? If "the total hospital circumstance (building, facilities, staff and personnel) is, to Christian eyes, a sacrament of the entire saving mission of Christ and the Church,"[24] is the sacramental nature of healing visible in the hospital's self-understanding?

If the staff is working for at least a stage four mode of hospital care, then their task involves examination of the hospital's image as projected to the community, the ways in which patients, families and staff members participate in decision-making, the wage and benefit structure in relation to justice, opportunities for employees to express their concerns and interests and the environment of various work units in relation to employees' health and welfare. All too often the hospital in general and the Christian hospital in particular has opposed efforts by hospital workers to obtain better wages or improve working conditions by employing the image of "community" or "family" to disguise a highly authoritarian model of management. Wage disputes, then, are viewed as matters of benevolent attitudes of higher administration or as family matters to be kept from public view. Certainly the pastoral team must direct much of its reflection and energy to these larger questions of justice for patients and staff within the hospital environment.

The Parish

In some ways the hospital as an institution may well resemble a parish in which the pastoral team functions much like a parish team.[25] But more

realistically the pastoral team will view the patient's parish and neighborhood parishes serving the hospital as resources to the hospital environment. In this way parishes and the hospital's pastoral team can forge an
integrated relationship which incorporates the sick person's vocation to the
rest of the Christian community with that community's responsibilities to
the sick and dying.

The hospital minister may be able to support efforts by local churches
to incorporate the sick into regular Sunday liturgies which focus upon the
Christian understanding of suffering, illness and dying. A liturgy of healing and communal anointing would then underscore the "interaction between the community and the people anointed, their mutual ministry to
each other." For if anointing confers upon the sick their vocation "to
sharpen continually the consciousness of the worshipping community
about all the dehumanizing components found in contemporary society,"[26] anointing within a community context calls the members of the
community to their responsibility in assisting the sick and dying through
the rites of passage, illness and dying. Within the parish context of liturgy,
preaching and teaching the symbolic meaning of anointing in broadening
the patient's and community's perspectives can well enliven all concerned:

> If sickness . . . [is a symbol] of the possible destructive disunity in the
> human person and of separation from community and from God, then
> the purpose of the sacrament of anointing is to provide the experience
> of the death/resurrection of Christ precisely in terms of this kind of
> alienation and fragmentation. Any pastoral care on the concrete level
> should emphasize that the plight of the sick and elderly is not senseless
> and cruel suffering. Rather, it can be a time of growth for these people
> as human beings and as Christians. Ministry to them must stress their
> ministry to the larger Church. . . . They remind the rest of the Church
> of the importance of life, health, death, and salvation as compared to
> the many trivial things which preoccupy people.[27]

Through such opportunities as liturgy, preaching and workshops in
the parish, the hospital team can assist the parish community in better understanding such central Christian truths as the paschal mystery and invite
parish members to assist in hospital ministry. This effort will result in
teaching the well of the parish the Christian meaning of sickness and
dying, not only to better understand what may someday happen to them
but also to counter the marginalization of the sick and dying rooted in attitudes of fear and resentment present in the larger society. Furthermore
such an effort should lead to parish volunteers who express their universal

call to ministry in the form of visits to the sick and dying. In training workshops the hospital team can acquaint the volunteers not only with basic skills of attending, listening and responding to the patient's needs but also with a framework such as the faith development scheme within which the patient's faithing can be fostered and promoted.

Summary

In looking at the patient, the minister, the family, the staff, the hospital and the parish, I have attempted to develop the faith development theory in some practical directions within the hospital settings. The hospital has much in common with the school, family and parish in terms of ministry. However, the positive forces which lend hope and excitement to those environments are missing in the hospital setting. Instead the minister must attend to the separation, marginalization and negative social attitudes toward the sick and dying. The minister's and the team's monumental task is precisely to provide meaning where it is absent and to develop community where it is denied. This strong ''reversal of values'' requires not just lively faith on the part of each member of the pastoral team but sharpened skills and theoretical models which can best guide patients, their families and hospital personnel in their personal and collective faith journeys. And in the midst of these tasks the minister must constantly attend to his or her own growth as a sacramental sign of Christ's healing power as well as a prophetic challenge to the demeaning realities of hospitalization.

7. THE ELDERLY AND MINISTRY

. . . and I want you to know that also I will not make age an issue of
this campaign. I am not going to exploit for political purposes my op-
ponent's youth and inexperience.

> President Ronald Reagan, Sec-
> ond Presidential Debate, 1984[1]

It might just be one of God's surprises for us, that he may use those
closest to death—nearer to that other life—to show the Church how to
break with self-centered purposes and goals and look to the good of all
and serve that good.

> Maggie Kuhn, founder of the
> Gray Panthers[2]

As we move from our discussion of the hospital setting to a look
at the elderly in our society, we find similarities yet striking differences.
Like the sick and the infirm, elders in our society are truly marginalized,
pushed to the edges of our consideration. However, the sick are only temporarily removed to the fringes of daily life, except in the case of the
dying. Elders by contrast are permanently removed in our modern, indus-
trial-technological society, disenfranchised from participation by the stereotypes of agism, by the ritual of retirement and by our emphasis upon
social and physical mobility.

As we examine elderhood, the variety, numbers and racial, ethnic,
sexual and religious differences among elders force us to avoid generali-
zations in talking about religious education and ministry with elders.
Nevertheless exploring ministry and elderhood raise questions to which
the faith development scheme might provide some clues. How are elders
"imprisoned" by social images of aging? In what ways are their needs
misunderstood by well-meaning, younger care-providers? What roles of
social and religious participation are open after retirement? How has the
church contributed to the marginalization of the elderly? And what avenues would ministry with the aging take?

Aging in America

Before we begin to answer these questions, we need to review the
tremendous impact elders have in our society. In the first place, the num-

bers of elders over sixty-five alone are staggering: 24,541,400 in 1980 and increasing more rapidly than the general population.[3] The elderly will comprise twenty-five percent of the population by the year 2000.[4] Fully one-fourth of the federal budget goes to the elderly in some form,[5] while the percentage of elders living in poverty has declined from 35.2% in 1959 to 15.7% in 1980.[6]

These increasing numbers reflect several developments in the past two decades which ironically have led to the marginalization and problematic nature of growing old. First, earlier retirement means more leisure time but removal from the "productive" forces of society. Second, longer periods of healthy life are a boon to all, yet the price for health is increased services, greater expenditures. Finally, the growing mobility of the American family coupled with earlier retirement can mean even further isolation from children and grandchildren.

In part our very approaches to elderhood skew our responses, for we invariably view aging as a "decline." Thus aging can be defined as "a decline in physiologic competence that inevitably increases the incidence and intensifies the effects of accidents, disease, and other forms of environmental stress."[7] Those over sixty-five, and even younger, experience physical changes that other age groups do not encounter in such intensity. Coupled with retirement and consequent drop of income, these physical changes result in a view of the elder person as less "whole" and thus less worthwhile. These perceptions in turn lead to myths about learning abilities, sexual interest, intellectual decline, senility, impending death and lifestyle. Aging becomes a symbol to the young of a loss of status, physical and financial security and importance.

Yet ironically the very social, psychological and even physical disabilities attributed to elders are determined more by socio-economic conditions than by aging itself. Those who have wealth do not automatically reach a "role-less" position upon reaching sixty-five, nor are they subject to many of the ravages of disease other elders experience. "So many of the penalties age inflicts must therefore be viewed as deprivations of social status rather than the absolute and irrevocable consequences of growing old."[8]

Aging and the Faith Development Perspective

As we take up the first dimension of faith development, symbols and images, we immediately confront the powerful, demonic structure of agism, "a process of systematic stereotyping of and discrimination against people because they are old."[9] In short, the image of the elders is one of a useless and unproductive, dying being.

In part this image is perpetuated by elders themselves as they experience their own losses. As a result the aging person can fall prey to the self-absorption characterized by Erik Erikson in his descriptions of the final stages of the life-cycle, particularly the struggle of Integrity vs. Despair. Integrity for Erikson is "the acceptance of one's one and only life cycle as something that had to be and that, by necessity, permitted of no substitutions," while despair, often masked by disgust and cynicism, "expresses the feeling that the time is now short, too short for the attempt to start another life and to try out alternate roads to integrity."[10] In our society of idolatrous youth worship, bleak pictures of despair often seem to characterize life after sixty-five.

The minister then must begin to re-establish former images of skills, contributions and relationships which each person retains in memory and to challenge the dominant images of aging. Instead the minister must foster among the aged and in the church and society new, creative images of the aged, recalling the command from Leviticus (19:22): "You shall rise up before the hoary head and honor the face of an old one."

In this sense fostering a more individuative faith stance becomes an important mode of breaking the elder's own pull to conform to the expectations and images of the larger society. Eugene Bianchi offers several helpful suggestions in this regard:

> In the difficult work of changing the image of old age, the elderly must first recognize the degree to which they have incorporated this image into their own way of seeing themselves. Positive, in-depth reflections on the possibilities for significant living amid certain physical diminishments can also help to restore dignity. . . . [E]ach individual must look to his or her gifts, which can be stymied by the stereotypes of old age or facilitated by enhanced dignity through reflection on the lives of great old persons.[11]

As Maggie Kuhn's comment which began this section reflects, elders have the time to explore the rich inner resources of the self and to offer to the rest of us the gifts of their time. In a society dominated by control and the need to control, this approach of "letting go" not only offers young people some relief to the relentless push of social expectations but also invites them into the religious vision of a God to whom we entrust every aspect of our existence. And certainly in their "vocational" role as grand-parent, elders offer an image of rich and lively faithing which can imbue young people with deeply religious attitudes toward questions of life's meaning and purpose.

A second aspect of the symbolic dimension of faith development concerns the religious understandings surrounding elderhood. In the first place, retirement is a well-established rite of passage and offers promise of leisure time, travel, renewal of friendship and other positive rewards. As a social event, retirement signals the end of one mode of productive activity, rewarded by society, and the beginning of something new. As economic conditions change, many not only look forward to retirement but retire early.

Here the church could well begin to construct a more positive image of aging by looking upon retirement as a religious event, a "sacramental transition" full of danger as in any rite but also full of promise.[12] Churches could develop religious rituals which allow the retiree and members of the family to reflect upon the meaning of their productive skills and their value to the community. Utilizing the faith development approach, retirement rituals could focus upon the vocational dimension of elderhood and give positive support for the sense of "uselessness," the fundamental Christian insight that "Christians are not justified or validated by their works or their achievements and credentials."[13]

In a broader sense, however, the religious dimension of elderhood would encompass the movement toward a more reflective, and more intensive, quest for God in one's own experiences, in service to others and in serving as a model of holistic growth. In the first place, while the losses which accompany elderhood cannot be glossed over or pushed aside, a spirituality of elderhood would see these very losses as the moments of transformation of matter to spirit, or, in the words of Paul, of putting on immaterial bodies for material ones. This process of allowing God to take over the direction of our lives down to the last molecule again reflects Chardin's vision of God acting through our "passivity," meaning not what we do not do but what we undergo or bear up under in our very selves.[14] As Eugene Bianchi sees this process, "It is as though the diminishments themselves serve as a purifying catalyst to allow a deeper transformation of the personality and a consequent worldly endeavor of greater value" as the elder emerges with a "richer quality and power for developing the world."[15]

A spirituality of growth through diminishment would seem particularly suited to a stage five faithing mode. Yet here the minister can well serve as the leader and guide in developing such a perspective on a stage three and four level, taking into account the more formal prayer life of stage three and the more reflective, interior modes of stage four. On a stage three level the minister can employ familiar prayer forms such as the rosary and prayers involving an acceptance of pain, suffering, infirmity to translate personal experiences into growth moments. A stage four approach would utilize reflection of God's use of diminishment in the transformation of the person and the world. The minister can also use forms of centering prayer to call the elder into more intense, deeper relationship with the God working through an aging body and to develop new abilities aimed at reintegrating the very aspects of aging which seem threatening and narrowing.

The minister and the elder need to create new meaning along with new images for the time which society now finds valueless. For example, Robert Katz, reflecting upon the meaning of aging from a Jewish perspective, posits a new image of aging as "the Sabbath of the soul. . . . As the Sabbath is the climax of creation, so the time of maturity represents the highest point of a man's development."[16] In this way the very reflection upon the "losses" of aging in prayer can provide the catalyst for faith growth from the conventional toward the individuative and from the individuative to the synthetic.

Finally these new understandings and images must find their expression not only in and through an active prayer life but also in the worship of the whole church at every stage of faith growth. If, in Urban Holmes' understanding, worship is grounded in memory and the elders are the guardians of a community's symbolic realities,[17] then liturgies must involve the memories of elders as well as nurture those memories through music, stories and dance. Ministers familiar with the particular gifts and needs of the elders as well as the dimensions of faith growth can create liturgical settings and expressions which enrich the whole community with the values and wisdom that elders bring to life.

A further reflection on the religious dimension of elderhood brings us to the appropriation of the central Christian mystery of death and resurrection and a Christian understanding of pain and suffering. On the one hand the reality of life after death can bring a certain comfort to those close to death itself. And yet the minister is challenged to go beyond the literal meaning of death and resurrection which accompanies a stage three understanding. A deeper, symbolic understanding of the paschal mystery in a stage four or five mode provides the elders with a prism with which to view their many small "deaths and resurrections," their struggles, pain, and sufferings as channels of redemptive power for the liberation of the world. With these understandings, the minister and the elders can provide important guidance and insight for other members of the Christian community in their own encounters with the full meaning of Christian life.

And finally, as in the case of the sick, by focusing the community's attention upon the elderly through the sacrament of anointing, the church counters the marginalization of elders and emphasizes their meaning for the community's own welfare. On the one hand, anointing is a sign of Christ's redemption in the brokenness of old age, a movement of reintegration in the midst of bodily, psychic, and social disintegration. At the same time, anointing provides the elderly with their unique vocation to the community: the revelation through their own lives that life has full and ultimate meaning in every moment. From their marginalized position in society, the anointed elders are the " 'precursors' of the kind of attitude toward aging that is needed by persons at all stages of life, for they may have confronted our human finitude more directly than most of us."[18]

In many ways, elderhood challenges our contemporary culture. At precisely those moments when our fast-paced society flings elders to its fringes upon retirement, elders can point to another dimension of living which embraces simplicity, loving service, times for prayer and worship. Such a challenge necessarily calls for a strongly individuative faith stance, a stage four perspective and at least a beginning of wrestling with the ambiguities which stage five describes. This vocation of world-challenge is reflected in the words of psychologist Ann Ulanov:

> Aging brings home to us what we have done or failed to do with our lives, our creativity or our waste, our openness to or zealous hiding from what really matters. Precisely at that point, age cracks us open, sometimes for the first time, makes us aware of the center, makes us look for it and for relation to it. Aging does not mark an end but rather the beginning of making sense of the end-questions, so that life can have an end in every sense of the word.[19]

The religious dimension of this understanding implies a larger commitment on the part of the elders to the whole human project and the whole human community. Elders are called precisely by their age with its physical losses and diminishment to enter into service of the community and especially in service to one another. In Bianchi's sense elders must "desire to stay at the center of events in order to transform power from its oppressive uses to a resourceful energy that works for universal betterment."[20]

Our discussions of images and vocation of elderhood lead directly to some reflections on perspective-taking in relation to faith growth. In this area the minister may invite elders to share stories about their own lives and their fears of aging and dying, of "letting go" and of the unknown. These sharings can be enriched by reflections on the gospel stories such as Lazarus' resurrection or Jesus' own fears of impending death, by discussion of the meaning of resurrection and other themes. Undoubtedly concerns about retirement, financial problems, institutionalization and other issues will surface. In such sharing not only will elders realize the commonality they individually have with others, but they also enter into the faith lives, problems and joys of others. Here knowledge of the faith-development scheme can effectively support and challenge elders in broadening their understandings of others in need.

Through a "life review" process elders can examine their past with a quality of acceptance and tenderness toward themselves and those people affecting their lives, and they can re-evaluate and reintegrate powerful events of the past as well. Other techniques may involve oral histories of periods and places which utilize the elder as a preserver of a rich tradition or life stories in which elders research their own or the family's life history. Here, then, the minister's own skills in listening can integrate the revealed fragments into a whole reflecting the graced life of each person. At the same time the minister explores the symbols and ideas shared by the elder as clues to the faithing involved.

Some form of life review can develop elders' capacity to take the perspective of family members and so provide the basis for healing broken and frayed relationships, for achieving forgiveness of self, of others, and even by others. Here the elder's images of God and Jesus may be an important part of the healing and forgiving process, and a caring examination of those images with the faithing modes in mind can prove helpful. Thus for some the punishing and rewarding images of stage two may crowd out more nurturing images, whereas for others, images of God as trusted friend or God as spiritual presence may reveal and promote growth in stages three or four of faithing.

Not only must elders gain a meaningful perspective on their past, they must chart a perspective on the future for themselves and for the society of which they are a part. They need a life *proview,* the imaginative projection of goals, purposes and accomplishments no matter what impairments or limitations are involved. On one level, such a "peek" into the future involves planning for the after-retirement years or for financial security upon a spouse's death. On another level personal happiness and elders' sense of vocation demand that the future be an active part of the present.

> One could almost say that the elderly, as custodians of the wisdom of the race, should be even more future-oriented than the young and the middle-aged, who are typically enveloped in immediate concerns, establishing or developing a career, providing for families, and rearing children. . . . Rather than withdrawing into the past or to the periphery of the present, the elderly have a profound responsibility and vocation to build the future, both for their fellow elders and for the whole human community.[21]

Thus the minister can challenge the leader at different faith levels not only to develop a personal, prospective perspective but also to take into account broader perspectives demanded by the sense of care for the global community. Thus for some a personal ministry to another elder or involvement with charitable works may be an appropriate reflection of a stage three mode of faithing. Others may examine the critical patterns and structures which cause injustice and oppression whether for elders locally and nationally or for other groups.

Another method of promoting a broader perspective for elders involves the use of models of elders engaged in a variety of challenging activities related to the future, from the praying power of the bedridden elder to the activism of the Gray Panther. Through stories, films, novels, music and art, the powerful images of elders seizing every moment of life provide energizing models of growth and hope. And as we have seen, the use of such modeling can be of crucial importance in the transition of elders from stage three faithing to stage four and can provide a personal and spiritual mentoring into stage five faithing.

A good religious education program is another way to develop these forms of perspective-taking in which elders can challenge one another to attend to other perspectives and incorporate these fresh viewpoints into their own reflections. The development of college and university efforts to recruit elders is a refreshing recognition of the needs of elders for continuing education. Whether elders are part of the regular college environment in which they encounter younger students and in turn are encountered or are served by special programs, such as the popular ''elderhostels,'' those ministring with the elderly can provide contexts for education which integrate faith growth with active learning. Intergenerational educational efforts are especially helpful from a faith development perspective.

Our comments on images and perspective-taking provide the basis for the critical dimension of participation in relation to growth in faith. Participation assumes its importance not so much in view of the need to keep active physically, mentally and spiritually, but more in relation to the need to feel valued, trusted and so "faithed in." To be "faithed in" by friends, church, community is the other side of "faithing" and thus demands the development of a sense of participation as a prelude to faith growth.

We have already noted the marginalization of elders in society with the result that "(the) old are increasingly removed from the centers of decision making that influence the welfare of all. . . . Recreational and social communities are built for the elderly, but such retirement communities lack direct political impact."[22]

This "forced" withdrawal builds the cultural stereotype of the elder as unwilling and unable to participate in the larger society. Ironically such forced withdrawal accompanies the increase of separate services to meet the needs of elders created by their very removal from participation in society. While elders are often involved in the direction or administration of these services, they are just as often left out. And the churches are as involved in this process of marginalization as other social agencies.

> Religious institutions seem to corroborate the general attitude that the old have served society enough in the past and are now entitled to retire from social commitment to spend their remaining years in private involvements. . . . In fostering the privatized life of the old, the churches also deplete the political influence that the elderly might be able to wield for the welfare of their own age cohort.[23]

Thus both ministers and elders need to challenge the perceptions involved in such marginalization and to direct energies toward providing opportunities for continued involvement in social, economic, political and religious organizations. And while one important motivation may be the full utilization of the talents and gifts of elders, more importantly such participation involves the development of the very mission and vocation of elderhood outlined earlier.

While providing opportunities for community involvement and participation, ministers must attend to two practices particularly insidious to a sense of participation: withholding the truth about physical, financial, or family matters and not demanding enough physical or mental involvement from elders. Both of these practices deprive older people of their involvement in matters of great concern and result in a loss of trust in themselves, in their environment, and ironically in those who try to shield them from the truth or protect them from exerting themselves.[24]

Ministers with the elderly, then, face two tasks centering around participation. In the first place, working through church and social service agencies they must provide basic assistance to elders to preserve their independence and promote their continuing involvement in society on a meaningful basis. The second task concerns the active involvement of ministers and elders to humanely provide for those elders who cannot provide for themselves and to carefully monitor church and secular institutions which provide care for elders. These tasks demand that ministers and elders work from a stage four or five perspective in relation to just and human care of elders.

Are elders treated as "wards," or are they provided with full human dignity? In the institution,

> . . . the knowledge that we have concerning the reversibility of many of the conditions that give rise to senility is most important. Does the nursing home work at such possibilities of reversal? Does it take the easy course of keeping patients too drugged? Does it provide space for privacy? Does it encourage contact with people outside? Does it allow patients to keep some of their prized possessions which can provide continuity with their past lives and help them preserve their sense of identity?[25]

In addition ministers and elders must make sure that the environments of such "homes" provide for faith growth. That is, are there opportunities to exchange perspectives, to share personal histories, pursue further education, including religious education, increase awareness of national and global events, develop exposure to models of developed faithing among elders, become involved in activities of the home or outside organizations as much as limits allow, challenge the stereotypes surrounding elderhood, develop a deeper and more reflective spiritual life? Are nursing home personnel aware of the developmental needs of elders in faith? Are these personnel open to such needs? And ministers with elders must explore and advocate alternatives to institutional care such as "home health services, outpatient occupational and physical therapy, meals on wheels, day centers, short 'recuperative holidays' in the nursing home . . . and intermittent short admissions."[26] These programs help foster the sense of independence and participation essential to a more individuative faith stance.

Finally, we must say a word about the dying elder. Eugene Bianchi puts the plight of the dying elder poignantly: "With little or no promise of recuperation, the older individual can fall into depression and despair. . . . In this situation, it takes extraordinary reserves of spiritual power to maintain a life of hope and creativity."[27] And it would be the task of the minister, then, to develop those reserves in relation to the elder's faithing abilities in understanding death, resurrection and anointing. In view of initial studies which show that elders at higher stages of faith development are more capable of consciously embracing the question of death,[28] ministers can make use of these "faithers" in their work with dying elders at less developed stages. In addition, as an interpreter of religious meaning the minister can provide the elder with the opportunity to find a final "place" in the "world" of meaning in which the elder lives, whether that is a world involving the magical manipulation of stage two or the ambiguous interplay of good and evil of stage five.

The Role of the Minister

Although we have already touched upon the role of the minister to elders, we also need to look at the minister's person in terms of images, perspectives and participation. Whoever ministers with the elderly must have developed a good sense of his or her own history and must be able to share a personal story in such a way that it relates to the stories of elders. The minister can also know stories about powerful elders who exhibit those qualities of authenticity, courage and resourcefulness which shatter the cultural stereotypes of elderhood and move toward stage four and five faithing.

Certainly the minister should have examined personal feelings, anxieties, fears about aging, death and the dying process as well as the various theoretical materials about death, dying and elderhood in general. In this way as the interpreter of the end times of elderhood, the minister can develop images of dignity and understanding for each elder in terms of individual needs and modes of faithing.

But in order to effectively challenge the self-images of elders and enlarge their perspectives on themselves and the world, the caring minister must gain entrance into the worldview of elders and walk around that universe of memories, glories and losses. Such perspective-taking requires discernment skills in attending to the ways of elders. A key question, an idle conversation or a seemingly thoughtless reminiscence may reveal deep concerns and enlarge the minister's entrance into the elder's perspective. Or body language may provide clues to grief and joy evident only to those who have spent time with elders and have studied the unique physiological, psychological and sociological dimensions of elderhood.

The minister has the further burden of challenging not only the aged around their own perspectives but most especially the larger community. This demands that the minister understand the perspectives of various groups within the community and utilize those perspectives in educating the entire community about the unique richness and vocation of elderhood.

Finally, the minister can help provide elders with a sense of participation and involvement in the community which helps them "finish well" the cycle of their lives through a call to "the stewardship of life itself"[29] in response to their strengths, limitations and faith stages. This will mean that as a minimum beginning the minister "locate the 'hidden' elderly in order to bring them into the parish and community life and help them obtain community and government services to which they may be entitled but which they do not receive."[30]

Elders Ministering to Elders and the World

Certainly one of the most promising dimensions of ministry with elders surrounds the involvement of elders to elders and elders to the community. In this context the understanding of the faith stages can provide elder ministers with a powerful tool for self-understanding and for understanding their service to others as a sharing in Jesus' ministry. Precisely because of their daily involvement in the paschal mystery of dying and letting go, elders have special charisms which must be used to manifest the loving God to other elders and to the bustling world which marginalizes elders. As ministers to others, elders can create prayer forms, liturgical expressions, special feasts which draw upon their own creativity and provide meaning and challenge for the faith growth of the elders they serve.

Elders have a unique contribution to make to the dimension of perspective-taking by employing their own experiences of aging in order to assist their peers. And in this area the faith stage level appears to make a difference in the understanding of their own aging processes, or "agesense." Using "agesense" as a measure of subjective feeling about aging, Dr. Richard Shulik found that those elders who are higher in their faithing modes "are far more sensitive to internal changes brought about by the ageing process" than other elders. In his study of elders he goes on to note:

> They [elders at higher stages] are also likely to be more articulate as
> spokesmen for their generation. They can provide a very vivid de-

scription of what the ageing process is like, whereas their peers at lower stages of faith development are relatively inarticulate in this regard.[31]

Referring to his earlier finding that elders at higher levels of faith development tend to be most capable of empathizing with others and understanding the nature of the world and the meaning of their place in the world, Dr. Shulik postulates: ''Just as their understanding of the outer world is more comprehensive and more differentiated, so also their understanding of their 'inner worlds' may also be more refined'' inasmuch as ''they may have 'incorporated' or befriended a greater portion of their subconscious processes.'' And Dr. Shulik found that elders at higher levels of faith development also show lower levels of ''pathological'' fantasies.[32]

Shulik's research suggests, then, that the elder minister who can be identified as reflective of stage five faithing will offer some essential perspectives on the aging process to other elders. Here ''agesense'' becomes a clue to the elder's faithing mode as well as a way of helping elder ministers articulate what others may sense but be unable to fully understand or to fully communicate to others.

For the community this means that elder ministers at higher faith stages offer images and become models or precursors of attitudes toward aging which can be developed in people of all ages. It will be important then to have elders develop and lead educational explorations of death and aging as well as incorporate their insights into the prayer and worship of the believing community.

Finally through their participation and service elder ministers can make great contributions to other elders and to the community at large. While the physical, emotional and mental health of the elder may limit involvement in some ways, the elder minister can find numerous modes of participation which consolidate and challenge the faith growth of elders. Thus the elder minister can invite elders at stage three into a one-to-one ministry involving, for example, tutoring children in a local school, helping a child at the day care center, visiting other elders unable to move about, or developing prayer and worship services. Elders at stages four and five can be challenged to engage in activities which involve justice issues for elders and for the community through lobbying efforts, educational programs or organizations like the Gray Panthers or the American Association of Retired Persons.[33]

One particularly important area of lay ministry for elders involves those elders unable to take care of themselves. Experiencing an often acute sense of *dependence,* these elders especially need to feel that they are participating in the larger community's development. In this sense the Christian elder, especially at the higher stages, acts as interpreter of the symbols of death and resurrection in explaining the particular vocation of the suffering elder. For by their patient suffering and agonizing losses dependent elders "edify" (literally "build up") the Christian community and help transform the community's understandings of suffering and loss through their (the elders') own lived experiences. Whether this is understood as "inexplicable mystery of God's will" (stage three), "growth through diminishment" (stages four and five), or "our participation in the redemptive transformation of the world" (stage five), all elders can achieve some sense of participation in the development of the believing community, even in the most physically limiting circumstances.

The Family

Throughout this discussion of elderhood, we have assumed the presence of family members who sustain and nurture the elder in so many ways. The minister sensitive to the growth and diminishments of elders will realize that as the elder changes, the relationships with family members change also. Utilizing this interactive model of family life,[34] the minister will both foster the continuing communication of family members as well as challenge the expectations and images of elders which family members have.

Thus the minister plays a key role in interpreting the symbolic dimension of elderhood to the family. The family needs information about the effects of any illness, disease or loss; but the family also must have information on opportunities for the growth of elders in such areas as health, education and housing. In addition to such practical information, families need support and aid in sorting out the difficult issues they face. In this regard, families are often more knowledgeable than ministers; ministers need to listen to families in their role as interpreters of faith growth.

As the family embraces new images of elderhood, their perspectives on elders broaden through their daily contact with issues of elders. In addition, family members occasionally experience feelings of guilt around their treatment of elderly parents or grandparents, particularly if this involves placing the elder in a nursing home. The skilled minister and especially the elder minister can serve as a humanizing, objective link in this painful process, by encouraging family members to adopt the perspective of the elder with all the loss involved and elders to understand the perspectives of loving and caring that family members are no longer able to provide at home. A knowledge of the family member's differing faith levels can help the minister communicate a Christian interpretation of the needs and losses involved.[35]

Finally participation for the family means continuing involvement with elders. Whether through visits, phone calls or letters, family members provide elders with a sense of continuity, meaning and joy essential to those elders brushed to the edges of family and community life. And in return the family's contact with elders reminds family members of the whole of the life cycle, even when elders cannot seem to discuss more than their continuing ailments. In a way through their own capacities for empathy family members are invited to participate in those very diminishments the elders experience and in so doing relieve the elder of the weighty burdens of aging.

In this process of enabling the family to minister to one another, the minister has one final role as the interpreter of death. Through the anointing ceremony, the funeral and burial services, the minister can recapture the meaning of the dead elder's life as well as the meaning of aging and indeed of life's purpose itself. Yet this must be done in a manner sensitive to the family's faithing process, especially to the children who may be experiencing the death of a close relative for the first time.

The Community

There are many areas in which the minister with the elder can contribute to the community's understanding of and involvement with the concerns of elderhood along faith development lines. In the first place, people of all ages must be challenged in terms of the images and symbolic stereotypes of aging and elders. Preaching and liturgies which focus upon elderhood, involve elders or amplify the Christian understanding of the fullness of every aspect of human life can reflect a view of aging as a witness to God's voice calling us to full being and personhood.

Certainly educational programs involving elders themselves can enrich the whole community. An intergenerational approach can include elderhood as one of several components in the learning situation. Following the faithing development scheme here might indicate times for story telling, retelling classic Bible tales in terms of the conflicts and growth with which the heroes and heroines had to deal, e.g. Sarah confronting motherhood. Or the minister might involve all age groups in dramatizing the great liturgical events of the year or presenting biblical stories as plays. Other approaches might include small group discussions of issues pertinent to elders and family such as death and dying, spirituality or neighborhood services; other groups might form around problem-solving techniques and advocacy approaches to situations afflicting elders and the community.[36]

Equally important, the education of ministers must involve courses about elderhood. While pastors and ministers are in unique positions to help elders, they often lack basic understandings and skills involving elderhood. Although the interest and numbers are growing, few seminaries and ministry training programs offer studies in elderhood as a constitutive component of training.[37] Such programs could well offer internships with elders as part of their field training.

Any parish approach to ministry with elders can best understand the views, needs and attitudes of elderhood by involving elders in every aspect of parish life according to the elder's faithing mode. In addition regular visits to homes of elders, nursing homes and retirement centers can not only support elders but also provide the visitors with greater understanding of their own faithing and growth throughout the life cycle. And through the visiting process elders are able to carry out their "vocation" of witnessing to God's presence in every human situation to the rest of the community.

Finally, the parish can act as an intermediary with the community's social service agencies, referring elders to the variety of services already available in the community. Parishes, in some form or other, can provide advocates for the needs of elders and critically examine those agencies which already care for elders. Or parishes and entire church communities can establish environments for elders which provide in addition to basic services the resources for the faith growth of elders at all levels of the developmental scheme.

One model of such an approach is The Shepherd's Center in Kansas City, Missouri. Established in 1972, the goals of the Center incorporate several of the dimensions of faith development:

1. To sustain older people who desire to live independently in their own homes and apartments in the community;

2. To provide retired people with an opportunity to use their experience, training, and skills in significant social roles;

3. To enhance life satisfaction in later maturity and enable self-realization through artistic expression, community service, caring relationships, lifelong learning, and the discovery of inner resources;

4. To demonstrate life at its best in later maturity so as to provide attractive role models for successful aging;

5. To advocate the right of older people to a fair share of society's goods, and to assist them in gaining access to services;

6. To contribute to knowledge about what is required for successful aging and to experiment with new approaches and programs for meeting the needs of older people.[38]

Independence, modeling, advocacy, new knowledge, self-realization, participation—these are all factors involved in faith development, especially in the crucial transition to stage four and beyond. Thus an institutional approach such as the Center's supports the possibility of incorporating faith development into a supportive and confirming as well as challenging environment for continued faith growth in elderhood. In view of the growing numbers of elders in our society, the church's ministry must foster the rich development and variety of ministry among elders, not only to one another but also to and for the whole church.

Summary

Throughout this and the previous chapter we have been exploring two dimensions of ministry which revolve around common themes of suffering, death, abandonment, dependency and marginalization in society. False images and stereotypes of illness and aging lock the healthy and young as well as the sick and elderly in attitudes and behaviors which affront the full dignity and worth of millions of people and vitally inhibit their faith growth. Ironically, social perspectives toward the ill and elders tend to be negative almost in proportion to our emphasis upon health and youth, two prominent preoccupations of contemporary Americans caught up in the energizing activities of modern life. The result of these images and perspectives leads to the removal of the ill and elders from our view and from active participation in the community's life, in effect assuring their marginalization to the fringe of society. The resulting loss of status and income, the accompanying loneliness and the loss of self-worth reinforce the stereotypes and closes the circle surrounding the place of the ill and aged in our society.

Yet this negative picture must be balanced by the new developments mentioned earlier. From the hospice to more holistic forms of medicine and from elders' discussion groups to political movements like the Gray Panthers, people working with the ill and especially elders themselves have developed programs and strategies to counter oppressive attitudes and social situations. Ministers too have become more aware of the individual needs, social obstacles, and unique vocations of the ill and elders. The faith development model can be an important tool in this development.

In that regard we have explored multiple ways to challenge the negative images, change the perspectives of the ill and elderly as well as the healthy and young and develop active modes of participation. Our focus has developed strategies aimed at removing obstacles to faith growth but more importantly has provided approaches to actively promote the faithing process, especially in the movement from stage three faithing to stage four. In part this development centers around re-examining the central Christian understandings of suffering, death and resurrection in terms of the sense of loss and diminishment inherent in any illness and in the aging process itself. This leads us to interpret the meaning of sickness and aging as arenas of life which reveal God's presence inasmuch as we "let go" of our own control and allow God's transformative spirit to enter our lives and the lives of others in the midst of bodily diminishment.

In this sense the "vocation" of the sick and elder challenges society's pretensions and preoccupations with health, youth, status and power. The mission of the sick:

> . . . is to call all back to an honest contact with reality: that God is renewing humankind by overcoming suffering not by abolishing it but through suffering itself. . . . "Sickness is a collision with human limitation, a harsh and uncompromising reminder of the reality of man's finiteness and of the emptiness of the pursuit of an earthly paradise."[39]

And in their vocation elders "are to us a witness of a 'cleaner' set of values, purged of the clutter of egocentric striving and open to the whisper of God calling us into being."[40] Or again, what elders "articulate . . . is that *life is worthwhile;* life is worth closing well not because of what has been achieved by an individual but because one's very being is of worth."[41]

In these processes of restructuring images and symbols surrounding illness and elderhood, of broadening social and personal perspectives and of fostering participation in the life of the community, all key dimensions of promoting faith growth, the church and the minister play key roles. And no matter what skills and resources the ministers may have, their own visions of themselves as whole yet broken and their own understandings of their faithing journeys will shape their enabling capacities with the sick and elderly and their willingness to challenge the members of the Christian community and society at large. In this sense ministers with the sick and elders must always remember that they are being ministered to at the same time as they are ministering: "So maybe, after all, there are old [and sick] men and women hidden from our troubled vision, whom we have to bring into the midst of our assembly so that they can cast away the darkness of our confusing existence and tell us top from bottom."[42]

In our next chapters, we will develop the discussion of marginalization and ministry one step further. First we will look at yet another institutional form of marginalization in contemporary society, the prison and ministry. Then we will conclude with the relationship between the church's ministry and social justice.

8. MINISTRY TO THE IMPRISONED

While there is a soul in prison, I am not free.
Socialist Eugene V. Debs[1]

The laws are really organized for the protection of the men who rule the world. They were never organized or enforced to do justice. We have no system for doing justice. If every man and woman and child in the world had a chance to make a decent, fair, honest living, there would be no jails, and no lawyers and no courts.
Lawyer Clarence Darrow[2]

Who in our society but the incarcerated are more systematically brutalized daily? Prisoners at this historical moment are the crucified in our society.
Prison Minister Sr. Joannette
Nitz, O.P.[3]

Up to this point in our discussions of faith development and forms of ministry, we have explored areas routinely associated with church life. In the last two chapters our concerns extended to the marginalized populations of the sick and elderly. In those cases we were looking at either those temporarily separated from the community or those marginalized by a reality outside their own control.

In the case of the prisoner, however, we face a new challenge, particularly in relation to the faith development scheme. In the first place, in place of sympathy for the afflicted the general public views the plight of the imprisoned as justly deserved. In addition, while cure, rehabilitation, restoration or at least care characterizes the institutions and attitudes of those serving the sick and elders, attitudes and actual policies of retribution, recrimination and in many cases malign neglect and brutality characterize the institutions of the criminal justice system.

More critically for our discussion, we can identify the penal institutions more in terms of the ways in which they *do not* support the faith development factors. The self-images and symbols of the prison system overwhelm any view of the person as a created reflection of God. Institutionalized punishment and isolation prevent opportunities for perspective-taking, and the prison's daily regimen provides no sense of

142

participation and responsibility. Prison personnel are not in a position to model more advanced stages of faith development. Nor does the development of community and a sense of independence find support in a prison environment. These challenges for ministry and for a growing faithing process provide an important test for Christian care and justice which the faith development model can greatly assist.

Before we examine the issues concerned with prison ministry, I would like to indicate the limits of the comments in this chapter. Although the important discussions surrounding capital punishment, prison reform, private ownership of penal systems and other issues certainly form pressing concerns for anyone in prison ministry, our focus centers on ministry in the prison context. And while important differences exist between the jail and the prison context,[4] our discussion will revolve around the prison as the central place for ministry. That will involve us in the plight of the prisoner, the prison environment, the minister-chaplain and to some extent ex-offenders, families and the community/parish. Before we proceed, however, we must quickly review some of the background of the prisoner in today's society.

Jail and Prison in America

Among the general public, the hardened attitudes of the 1980's toward those in prison rest on several recent trends and perceptions. From 1960 to 1974 *reported* crimes tripled from 3,360,000 to over 10,000,000 and since then increased another thirty percent from 10,000,000 to 13,295,399 in 1980. The state and federal prison population has grown from 204,211 in 1973 (96 for every 100,000 people) to 353,167 (153 for every 100,000) in 1980. When we add the number of those awaiting sentence or serving sentences under one year, about 16,000, and those in local jails, 158,394 in 1978, over half a million people are behind bars, placing the United States third in the world after the Soviet Union and South Africa in the number of incarcerations. Funding for police, courts and correction facilities has increased dramatically from $4 billion in 1965 to $26 billion for fiscal year 1979.[5] Correspondingly jail and prison construction has proceeded apace, while more than thirty states are currently under court orders to correct overcrowded and unconstitutional conditions.[6]

Currently the average sentence in the United States is four years, compared with thirty-five days in the Netherlands and less than a year in Sweden.[7] Support for the death penalty has increased dramatically from thirty-eight percent in 1965 to seventy-two percent in 1985,[8] with Catholics more likely to support capital punishment than Protestants.[9] This increase in attitudes has accompanied an increase in the number of death row inmates, up fifteen percent in 1983 over 1982 for example; and similarly, after a ten year moratorium ended in 1977, the number of executions has increased, from one in 1977 to twenty-one in 1984, eighteen in 1985 and 1986 and twenty-five in the first ten months of 1987.[10]

Media accounts fuel public perceptions of increasing crime, violent criminals and rioting prisoners and fashion images of crime as inherently violent and of the criminal as poor, young, ignorant and a minority person. In actual fact, statistics from the National Victimization Survey of the Census Bureau has indicated that from 1973 to 1981 the total level of crime remained relatively stable. In addition, in the past decade over ninety percent of all serious crime reported by the FBI has been non-violent property-related crimes; homicides constitute only one half of one percent of all serious crime. And of those eventually serving terms in jail or prison, fifty percent have committed non-violent crimes.[11]

Furthermore as numerous studies indicate, middle and upper-class whites avoid jail and prisons for their crimes while the poor and minorities are overrepresented there and on death row:

> *For the same criminal behavior,* the poor are more likely to be arrested; if arrested, they are more likely to be charged; if charged, more likely to be convicted; if convicted, more likely to be sentenced to prison; and if sentenced, more likely to be given longer prison terms than members of the middle and upper classes. . . . In other words, the image of the criminal population one sees in our nation's jails and prisons is distorted by the shape of the criminal justice system itself.[12]

In the author's analysis, this conveys to the public the message "that the greatest danger to the average citizen comes from below him or her on the economic ladder, not from above."[13]

Faith Development and the Criminal Justice System

In this brief review I wanted to indicate the background against which the minister to the imprisoned works. In particular, the distorted images of crime and criminals which inform the public reflect to prisoners and those working with them powerfully debilitating images of the human person and false understandings of the "fairness" of the criminal justice system.

Furthermore, the very philosophies of imprisonment rest on assumptions detrimental to the kind of faith growth we have described: toward greater responsibility, toward a self-chosen community, toward enhancement of the person, with opportunities for faith sharing and challenge within a supportive environment, with chances to take the perspectives of others and with times to perceive oneself as "entrusted" with responsibility. Whether they express "purifying punishment," physical and psychological deterrence or "treatment," the prisoner is seen as someone not in control and thus not basically responsible. All these models deny that prisoners can make moral choices, can assume responsibility for their lives and can grow humanly, spiritually.[14]

Since the goal of the institution in whatever form seems to be the maintenance of order in view of the criminal "nature" of the inmates, Christian values of repentance, forgiveness, respect for the person, mercy, love and justice have little opportunity to develop the mature "faithing" we looked at in earlier settings. Inasmuch as the institution itself incorporates some form of reward and punishment in its daily operation, the modal "faithing" form of prison life fits the description of stage one faithing or at best the stage two view in which prisoners and staff adopt a "you-scratch-my back, I'll-scratch-yours" approach to one another and the institution.

Even prison architecture reinforces dependency patterns and low self-esteem:

> The architecture and layout of most traditional prisons not only prevents the inmate from expressing his reactions but magnifies his perception of not having behavioral control. The employment of the cellblock observation system reinforces the inmate's feelings of subordination to staff and emphasizes his inability to influence the structure of his environment. . . . As a former convict so eloquently stated, " . . . one's individuality, independence, sensitivity, and responsibility for self are systematically assaulted. . . . "[15]

In addition, the majority of prisoners are not affiliated with religion and view the institutional church and its representatives as hypocritical. Those who maintain some religious expression often continue a stage one or two approach to their imprisonment by looking upon their imprisonment as God's judgment against them. God becomes the father figure or the unjust despot, and they attribute responsibility for their actions to the devil or an evil spirit rather than themselves.[16]

In view of all these factors the prison minister faces formidable obstacles in carrying out the gospel mandate to visit the imprisoned, especially in a faith development framework. However, several promising reform measures and experiments, especially a "just community" concept using Kohlberg's moral development patterns, show that in some cases a correlative faith development model can be successfully employed. And at its least such a model helps the minister anticipate difficulties in prison ministry as well as better understand the ways in which the institution reinforces patterns of stagnation and regression in faithing, especially in relation to our key facets of cognitive conflict in symbols and images, perspective-taking, and sense of participation.

Prisoners and Prisons

The first questions we need to raise about the images and symbols surrounding people in prison involve the very process by which they got there. Our images of criminals are "selected" in large part by what we decide to define as crimes and by the ways in which the criminal justice system filters out middle and upper class people. Thus our images form around those who are left, the poor and minorities, while large areas of harmful activities such as air pollution, unnecessary surgery, occupational injuries resulting from plant negligence or consumer deception practiced by white, middle and upper-class people are often overlooked or treated as civil rather than criminal matters.[17]

These distorted cultural images find concrete expression in the embodiment of the criminal justice system, the jail and prison. From the moment of arrest through sentencing and imprisonment, the "prisoner" is continually attacked emotionally, psychically and spiritually until some form of the image of criminal sticks no matter how strongly resisted or how innocent the individual may be. Eventually the self-image of most prisoners combines a fatalistic determinism about their fate, a profound sense of failure to shape their environment, a loser mentality and the stance of the "Manly Man" (or woman).[18] When they see countless others escape detection and prosecution, prisoners often experience a strong sense of injustice and thus an unwillingness to admit their wrongdoing. At the same time, the desire for respect, for some measure of control over one's life, for equality, emerges in a variety of ways for prisoners, such as surly behavior, slow-downs, passive resistance, self-destructive and violent acts or even riots. While we cannot overlook prisoners' responsibility for their own actions, we can begin to see the ways in which prisoners construct their self-images around perceptions shared by the public, guards and the entire criminal justice system.

Then too the prisoner is cut off physically and psychologically from contact with other persons in all varieties of life who could challenge this poor self-image, and the "walls" of separation from "decent people" reinforce such an image by surrounding the prisoner with others much like himself or herself in background and mentality who must all conform to the prison's expectations. Prison "society," then, reinforces an already low image of self and of other prisoners. A hint of the stage two mode of faithing emerging from this environment breaks forth in this prisoner's comment: "You know how it is in this dog-eat-dog world. You got to take the other guy before he takes you."[19]

In addition, since prisoners do not see their punishment as just, well-intentioned or "purifying,"[20] then their perceptions of the prison, coupled with their treatment by the correctional authorities, only reinforce the symbol of the prison as a stage one punishment or a stage two arena in which one "cooperates" to get minimal individual needs met. Such a survival ethic pulls against any call for community and concern for others' welfare.

The prison minister then faces a formidable task in challenging the prisoners' self-images and views of the prison environment and must begin with a Christian anthropology which reshapes those perceptions. Such an anthropology begins with the assertion that crime is "fundamentally a violation between persons and relationships,"[21] rather than against the state. From such a perspective, the "solutions" to a correctional system from a Christian viewpoint would involve factors of forgiveness, reconciliation, healing, social justice and restitution. Such a model includes an image of the "criminal"-prisoner as a free, responsible and so *accountable* human being and involves some form of response to the victims of crime as well. These components support the critical evaluation which a faith development scheme calls for in terms of developing a mature faithing of responsibility to oneself and to the community on at least a stage three or stage four view.

In addition the images and symbols of a Christian anthropology incorporate an understanding of the criminal/prisoner as a true reflection of God's image, in as much need of reconciliation, liberation and transformation as the rest of us. Beginning with the liberation of the Hebrews from Egyptian rule through to the imprisonment of John the Baptist, Paul and Stephen, the biblical account is one of liberation from bondage and oppression of the person in any area. Quoting Isaiah in the temple (Lk 4:16–31) Jesus proclaims the release of the captives as a central part of his mission. He dies the death of a criminal and accepts the criminal at his side into his kingdom. The prophets and many of the apostles found themselves in jail, often as much for attacking the property arrangements of their societies as for proclaiming a religious message. Given the disproportionate numbers of poor and minorities in our prison system, these biblical images, while not necessarily justifying nor romanticizing the "crimes" which prisoners have committed, provide a check against which the prisoner can counter the destructive self-images conveyed by the worldview of the criminal justice system itself.[22]

For prison ministry such a Christian anthropology and biblical analysis might find direct expression in a variety of forms, from liturgies to prayer groups and Bible study sessions which challenge the destructive self-images built into a stage one punishment or stage two "con-man" view of prison society. In addition, classes, workshops and retreats which encourage the prisoner to view himself or herself as gifted and talented, with other modes of self-expression than violence, reflect this theological view. Such experiences develop more positive self-images and, in view of the numbers of poor and minority prisoners with little educational background, provide skills, attitudes and perspectives needed for any future resumption of "normal" life outside prison.

Finally, prisoners need to understand how the public currently views criminal activity and prisons and the role that jail and prisons serve in the larger society. Such an analysis outlines how the criminal justice system serves certain interests better than others and has definite biases. These stage three and four perspectives can serve as a step in consciousness raising among prisoners which leads to reforms within the prison system and prepares them to understand the social system once they leave prison.

Using some of these tools, the prison minister can develop new approaches which complement the ways in which prisoners routinely share their stories among themselves. When the minister adds the biblical outlook we saw above, prisoners can express their "sharings" in a suitable faithing context as well. Listening carefully to each other and hearing their stories at the different developmental levels, the inmates themselves sponsor one another's sharings. In addition, the minister can utilize accounts of prisoners such as Malcolm X, Dietrich Bonhoeffer, Martin Luther King, Jr. and others to help prisoners interpret the significance of their imprisonment within a larger context of meaning and to provide models for more reflective lives and faith stances.

Beyond participation in such small sharing groups, the minister can foster forums for exchange between prisoners and citizen volunteers who

visit the prison to learn about prison life and to serve as a support for inmates. Such visitors furnish inmates with yet another context to share life
stories and often assist prisoners in obtaining basic necessities, contacting
relatives and so forth. More importantly, these outsiders demonstrate a
form of concern by the outside community and model more developed levels of community, cooperation and social living than the modal levels of
prison which afford little developed perspective-taking.

Since most prisoners realize that only some ten percent of all "criminals" find their way to jail or prison, they tend to feel that they are the
"victims" of a biased system. Thus empathy with people in the community and trust in the community's representatives become difficult. In
turn, the empathy required to develop a sense of community within the
prison, while possible to develop, needs much nurturing. Yet the more the
minister can promote such experiences and encounters with visitors the
more such capacities can develop.

In addition to the exchanges with outsiders, the prison minister can
foster sharings between inmates and prison staff. Initially rooted in distrust
on both sides, such exchanges where developed have promoted a much
more humane context for prison life. Again, the minister utilizing a faith
development model would facilitate such exchanges with a goal toward
greater understanding, especially of more community-oriented perspectives.

Beyond these individual exchanges of perspectives, the minister must
assist prisoners in viewing their place within the larger structure of society.
Far from justifying the existing criminal justice system, such an analysis
would incorporate theological and political perspectives of liberation in
discussions of violence and non-violence, conflict resolution and communication skills, the legitimate and illegitimate use of force locally and
even internationally. These aspects of an education program would possibly be seen as "subversive" by some prison authorities, and yet such
analyses provide alternative perspectives and groundings for behaviors
other than the violence and retaliation of prisoners against themselves, one
another and prison staff. In addition inmates need to understand how factors such as poverty, race and class have shaped their lives to this point.
Only through some such understanding can new behaviors and attitudes
develop which support more developed faith growth.

Still another approach to perspective-taking involves ways in which
inmates are enabled to take the perspective of their victims or the community harmed by the crime. A number of programs such as the Victim
Offender Reconciliation Program or the Community Service Restitution

Program[23] rest upon the premises of offender responsibility and response to the victims of crime. The Christian view of the person behind such programs sees the offender as both responsive and capable of moral responsibility. Thus not only do restitution and reconciliation attempt to satisfy the claims of justice, but they further involve offenders in the victim's and community's worlds. Where such programs are possible, they promote perspective-taking which challenges the faithing modes of prisoners, victims, and law-enforcement personnel and promotes a stage three orientation toward personal responsibility and community.

Perhaps in no other area of prison life are the differences between civilian and prisoner felt so keenly as in the loss of participation in the decisions which affect one's very person. No matter how well justified "objectively," that loss represents the deliberate efforts to remove prisoners from playing a role in any form of "community." And yet, ironically, we expect released convicts to resume social roles in the larger community when deprived of such roles in prison. From our developmental perspective, the *capacity* for community participation and the sense of responsibility rest fundamentally upon the factors of perspective-taking, moral decision-making, symbols, world coherence and views of authority which encompass the faith development scheme. When these elements are not only *not* supported along developmental paths but are reduced to the lowest stages, we should not be surprised that "reform" and "rehabilitation" achieve so little positive results.

Most of the people found in jails and prisons have not participated in many of society's benefits in the first place. Prisoners' fatalism and lack of personal responsibility reflect the actual situations in which they found themselves all their lives. Prison merely represents a more extreme form of their earlier marginalization. As they pass through each step of the criminal justice system, prisoners are simultaneously viewed as fully responsible for their "criminal" acts but irresponsible in terms of the most basic decisions of daily life. In relation to the need to feel valued, trusted and "faithed in" as a prelude to more developed forms of "faithing," prisoners have been systematically cut off from the very sources, family, friends, church, community, which could supply such trust and must now struggle alone to develop any sense of trust in themselves or others.

Here we have the fundamental contradiction of the criminal justice system: rooted in an abstract sense of personal responsibility for actions, the system systematically reduces any arena for the exercise of that responsibility. Given that most prisoners do not view themselves as free but as "forced" in some degree to commit crimes, then the absence of any exercise of freedom only reinforces the image of oneself as not free.

> [T]o a great extent, one is free only to the extent that one believes himself/herself to be free. . . . The regimen of prison life, rather than encouraging the use of freedom and fostering responsibility, makes convicts dependent on authorities for their every need, and the capricious use of authority in prisons enforces prisoners' belief that what happens in their lives is indeed beyond their control.[24]

An equally degrading aspect of prison life which works against responsible participation centers around the meaningless work which prisoners perform. If there is any work, most jobs involve no marketable skills or training and bring in only pennies in earning power. Thus "a person leaving here skill-less and penniless has but one choice (i.e. to resume a life of crime), and so society again becomes a victim."[25] Furthermore lack of meaningful work and the poor pay encroach upon self-worth and a sense of dignity in a society in which we measure our worth by what we do.

Finally, lack of political participation and responsibility accompanies the denial of personal and economic participation in prison life. While the denial of full citizenship rights can be justified to some extent, prison prevents most prisoners from involvement in any governance of their environment. If democracy rests upon responsible involvement in political life, prisons systematically suppress the development of such a capacity, often forbidding prisoners political magazines, access to political analyses, etc., especially when these involve prison reform. In terms of the faith development scheme, the development of at least a stage three form of faithing would require some sense of involvement in group governance and community responsibility.

At a minimal level, the kind of sharing groups mentioned earlier also involve a sense of participation in telling one's own story, whether from an explicit faith dimension or not. In addition, the prison minister should view the continual struggle of inmates for simple privileges over uncensored mail, television or exercise as not only matters of more humane treatment but also as the prisoners' drive to exercise some control over their environment and thus to express some responsibility in prison society. Participation in these minimal decisions supports the development of more adequate modes of faithing.

A broader and very exciting approach to responsible participation emerges from the "just community" experiment tried in a small setting in Niantic Correctional Institution for Women, Connecticut, in the late 1970's. There two researchers with experience in the corrections field, Joseph Hickey and Peter Scharf, established cottages of prisoners who governed their immediate environment using Lawrence Kohlberg's moral development model. While the larger, philosophical issues of corrections are beyond our concern here, the basis and outcomes of their experiment are an essential dimension of the faith development approach that a minister or team of ministers could use.

The "just community" approach in a prison setting assumes that moral development is possible beyond a stage one punishment or stage two "you scratch my back" approach. The model also assumes that prisoners, even long deprived of opportunities to exercise choices and exhibit some sense of freedom, participation and responsibility, respond to such an approach as genuine and critical to their self-development and their return to the larger society. Hickey and Sharf's application used the daily dilemmas of inmates in the cottages to discuss their moral implications and to challenge inmates to more "adequate," i.e. higher stage, decisions.

With the cooperation of the Connecticut Department of Corrections, Hickey and Scharf trained a small staff and invited a select group of inmates to join the "just community" cottage. The inmates and staff established a "constitution" which set out the rules of the cottage. Regular community meetings provided the arena in which the rules were enforced and maintained while conflicts were resolved or at least articulated. At marathon sessions inmates renegotiated the constitution while they dealt with individual and personal issues in small groups. Throughout all these processes, the goals of the two "interveners" included creating a context of trust, training inmates to be peer counselors and take the perspectives of others, facilitating moral discussion and helping inmates remain faithful to their commitments and agreements. Developmentally, Hickey and Scharf sought to create a prison community associated with stage four of Kohlberg (three of Fowler). The development "of an autonomous moral community . . . in which the inmates could form a mutual contract to aid one another was seen as a critical goal. . . . [U]nless the prison can be transformed . . . into a place with a common sense of community and concern little could be expected in the way of altered lives for inmates."[26]

The authors recognize the difficulty in establishing the basic trust among themselves, inmates, staff and the prison administration. In addition, there are inherent conflicts between the prison bureaucracy based upon rules established outside the control of prisoners and the prisoners'

own set of rules democratically established in the dialogue of moral decision-making. In addition, a built-in social inequality exists between inmates and staff. And finally, the legal system does not support basic rights
for inmates. Consequently distrust pervades the attempt to establish a just
community at all levels.

And yet the program was a success. As opposed to inmates in other
settings who saw prison rules as punishment or sanctions imposed by the
staff, those in the program perceived the rules they had established as fair.
The program worked best when it consisted of at least half of the prisoners
at Kohlberg's stage three (community based upon expectations of important others) or above and when those inmates identified with the positions
of the program staff and were respected by other inmates. Their findings
support Kohlberg's claim that moral change is associated with the perception of justice in the environment and that the social environment of the
prison can be used as a means of political re-education.

> We are convinced . . . that the application of self-governing processes
> in prisons . . . provides the best hope for a morally defensible penal
> system in which the individual is treated not primarily as an instrument
> to social order but as the very justification for that order. . . . Pris-
> oners, like humans everywhere, generally respond in morally positive
> ways, particularly when they perceive their environment as fair and
> just and when they see that this experience can produce growth in
> moral terms.[27]

The implications of the model for prison personnel seems obvious.
Unless they are convinced that they can trust prisoners to develop a self-
governing system within limits, a genuine community of trust and concern
cannot develop. In the Niantic experiments, the staff often found themselves caught in hard dilemmas when inmates would entrust them with
knowledge which, if revealed to the prison administration, might bring
harsh punishments. The just community approach can only work when
inmates can trust staff with confidential information and when staff trust
inmates to make responsible decisions when dealing with the misdeeds of
fellow prisoners.

Hickey and Scharf also address themselves to one other form of participation which we examined earlier, the work which prisoners do. They
acknowledge the status of prisoners as "economic chattel" and agree that
a prison industry which used unpaid labor to make competitive goods
would be economically and morally unacceptable. The solution they pro-

pose involves the incorporation of private industry into the prison system with appropriate pay scales. Such an approach would lead to "(1) fair wages for their work . . . (2) on-the-job experience in a modern, efficient business operation; (3) meaningful vocational training which instills a skill demanded in the civilian labor market."[28] In this way prisoners would see themselves as contributors to the nation's economy and would have the economic base to develop a program of restitution to their victims, an appropriate form of perspective-taking from the view of faith development.

The authors also suggest the possibility of using this industrial base in the prison to develop labor unions as a basis for securing political rights and participation for prisoners. Although a more controversial suggestion, this possibility further develops the sense of participation and self-worth so basic to a return to full civilian life.

Finally, in combining prisoners' participation in economic and political life with a sense of responsibility for their crimes and their own welfare, Hickey and Scharf suggest that self-determined task sentencing "designed to provide restitution to crime victims" form the basis of the criminal justice system. In this scheme prisoners repay to their victims or victims' families a prepaid assessment based on the severity of their crimes and "include an additional fine to satisfy society's need to punish as well as reduce the cost of court." In this way release would not be based on "playing the rehabilitation game" but rather "on repayment of a debt owed his victims and society through honest labor."[29]

The proposals outlined briefly in the full just community concept incorporate the faith development factors: symbols of prisoner and prisons, perspective-taking and sense of participation. Although there is no guarantee that growth in faith would occur in such a model, the elements which militate against faith growth would be largely removed. In place of the "degradation ceremonies" and dependence of the existing system, prisoners would be encouraged toward greater independence and responsibility through setting the terms of their own sentencing, making decent wages and providing direct restitution to victims and society.

And the role of prison staff would change too.

> Placing the responsibility for the duration of their sentences in the prisoners' hands provides the mechanism for a viable system of inmate rights and thereby forces a shift in the relationship between the institution and the prisoners. . . . Prison routine would necessarily orient to the needs of its private industrial component, and the correctional officer would be responsible for the protection of a vital labor force

rather than the custody of a resentful mob. . . . Within this frame-work, shared decision making would be legitimized, and a type of de-mocracy . . . could flourish.[30]

Although the prison minister individually cannot bring about such sweeping structural changes as Hickey and Scharf ultimately call for, the model serves as a background against which ministers can measure the strategies and approaches of their ministry. The model links together the issues of self-esteem and self-image, perspective-taking and participation/responsibility and reveals the important ways in which the prison environment can promote or hinder faith growth. Without excusing prisoners for their actual crimes, the just community concept shows that prisoners can view themselves differently and prepare themselves to assume a re-sponsible place in the larger society. When the minister combines the just community model with elements of faith sharing and a theology of im-prisonment, forgiveness and reconciliation, he or she can develop a pro-gram and environment in which faith growth can begin to sustain itself.

Several other approaches offer promise of developing the faith de-velopment factors we have utilized, particularly in view of a Christian un-derstanding of crime as a breach in relationship. Such programs would include probation, restitution, community service, temporary release, halfway houses, parole and other measures of community-based correc-tions. All of these means should involve some measure of participation/responsibility and perspective-taking in which the "criminal"/prisoner views the effects of his or her actions upon the victims and responsibly participates in building up a sense of faith and trust where these have been badly shattered. In summary the faith development scheme, then, serves to promote a more responsible approach to the criminal justice system, whether carried out in a just community model, community-based correc-tions systems or some form of restitution to and reconciliation with vic-tims.

The Prison Minister

The prison minister today faces a number of crucial questions sur-rounding his or her role of service to prisoners. Chief among these ques-tions is whether the prison minister is an agent of the system or an agent for transformation of prisoners and prison systems. This inquiry implies fundamental theological issues as well:

Prison chaplains are caught in the middle of classical theological teach-ings on the role of freedom in human decision-making, prisoners' self-perceptions and the growing body of evidence that crime is strongly influenced if not caused by social and economic forces originating outside of the individual. Chaplains who try to resolve this tension by resorting to a hard-line traditionalist stance on free will are apt to be uneasy with its failure to take account of communal responsibility for crime. . . . On the other hand, chaplains who accept deterministic explanations for crime . . . are likely to find that . . . they are of no help to prisoners because they thereby encourage their dependence, their lack of freedom, and fail to point the "way" toward individual transformation.[31]

As in other areas of ministry the prison minister must look at personal feelings, fears and stereotypes of prisoners and prison life. Since in general the prison culture is one foreign to most ministers' backgrounds, the minister must learn the very "language" and vocabulary of prison life, the different backgrounds of minorities, the "culture of poverty" with its differing expectations and needs. The introspective approaches of most middle-class pastoral counseling, communication patterns, prayer and spirituality do not reflect the thoughts and feelings of most prisoners. Thus the first need for ministers involves a critical examination of personal self-images and perspectives of prison life and demands that the minister lay aside middle-class perspectives, methods and expectations. The minister should be operating from at least a stage four faithing mode. In addition, the minister must be willing to share his or her feelings, anxieties and personal story and should know the stories of those who reveal the qualities of courage, independence, self-authority and faithing which can support those in the prison environment.

While the minister begins with Jesus' exhortation to "visit the imprisoned," prison ministry today requires that ministers have a broad understanding of the criminal justice system, the social origins of criminal activity and the place of social justice in prison ministry. In the current context, the minister must challenge, complement and enlarge the traditional image of ministry as support and comfort with a vision of ministry as advocacy *for* as well as service *with* prisoners. Furthermore such an advocacy role requires the minister to assume a much more critical image of the prison and criminal justice systems.

If the prisoner thinks that you [the minister] believe that he belongs there, that he should be in prison and that what needs to be done is to make it a little less oppressive, a little less destructive, but that basically it's right for that person to be in prison, then the minister is looked upon as a cop. . . . I think there is very little possibility of a human, much less a pastoral, relationship with that individual.[32]

In this first task, then, of reappraising images the chaplain/minister must attend to the ways in which the prison system wishes the minister to perform in a stage three mode of conformity as opposed to more of a stage four manner of prisoner advocacy and change. A social analysis of the causes of crime and a historical overview of the history of the penal system can shape more humane images of prisoners themselves and more critical views of the criminal justice system.

Inasmuch as prisoners see the minister as an advocate, a conscience to the larger society, the minister can assume another important role in the life of prisoners, namely that of *interpreter* of a more humane reality than prison life and of hope for their own future lives. As interpreter, the minister can help prisoners view their lives in categories other than fated punishment, God's just wrath and other images of a stage one or two mode of retribution. Rather the minister can call forth images of forgiveness and reconciliation, abandonment to God's providence, transformation and responsibility, justice and change, and community and concern for others' welfare as long as these are grounded in some of the changes in self-image, perspective and participation of prisoners mentioned above. Otherwise the gospel will fail to be heard in the midst of the hell of prison life.

The reappraisal just discussed leads necessarily to an enriched capacity for perspective-taking on the part of the prison minister. To be effective with prisoners the minister must be identified with them, must understand the trauma of arrest, trial, sentencing, lock-up and imprisonment. In addition, the minister must understand the prison routine and structure from the perspective of the prisoners, from the "bottom up," in view of the prison's punitive or "conning" mode of operation rather than just from the staff's perspective of "rehabilitation" or "therapy."

The world of prison life only magnifies the cultural differences among prisoners and between prisoners and minister. By listening to the stories of prisoners, sharing with other prison ministers and prison personnel and reading accounts of prison life, the minister can begin to set aside the filters of middle-class life, to understand the inequities of the criminal justice system and the oppressive nature of prison life and enter into the prisoners' worlds.

In gaining an understanding of the prisoners' perspectives and cultures and of prison vocabulary, the minister can support yet challenge those perspectives toward more complex and developed outlooks on themselves and society. In addition, the minister must also challenge the perspectives of staff, prison administrators, judges and the public at large in view of the current mood of the country toward criminals and prisoners. Through their writing, speaking opportunities and other outlets chaplains and other prison ministers need to foster a sympathetic understanding of prisoners' needs and potentials and of the necessity for drastic reform in terms of the human indignities and economic waste of the prison system.

Ex-Offenders: Ministered and Ministering

One of the most important aspects of prison ministry involves the follow-up to those released from prison. The dependence, survival mentality and brutalizations of prison life leave deep scars that take years to undo. If the Niantic experiments in just community showed anything, it was that any positive changes effected in prison had to be supported later:

> [W]ithout such support, it is unrealistic to expect meaningful alterations in behavior. . . . [T]he Just Community program offered a beginning for inmates to assume new meanings in their lives as well as new ties and a sense of community. When future ties and community were available and accepted, the inmates' changes became permanent.[33]

Ministers can best sustain the developmental changes which occurred in prison if the people and contexts surrounding the ex-inmate promote a stage three or four faithing mode of group expectations and interpersonal relationships combined with movement toward independent thinking and behavior. Thus people working with halfway houses, job opportunities and living situations for ex-offenders need to take the faith development scheme into account and to continually help the released person interpret the "new world" in stage three or four level terms rather than the stage one or two modal level of prison life.

In cooperation with other ministry programs, the prison minister can establish settings in which ex-offenders share their own struggles and sustain one another. In this context, "faith" stories can and should emerge, including the stories of those imprisoned and marginalized precisely because of their attempts to carry out the convictions of a strong faith. In addition, ministers can promote opportunities for perspective-taking and participation through education, dialogue and sharing with sympathetic groups, and service projects.

Several of the over 10,000,000 ex-prisoners who made a successful transition into civilian life have themselves become prison ministers or offered their services to those in prison ministry. Their understandings and their acceptance by inmates make their services invaluable in ministering to prisoners and advocating the changes needed to create a more faith-conducive setting in prison. Certainly they understand well the fears and sense of abandonment which the rapid tempo of "release" brings and the temptations to return to the only life which feels familiar, that is, more crime. In sharing their own stories and challenging prisoners to take varying social perspectives into account, the ex-offenders help prisoners face their release with a more realistic and promising hope of staying forever free.

Families and Friends

Throughout the prison life family and friends have served as the one link with the outside world which reminds inmates of such values as care, faithfulness and love. Yet the families and friends themselves often feel the traumatic effects of arrest, jail and imprisonment as much as the prisoner. The minister can become a critical life-link here, particularly in the cases of separated spouses. In the face of society's images of criminals and prisoners, the minister's interpretations of the gospel's messages about liberation and God's forgiveness are crucial in helping friends and family understand their own views of their loved ones. In addition, the minister can provide families with understandings of crime and imprisonment which go beyond attitudes of "punishment for a bad life" or "resignation to God's will" and involve more complex analyses of the criminal justice system and prison life.

In view of the generally negative impact of prison life upon inmates, the minister can also help the family understand the prisoner's view of prison life and the effects of prison's depersonalization, dependency and regementation. With the minister's guidance, the family can keep and construct positive images which support the prisoner as an independent, faithful, trusted person to counteract the survival and dependent modes of the prison.

In addition, the minister can continually encourage family and friends to participate in the prisoner's life through letters, calls and visits. Just as importantly the minister can involve these interested people in efforts at prison reform at whatever developmental level is appropriate. Whether supporting one-to-one contact by other civilians in an interpersonal mode or joining a social justice group working for structural change or both, family and friends can become the most motivated people in ministry to the imprisoned.

Finally, as mentioned earlier, when the prisoner is released, prison ministry must extend to the creation of a supportive environment using family and friends as the first and primary resources of the community. Here the minister assists the former prisoner and his or her loved ones to reformulate their images of one another, share new perspectives and participate in one another's lives and in the life of the surrounding community. The minister who knows the faith development scheme can help match the faithing modes of the ex-prisoner, family and friends to enhance their relationships while promoting more communal and individuative stances by all.

The Victims of Crime

While we have concentrated most of our discussions on the plight of prisoners in our society, a Christian prison ministry must include a concern for the victims of crime as well. In Jesus' popular parable of the Good Samaritan, we have focused upon the Samaritan rather than the person whom he helped. All too often overlooked in our surge to punish the criminal, victims respond to their treatment with fear, anxiety, mistrust and deep feelings of rage and resentment toward those who threatened or injured them and their loved ones.

Rooted in a theology of reconciliation and forgiveness, ministry to victims may well begin in the swell of images the victim has of himself or herself and of the ''thief, attacker, mugger, murderer.'' Initially comforting the victims in their grief and loss, the minister also needs to support the positive images of themselves that victims have as they try to sort out answers to ''Why me?'' or ''Did I deserve this?'' Again, different faithing levels will precipitate out different responses, but the minister should challenge feelings that the crime was punishment for a bad act, God's will or some other inappropriate understanding.

Most fundamentally, the crime has initiated a deep mistrust in the victim's responses to others in society and often triggered stereotypes of offenders. In this area, the minister can restore that sense of trust by challenging the stereotypes and personalizing the offender to the victim. Stereotypes operate most freely in a stage two mode of ''faithing'' while personalizing the offender at least moves the mode of interaction to a stage three interpersonal level. Ideally, the minister can then propose more critical discussions of the social and economic forces which produce such crimes, when and if these apply.

If at all appropriate, ministers can invite victims to participate in such programs as the Victim Offender Reconciliation Program mentioned earlier.[34] Or victims and their families can engage in some form of participative program with other victims, with local prison improvement groups or with prison visitors. Regardless of the outlet, the prison minister can shift the victim's focus from the initial shock, anger and resentment against the offender to a broader perspective of forgiveness, reconciliation and social justice toward imprisonment. Understanding of the victim's faith level helps the minister discern the initial responses of what appears as stage two "revenge" as a preliminary stage toward a Christian response of restoring violated relationships between victims and offenders on a stage three interpersonal level or toward a more critical level of social analysis and struggles for change of stage four.

The Staff

As much as the prison minister works with prisoners, the responsibility for setting the tone of the prison environment, for enforcing prison rules and thus for establishing the context for any kind of faith growth lies ultimately with the prison staff. Prison ministry necessarily includes ministry to these people, since the stresses, tensions and even inmate threats which they experience affect not only their encounters with prisoners but also with one another and family members.

On one level, then, the prison minister can initiate faith sharing groups, Bible discussion groups, educational opportunities, social celebrations, and retreats as in other staff settings examined earlier. In whatever contexts, however, the minister should move the focus of the staff toward their interaction and relationships as part of a community caring for one another and for those of whom they have been put in charge. The more the minister can establish these bonds and help the staff establish working relationships which reinforce each staff member's value and independent thinking and acting, the more these processes will help the staff adopt such practices toward and with prisoners.

In addition to supporting the staff members' positive images of themselves and of prisoners, the minister must challenge the prevailing models which underlie many prison philosophies. Whether those involve deterrence theory, behavior modification or medical/therapeutic treatment models, they violate the central concepts of dignity of the person and human freedom. The minister can become the interpreter of a gospel vision of freedom, responsibility, justice and dignity through the espousal of a coherent theological basis for prison life.

In the context of personal sessions, informal meetings or workshops, the minister can work with staff to share their perspectives on crime and prisoners and to develop more comprehensive understandings of themselves and their roles. In addition, these contexts can provide staff with broader understandings of the social and economic conditions which shape criminal behavior in the first place. While difficult to develop, prisoner and staff exchanges can foster greater understandings and enlarge perspectives. But if prisoners think that somehow such honest exchanges will be used against them, then there can be little basis for real sharing of views.

Finally, the minister has to deal with most staff members' inexperience in forms of democratic decision-making along a just community line. In addition, the basic social inequality in the staff-prisoner relationship makes any sense of participation difficult to achieve. Yet Hickey and Scharf found that when staff used inmates at higher levels of moral development to interpret and communicate their modal levels to lower stage inmates or presented higher-staged reasoning to counteract the stage two ideas of many inmates, with a "great deal of time and patience" the results were successful.[35] Thus if the minister can motivate and train a small number of staff in the "just community" approach, some of the factors of symbols, perspective and participation which we have studied earlier can become effective tools in developing both a more humane prison system and an environment in which faith growth can take place.

In developing an environment more conducive to true faith growth the prison minister must be aware of the problems involved. Staff may well resent the minister who emerges as a strong advocate of changes for prisoners but who does not address the job concerns of staff. Low salaries and inadequate compensation lead to disillusionment and high turnover rates among staff. In addition, the staff who do join in the kinds of sharings, perspective exchanges or experimental programs in participative decision-making essential to the tasks will experience the conflicts between their new attempts and the pull of the present structures of the prison environment. The minister working from the faith development scheme can contribute to improving any prison environment by working closely with staff in these areas.

The Community

Although the prison minister's primary role involves the prison environment itself, the minister must develop relationships with other ministers and volunteers in the community to continue the work of prison ministry on a broad basis. The most challenging dimension but the most fundamental involves changing the images which the general public has of "criminals," prisoners and prisons, and ex-offenders. In many ways, the criminal becomes the scapegoat of the community's moral outrage, and once imposed the stigma is rarely removed.

The foundational experience for people in the community, and more particularly in the parish, school or family, lies in developing a theology of crime, imprisonment, and release rooted in the dignity of the person, the restoration of broken relationships and the pursuit of justice for victims and criminals. Such an approach means that we carefully examine the uses of "justice" in the criminal justice system and the ways in which Christianity has supported the harsh and inhumane treatment of prisoners in the past. This theology would apply especially to capital punishment, for in that context the possibilities for transformation, reconciliation and liberation are completely eliminated.

Then depending upon the developmental levels encountered in parishes and the community, prison ministers can develop suitable ways of challenging people's perspectives on crime and prisoners. In addition to education, the more ministers can personalize the lot of prisoners and have prisoners share their stories and parts of their lives, the more people in the community will comprehend the world which produces crime and the changes needed in prison life. Visits, calls, "pen pals," evenings with criminal justice officials and ex-offenders all offer some ways in which ordinary people can find their perspectives challenged and gain a better understanding.

Finally, ministers can develop the myriad ways in which Christians can take part in the whole range of prison ministry. Visits, calls and letters will involve many in the one-to-one personal dimension preferred and understood by those at stage three in their faithing. In addition, volunteers are needed at halfway houses, in community service agencies and work release centers to help minister to prisoners. Others might become involved in Victim Offender Reconciliation, Community Service Restitution and other successful programs used around the country.[36]

On another level of faith growth, programs of social analysis and social justice skills allow volunteers to develop proposals for changes in criminal justice by lobbying, developing legislation or inspecting jails and prisons on a regular basis. In whatever ways ministers prepare volunteers for their parts in prison ministry, all volunteers should experience the faith development scheme in some way so that they can better understand those to whom they minister, attend to their own faith growth and work for needed changes.

Summary

As we have examined the various dimensions of prison ministry, we have linked any form of Christian ministry with a call for critical changes in the criminal justice system. In no other area of ministry has the need for systematic change been more obvious. Yet traditionally ministry to prisons has involved the minister in viewing the prisoner as "the fallen one" who must face the error of his or her ways and thus be "redeemed," which has meant becoming acceptable to middle-class society. Our very concept of ministry here has changed:

> Certainly it cannot be denied that any viable Christian response to pris-
> ons must consider the individual tragedies of prison—the broken, often
> hopeless, and (properly defined) sinful lives of the prisoners them-
> selves. However, at the same time, prisons are equally, if not so ob-
> viously, destructive in the lives of those who build and support them,
> and the need for the existence of prisons is a sign of profound disorder
> in the structure of society. . . . Prisons likewise pronounce judgment
> on a way of life which relies upon their continuance. . . . Christian
> involvement in prisons then is really a ministry to people on both sides
> of the wall, for there are many kinds of prisons.[37]

The prison minister is necessarily engaged in a broad undertaking, often with few resources in a ministry not well supported by the public or sometimes even by the church. Nonetheless the gospel mandate calls all Christians toward a part in such ministry, from the challenge of Amos to "see that justice prevails in the courts" (5:15) to Jesus' proclamation of his mission, quoting Isaiah, "to proclaim liberty to the captives" (Lk 4:18–19) and his injunction to "visit the imprisoned" (Mt 28:32) and in doing so visit him.

In the context of this ministry to today's "crucified in our society," the minister can utilize the faith development scheme in ways which support and strengthen the efforts of so many others in this system. On the one hand, the scheme well describes the stage one and two modes of symbolizing, thinking and understanding which prison life and indeed the whole criminal justice system construct around the accused and prisoners;

their own world view gradually accommodates to these schemes. At the same time, the faith development model shows areas of great promise around images, perspectives and participation such as the just community experience which do incorporate modes of faithing aimed at promoting more developed and hence more mature forms of growth. Such growth not only promotes the prisoner toward greater freedom, restitution and responsibility and the victim toward forgiveness and renewed trust, but also helps the minister reshape his or her work from the one-dimensional context which the prison system wants to a broader context "in understanding the forces around us through a multi-dimensional ministry of advocacy with both individuals, the community-at-large, and broader policies adopted by our government." Through such a vision we expand "to a more healthy and healing ministry of Christian intervention" and "greatly strengthen the powerful presence of Christ in offering reconciliation and peace to a broken and suffering world."[38]

9. TRANSFORMATIONS IN JUSTICE

The body of Christ should live out for all to see the meaning of being trustworthy stewards of God's creation. This will be seen in how we view our possessions, in our style of living, in how we respond to global economic injustice, and in how we show love for one another by sharing ourselves and what we own. If we belong to one another spiritually, then economic bonds must join us. And if we have been deeply touched by God's compassion, we will naturally feel a call to help the hurting world God so loves.

Senator Mark O. Hatfield,
Oregon[1]

You are not making a gift of your possessions to the poor person. You are handing over to him what is his. For what has been given in common for the use of all, you have arrogated to yourself. The world is given to all, and not only to the rich.

St. Ambrose[2]

In Christ, women and men, oppressed and oppressor, are set free to work together on behalf of the liberating purpose of God. . . . The Christian community is called to be a sign of that new humanity where new relationship and life-styles can emerge.[3]

Letty Russell, *Human Liberation in a Feminist*

Perspective

In the next chapters we arrive at discussions on justice, spirituality and worship. Obviously we are re-examining some views examined earlier. Yet we need a more concentrated focus here inasmuch as all ministers struggle with questions of justice and the spiritual life in their work and in their own lives. The guiding themes of this discussion will be that all ministry is social and is rooted in each minister's spirituality and worship as well as the spirit of the culture. But in addition we will enlarge upon the justice, spirituality and worship questions primarily for ministers engaged in those areas, whether toiling in city food banks, lobbying for political change, guiding a high school retreat, leading community worship or engaging in a host of other ministry activities.

The social dimension of ministry is unmistakable, since every form of ministry projects some model of the relationship between church and society.[4] Thus every form of ministry either continues the existing patterns of social relationships, modifies or ameliorates them, or attempts to change them in some way.

Similarly, each minister roots his or her work in one's own spirit, crafted from personal experience, contact with the churches' teachings about union with God and the implications of that union for daily living. Unless the minister carefully examines the forms of that spirituality in light of his or her own gifts and the openness of the Christian spiritual tradition, much ministry merely duplicates the skills and services of the broader society without the transformative love at the heart of any "ministry" to others.

Already in our discussions of the sick, elders and the imprisoned we have seen how the spiritual debilitation of institutions and the injustices of images and attitudes shrink the area for faith growth, twist spirits and prevent the restoration and development of creative relationships. The faith development scheme offers helpful guides here. First, the theory allows ministers to evaluate the modal level of the institutions within which they work and ask how much those structures support faith growth in terms of openness to the independence, mutuality, participation and full dignity of all peoples demanded at the higher stages of faithing. Then in addition, the theory helps ministers critically discern the whole range of justice works, spiritualities and worship expressions we see around us today for their appropriate support of people at different developmental levels. Finally, the faith development approach can assist ministers in assessing their own growth in justice and spirituality.

Background

As we look at the complex interdependence of our world today and the ways in which we can participate in world events through modern communications, the striking injustices of hunger, poverty, war, racism, sexism and forms of violence call us as Christians to new forms of action and involvement. The recent fall of dictators in Haiti and especially the Philippines resulted from not just the advice but the active political involvement of church people and church leadership. Religious organizations in the United States have established lobbying and social justice efforts which focus upon economic change or peace conversion. Groups such as the Center of Concern, Network, Bread for the World, Sojourners and others all express a new self-understanding on the part of the Christian churches which reflect this perspective:

> Action on behalf of justice and participation in the transformation of the world fully appear to us as a constitutive dimension of preaching of the gospel, or, in other words, of the Church's mission for the redemption of the human race and its liberation from every oppressive situation. . . . The mission of preaching the gospel dictates . . . that we dedicate ourselves to the liberation of man even in his present existence.[5]

At the same time new yearnings for spiritual growth and ways of worshiping blossom in a culture steeped in widespread patterns of materialism and indiscriminate consumption. With the decline of much popular piety, certainly in the Roman Catholic Church after the Second Vatican Council, the need for new forms of spirituality and worship has spawned a variety of expressions such as the cursillo, charismatic groups, Christian encounters, prayer centers, journaling workshops, Jungian psychology and studies of Eastern forms of meditation and diet. In part these new forms and spiritualities are reactions to the emphasis upon technique and methods rather than goals and purposes in our technological society. And certainly many forms of "spirituality" and "worship" seem excessively self-centered, appropriating the language of personal fulfillment as a wall against the injustices of the surrounding world.

Yet the most exciting aspect of these renewals in justice, spirituality and worship lies in the recognition of the intrinsic relationship among them. As Senator Hatfield's remark at the opening of the chapter indicates, there is an intimate connection between our spiritual and bodily unions in Christ. We are engaged in a "justice spirituality," which involves not only the transformation and conversion of persons but necessarily the transformation of structures as they shape and form the persons within them.

While this becomes especially evident at stages four and five of the faithing model, this consciousness must pervade ministry at all developmental levels. In our formative faithing years, we reflect the "spirit" of our parents and our culture, and in our mature faithing we move toward a more authentic spirit which reflects the gospel concern for all peoples, especially with a "preferential option for the poor" following Jesus' example. Our religious task becomes a "political" task in our concern for the welfare of others:

Social spirituality and ministry will, therefore, find its expression in "politics," which means here the social activity to struggle for and promote justice in social relations. Since this struggle goes hand in hand with evangelization, all Christians have a duty to participate.[6]

In these final two chapters we will concentrate on the meaning of such a "justice spirituality." Since the scope of ministries in justice, spirituality and worship are so broad and since we have covered several dimensions of these areas earlier, we will not use the factors of images, perspectives and participation in this discussion. Nevertheless, the reader will notice how much a part of the discussion they implicitly remain.

Justice in the World ———————————————

The church's new understanding of itself as an active agent in a world of complex social relationships has brought with it a series of arguments about the relation between church and state, religion and politics and the role of clergy, which reflect differing views of the church and its mission. Many today still see the church as "above" or "apart from" society, concerned primarily with the salvation of souls. But the trends we looked at above reveal a much more profound involvement of the church *in* the world, dedicated toward the welfare of the whole person and of all persons. And finally, much of the conflict surrounding the roles of the church in the world centers around different developmental understandings of the mission of the church and the images of Jesus. Where a stage three understanding calls for active involvement in acts of charity to meet the needs of those worst off in society, a stage four or five understanding would demand the elimination of the very conditions which led to marginalization and deprivation of people in the first place.

The relationship between justice and faith development lies in the understanding of justice as a dynamic aspect of human relationships demanding the imaginative capacities to step into others' perspectives and to envision alternative possibilities. We have defined faith as a mode of being-in-relation to self, others, nature and God and the imaging of those relationships in concrete terms. This relational character is underscored when we define justice biblically as "fidelity to the demands of a relationship" with God, others, nature and self.[7] Thus if faith places us in trusting relationships of commitment and loyalty, justice measures our "faithfulness" to the demands which arise from those relationships.

The understanding of faith from the faith development scheme is at the very heart of this definition of justice. Consequently, such an understanding of faith-justice means each person necessarily *acts out* justice or injustice in every relationship whether in the personal interaction of daily encounters or in the social relationships of institutions and structures of which each is a part:

> Faith can never be a matter of disembodied words. It must be incarnate in *praxis* (faith-in-action). Faith is a transforming acceptance of the Word, which challenges us through the cries of the poor and oppressed. . . . Faith is not a passive waiting upon God's decision to act; rather, it seizes the initiative and reshapes the world by its God-given power. . . . It is active engagement in the service of the Kingdom of God.[8]

In part such an understanding of the faith-justice relationship underscores the developmental nature of justice, both historically and personally. Although we are looking primarily at the personal side of this development, we can note that the understanding of justice has grown from its interpersonal and contractual dynamics (commutative and distributive justice) in the late nineteenth and early twentieth centuries to a call for a change in social arrangements themselves (social justice). Likewise the equality demanded by justice in the social order has developed from an equality of citizenship and laissez-faire economic policies to equality of opportunity and finally to some basic material equality. So in our time the service of faith

> . . . requires promoting just systems which distribute the 'benefits of culture' with some measure of equality so that at the very least each human person may creatively exercise his or her personal freedom in the process of providing for himself or herself and for dependents, or, if that is impossible, being provided for.[9]

Before we examine the implications of the faith development scheme for justice actions, we need to reflect on the sources of these new understandings of the faith-justice relation. For in this way, the *content* of faith will shape and be shaped by the *developmental structure* of faith.

Certainly the renewed interest in scripture among lay people generally reflects the impact of research and scholarship on the person and mission of Jesus. Thus Jesus' own description of his mission informs anyone working in ministry today, especially in the justice area:

The spirit of the Lord is upon me, because he has anointed me to preach good news to the poor. He sent me to proclaim release to the captives, and recovery of sight to the blind, to set at liberty those who are oppressed, to proclaim the acceptable year of the Lord (Lk 4:18–19).

The key to the fresh look at Jesus and his mission which biblical studies have unearthed lies not just in Jesus' words or the words of the prophets but also in the images we have of Jesus. As long as our images were controlled by church authorities intent on assuring that the faithful followed the conventions of the church, the dominant images of Jesus' service tended to be those fashioned from texts of submission and one-to-one encounters of healing.[10] Or Jesus was envisioned as a "nice guy," "friend" or "super-star" who worked miracles and taught messages of love and concern for individual welfare.

The emphasis upon Jesus' challenges to authorities of his day, his understanding of his role as "suffering servant" and the nature of his death as a criminal all point to a powerful image of Jesus' mission as liberation of the oppressed from every oppressive structure: "[T]he kingdom of God . . . is an inclusive gathering of people that reaches out in a reconciling manner, like a net, to those who have been marginalized."[11] In turn, this "reimaging" of Jesus as "the justice of God" structures the images of what Christians see as demands of their discipleship: "new things do not become part of the behavior of Christians unless they are seen in the behavior of Jesus after whom devoted Christians pattern themselves."[12] Finally, this restructuring of images challenges the socio-economic context of the Christian, for our interpretation of Jesus' message depends on our place in the structure of society. The demands of biblical justice today require that we take the perspective toward social relationships of the least advantaged, the marginalized of society. Thus dramatic, new images lead directly to changed perspectives and a call for increased participation.

Two other areas have helped expand the meaning of the faith-justice relationship. The first involves an awareness that the primary focus of moral evaluation has shifted from persons as individuals to the structural patterns of social existence in community. This shift reflects our understandings that persons are responsible for more than their personal acts in terms of the social activities of which they are a part and that the corporate acts of peoples proceed from structures and institutions.[13] We are shaped by the very structures in whose names we act. The second important thrust toward a more comprehensive view of justice emerges from the social teachings of the Christian churches, for example in the unfolding development of the Roman Catholic social encyclicals. Particularly since 1963 those teachings have become increasingly critical of all existing social arrangements in the name of the full equality of all peoples.

The Development of Justice-in-Faith ———

For those working in peace and justice ministry the faith development approach applies the biblical, critical understanding of justice in particular ways. The basic thrusts involve first a movement beyond one's own immediate needs into a sense of community (a stage two to three transition), then a movement beyond personal interaction to structural analysis (from stage three to four), and finally a movement beyond the selectivity of one's own group and a "parochial universalism" to the inclusive community of all peoples (toward stages five and six). Throughout these developments, the imaginative capacity to enter into the worlds of other peoples and groups and envision reality from their perspectives plays a key role.

At stage one, justice in the child's faith life will be expressive of his or her more immediate needs and thus be largely imitative. Within that framework adults can involve children in food drives, support for charitable organizations, saving allowances for the needy and gathering information about other groups different than their own. Parents can encourage and entice children to help with chores and other activities in which children develop positive attitudes toward others, respect differences, take responsibility, use resources carefully and foster a sense of community even around the world. All these activities and others, such as visits to the aged and hospitalized, can enlarge the child's capacities for viewing people different than those of his or her own group.

Since the images in stories and fables about animals and plants greatly influence children at this stage, ministers and others must become much more aware of the attitudes about caring, sharing and fairness which children pick up through reading and television. For example, a few viewings of "Mr. Roger's Neighborhood" and "Sesame Street" reveal that pro-social attitudes which portray values of caring, sharing and fairness are much more in evidence on "Mr. Rogers" than on "Sesame Street," for all the other strengths of "Sesame Street."[14]

As the older child emerges into stage two faithing and the world expands to include school, community and through modern communications even people and events from around the world, the family can encourage the child to assume more responsibility around the home. The various groups to which the child belongs such as Cub Scouts, Brownies, and so on can involve the child in care for people with problems, such as the aged, handicapped, the poor in the neighborhood. At this stage when a child has the capacity to take another's perspective, involvements in charitable collections, visitations and community activities give the child a sense of responsibility as well as some experiences of the life and struggles of other people. Although children at this stage often respond to people who are different with cruel statements and actions, the justice minister can lay strong foundations for the sympathy, empathy and finally justice concerns of later faith life by identifying others who are different as members of a more inclusive community of all persons whom God loves.

Since stage two faithing involves a driving need to categorize reality and provide order to causal events, ministers, parents and other sponsors must work to mitigate stereotypes or prejudices and instead provide children with new opportunities to expand their categories, to listen to stories of others and to challenge the narrow focus of their own group. Some concrete expressions such as pen pals, cultural exchanges, and learning new languages and customs are helpful, as are opportunities for service in the neighborhood and community.

An interpersonal world and the general acceptance of the social and cultural status quo shape the sense of justice action at stage three. Precisely at this stage personal involvement with individuals among the aged, the handicapped and the poor will be an important way to develop a critical sense of justice which later asks *why* people are treated this way. For example, the motto of United Way, "People Helping People," expresses one method of visualizing such a personal approach to "social action" through agencies and institutions.

At this level the main developmental tasks around justice center on extending the concepts and practices of community and personal responsibility toward more inclusive membership than just those of "our group," "our religion" and "our country." The possibilities through volunteer assignments and service clubs are endless. And the minister can extend the dynamic of friendship across racial, religious and national boundaries to include people in groups and countries different than one's own. This exposure to other people's cultures and values can expand the boundaries of social awareness and capacities for perspective-taking so important to a vision of social justice at higher stages of faithing.

Since the personal qualities of individuals attract people strongly at this stage, the justice minister must take special care that the charisma of strong leaders is measured against the biblical concern for the poor and oppressed. On the other hand the personal integrity of the minister and the images of Jesus helping others are more powerful motivating forces for justice and peace involvement than church statements and party platforms. Personalizing the particular justice concern in concrete cases enables the stage three person to see how his or her actions can make a difference and improve people's lives.

In helping make the transition toward a more structural understanding of justice, the minister can work with the one-to-one involvement with the aged, poor, imprisoned or handicapped, for example, and initiate discussions around the causes of the poverty, hunger or oppression which afflict marginalized people. In addition, the minister must challenge the secular and religious symbol systems which continue to support systematic injustices and violations of real peace. For example, the ways in which great heroes and heroines are invoked for various causes must be authenticated. For whoever controls those symbol systems, especially in the area of language, has access to great control over what attitudes, motives and activities are legitimated for people faithing at stage three levels. For example, all too many male clerics have difficulty in understanding the subtle ways in which sexually exclusive language perpetuates sexism.

In addition, since a stage three understanding fails to sense the structural level of injustice and social sin, it becomes easy to blame individuals or groups for structured patterns of racism, sexism, poverty, hunger. Thus the poor are castigated as lazy; all men are labeled sexist. When these symbols play their role in the values, attitudes and beliefs of stage three faithing, they become powerful supports for further systemic injustices. Or personal solutions are proposed for structural issues, compounding the problems. Christmas baskets for the poor or sensitivity sessions between whites and blacks may be helpful, but they hardly address the structural issues of poverty and racism.

In making the transition to a more developed sense of justice, the biographies of people working for justice, a "reimaging" of Jesus and his work, discussions about causes rather than symptoms of social issues can all help the justice minister in work with individuals and groups. Since the "faithing" levels of people in any one group are not immediately evident the minister must spend some time discussing with people their perspectives on issues. Some will volunteer "just to help out," while others will evidence a concern for bringing about changed circumstances. Whatever the background the minister needs to match the activities and understandings with people's developmental capacities.

Probably those most involved in any movement for change will reflect some aspects of a stage four mode of faithing. That is, they will begin to articulate a sharp sense of what *ought* to be, of a real equality among peoples, of due process regardless of status and lifestyle. In addition, their reflections on the church and the biblical accounts of Jesus and the prophets may well have sharpened their sense of the kingdom as the root metaphor for the transformation of society as well as personal transformation. In much the same fashion as we indicated earlier, the full understanding of justice as fidelity to the demands of personal *and* social relationships begins to provide profound roots for meaning and motivation to the individuating faither of stage four.

Yet the justice minister faces a formidable task at this juncture. Inasmuch as the church itself is an institution, it reflects many of the injustices found in other social structures. Precisely because of the profound sense of injustice which the individuative faith stance embodies, the church as institution may seem too caught in its own sinful structure to be an instrument of true liberation. If the church is to have an impact on those who view justice in this fashion, then it must offer powerful, new images of traditional understandings which draw people into deepened, broader and critically self-chosen commitments. Inasmuch as stage four faithing finds expression in ''clear and distinct'' ideas, in systematic thought, then concepts such as ''kingdom,'' liberation, equality, freedom, ''shalom'' can become the goals of new understandings of what it means to be human.

In the role of sponsor of critical questioning, the minister must be comfortable with challenges to any status quo, even those which involve his or her personally held beliefs and commitments. And the justice minister must acknowledge the class biases which he or she brings to the understanding of ministry at this faith level. The minister and others working with justice issues must become fully aware of the cultural differences between themselves and the people they work with and willingly acknowledge their own limited visions of what justice demands. As the minister takes up the challenge of the ''preferential option for the poor'' at stage four, he or she must prepare for resentment, misunderstanding and anger from the people ''helped'' in ministry. The minister must remember that he or she works *with* the poor, not *for* the poor. And the minister will also identify the ways in which the middle-class background of most people in ministry shields them from a critical analysis of the society which benefits them. The ministerial need here revolves around the necessity to get beyond the confines of one's group as the basis for understanding other groups.[15]

Next the justice minister must articulate in a revolutionary way the relationship of the gospel and the church's teachings to the demands of a justice which addresses the complexities of social structures. This will help those at stage four develop a critical understanding and utilize social analysis as a tool for structural change.

> Having made a diagnosis of the structural causes behind social injustices in the world, the Christian community is in a strong position to do something to advance the Kingdom of God. This will involve, among other things, taking up a prophetic stance in the world on behalf of the poor, deprived, and oppressed. . . . The Christian community, in the light of social analysis, will have to denounce and "call by name every social injustice, discrimination, violence inflicted on man against the body, against the spirit, against his conscience and against his convictions."[16]

In many ways, the poor and disadvantaged themselves often exhibit a perspective more advanced than their oppressors who live comfortably by the injustices of the status quo. For the marginalized must not only understand the views of their group in order to establish their own sense of identity; they must also take the perspective of the oppressor, the "other," into account in determining their own behavior, values and beliefs. Thus the oppressed will most likely have a sharper sense of social injustices and often the causes of those injustices than middle-class people working in justice concerns. The task of the minister is to facilitate people working in justice to see history and society "from the bottom up," the underside.

Perhaps at this point we must reflect on the importance of the diverse perspectives that justice takes with different groups. Thus Carol Gilligan's pivotal work in developmental theory relating to Kohlberg's stages of moral development has shown that women utilize different language to describe the same realities we have ascribed to the word "justice." Categories such as "care," "concern," "healing" imply the relational quality of justice which the language of "claims" and "rights" often neglects in rather abstract analyses. Gilligan found that women tend to think of the persons involved in each situation more than men do.[17] This developmental difference is extremely important for the justice minister to keep in mind, since what might at first appear as a stage three interpersonal mode of justice faithing may well reflect a much more advanced four or five level of comprehensive compassion. Again, this means a continuous examination of *whose* symbols, perspectives and participative experiences are operative at *what* faith development level.

Unbiased social analysis, then, becomes a key tool for working with justice and "care" issues at stage four and beyond. At the same time, the stage four faither's ability to analyze and clarify leads to a number of dangers to which the justice minister must be sensitive. The drive to view reality in clear and distinct categories often means that the purity of ideals like justice, freedom and equality will dominate and crush the ambiguities of real situations and the complex motivations of individuals. In the name of such noble goals the stage four faither can find himself or herself involved in a crusade, blind to the complexities of individual differences and unaware of one's own involvement in evil. Thus Tarrou, in Albert Camus' *The Plague,* only later comes to realize that his crusade against capital punishment has involved him in the very hatreds he attempted to abolish.[18]

This tendency not to see the beam in one's own eye, not to understand the extent of human sinfulness in one's own motivation at stage four, often leads to an inability to admit the legitimacy of some claims of the other side in a struggle. Under the force of a compelling idea, the innocents often get caught in the crossfire. Even within the justice group, fascination with the pull of the goals of peace, justice and freedom can override the process of justice. During the civil rights struggle in the south white activists often kept blacks in menial roles because they weren't as well educated or trained; in peace groups men have tended to dominate over women in the name of *all* humanity.

Another danger for justice work at this stage involves the imposition of one's own convictions or the convictions of one's class upon all others in the name of what seems a pure ideal. Such "parochial universalism" attempts to squeeze all human experience into the clarity of ideals by seizing on the "either/or" dichotomy. Fowler notes the discrepancies among certain liberation theologians operating at stage four in articulating a theology of human liberation which draws such sharp contrasts *between* rich and poor, white and black, men and women, first world and third world: "Is it either wise or Christian to affirm, even for ideological purposes, that the line between oppressed and oppressors . . . can be drawn between persons and groups?"[19] Often this perspective confuses the kingdom with the social agenda of a particular political party or group.

The task of the justice minister in this case involves nudging the strongly ideological faither toward a more comprehensive understanding of actual situations, toward an understanding of human liberation which includes rather than excludes all groups, which takes ambiguity into social analysis, which tempers justice with mercy and forgiveness. Obviously this transition to stage five in peace and justice will accompany a personal wrestling with issues of suffering, pain and ambiguity in one's own life. As the justice worker comes to understand the unconscious aspects of his or her own motivation, the dark and hidden sides of personality, the ambiguities and hidden sides of the social structures will emerge for analysis as well. In this way the spiritual life, as we will see, is but an inner reflection of the justice perspective of the faither.

It is Dr. Rieux in *The Plague* who exhibits a stage five faithing in the struggle against disease and death when he reflects that it is ''better to cure than to know.'' For at stage five a clearer sense of one's own sinfulness, one's own dark side lets one see the dark corners and overlooked areas neglected in the ''clear'' vision of stage four. The need for clarity and control at stage four gives way to a sense of relinquishment at stage five. Such a view gradually transcends the biases of economic, racial, class and even religious self-interestedness. Thus justice claims cut across neat lines of oppressor/oppressed, right/wrong, black/white, male/female. A sense of personal fallibility and the limits of solutions to human problems involves mercy, forgiveness, reconciliation and universal love in the struggle toward justice and peace.

Since evil and sin are perceived even more clearly in social structures and human motivation at stage five, sin becomes more strongly identified as misused human freedom, a turning away from God and God's righteousness in human relationships. In this way, liberation confronts the oppressed and the oppressor with a need for personal transformation as well as structural change. The stage five faither becomes ever more aware that justice claims are not just ethical demands but religious obligations, rooted in our intimate relationship with God. This perspective will often lead to the pain of compromise instead of the clarity of victory, to a sense of what is most achievable in view of conflicting claims and of what one relinquishes as much as what one demands.

While the justice minister challenges those in transition from a more ideological stage four faithing to grasp a more comprehensive understanding of justice, the stage five person needs support and nourishment in the lonely vigil he or she adopts in attempting to do justice to various sides of an argument. Those wrapped in the flag of the glorious cause feel betrayed by those who ''aid and comfort'' the enemy out of humanitarian motivation. Yet that may be the call at stage five.

The justice minister can foster communities of support in which struggles are shared, in which people can find acceptance of limitations and vulnerabilities. Thus the minister needs the skills of self-exploration in addition to social analysis in order to handle the dark side of the self while exploring the underside of reality and the limits of any group's proposed solution to social issues. Such communities will incorporate new visions and new symbols surrounding justice and peace which express the affective as well as the cognitive dimensions of self-understanding and social analysis.

In the transition to a stage six faithing mode of justice, the worker for justice not only comprehends the essential unity of all being but acts on that unity. The minister can see the transition or experience it when the tensions between what one knows ought to be done in justice and what one does actually disappear and one acts with a clear sense of what is best for the community of humanity. The temptation at stage five is to think one is engaged in such activity while still servicing partisan and group goals. Obviously, such a comprehensive grasp of the truly "universal good" in action demands an understanding and perspective-taking purified of self-interest which is beyond the capacity of any individual. At this point of faith-in-action the graced nature of personal transformation becomes evident. One is able to love all persons only because one experiences God's transforming love first, and the injustices and violence done to any human being are keenly felt in one's "compassion" or "suffering with" others and active solidarity with the poor and oppressed. Perhaps the justice minister can only point to such people as embodying the account in John: "Love will come to its perfection in us when we can face the day of judgment without fear; because even in this world we have become as he is" (Jn 4:17).

Summary

These brief reflections on justice ministry have pointed to the gradual broadening of the sense of community in the faith development framework. At the same time, we noted that the church's new demands for social transformation and the liberation of the oppressed as a "constitutive" dimension of the gospel impel the justice minister to foster and develop stage four criteria in justice work as much as possible. This does not mean a neglect of the one-to-one service to individuals which has always been a part of the Christian response to injustice and violence. Rather, the faith development analysis reveals that the fruition of justice will be expressed best in any work which moves toward change and transformation of oppressive social structures. Likewise, the criteria of stage five reveal the need to continually challenge the "either/or" approach of a stage four view of social change with understandings of personal sinfulness, a capacity for relinquishment and the place of mercy, reconciliation and forgiveness in justice work.

In sum, the goal of justice ministry lies in the transformation of *all relations* at all levels, personal and social, toward the compassionate love of all. What the faith development scheme reveals are the ways in which individuals and groups can respond to the gospel call for transformed relations at various points in their personal and social histories. Finally, our discussion of justice has shown the interpenetration of justice and spirituality in building up the just community. Work for justice ministry demands renewal and resilience of the spirit for its very continuation in the pain-filled, frustrating, and often defeating activity for change. Most basically, the life of the spirit provides the very meaning and motivation for the kind of work justice demands at any level. To that aspect of faith-in-action we now turn.

10. THE SPIRIT IN THE WORLD

Contemplation is a mystery in which God reveals himself to us as the very center of our intimate self!

Thomas Merton[1]

Meditation teaches us to be solitaries who embrace the world in a more altruistic way. . . . The cultivation of inwardness frees us to relate more creatively with others. . . . These meditations, therefore, have an ethical thrust, an orientation toward a more peaceful, just, and caring world. . . . [E]thical sensitivity and compassion arise naturally from those deeper chambers of the soul where we encounter our common humanity and our mutual responsibility.

Eugene Bianchi, *On Growing Older*[2]

You know, in the old days, before all the changes, I used to go to Mass and it seemed like prayer, at least most of the time. Now I go and spend a good deal of time looking at my watch. Something's missing in the new liturgy. . . . [I]t doesn't seem so holy anymore—and I don't pray as well at Mass.[3]

All Christians find the source of their faith life and their life in the world through their relationship with Jesus Christ. For many Christians today spiritual renewal revolves around personal and group prayer, reflections, journaling, spiritual direction, retreats, worship and other instruments of spirituality which reflect the understanding that everyone's spiritual journey uniquely expresses her or his individual needs, experiences and gifts in the context of the Christian tradition. Spirituality in our day necessarily calls each Christian to a unique response to God's self-communication in love, a response which incorporates the whole person and a concern in care and justice for the whole human community and the globe itself. In this chapter we will begin with some introductory comments on recent changes in the area of spirituality and end with some reflections on the community's expressions of spirituality in worship.

Background

What a contrast with our understanding of spirituality only some thirty years earlier! At that time, the "spiritual life" implied a retreat or withdrawal from the regular rhythm of daily life. The "spiritual" contrasted with the "bodily" or "earthly," and we measured the health of the spiritual life by the number of rosaries, vigils, novenas, benedictions, retreats we made, the spiritual books we read or the confessions we made all isolated from our relationships and activities during the rest of our lives. Thus our "spiritual life" was a compartment which we entered on various occasions during the day, week or month, and where usually we followed rituals and formulas developed by others out of their unique experiences and understandings. Most importantly, this understanding of the "spiritual life" focused on other-worldly goals such as "mystical union" rather than the processes of growth and renewal and was concerned with the "salvation of souls" rather than the liberation of peoples.

Fortunately we have replaced this highly structured and isolationist approach with an understanding of spirituality as "the sum total of responses which one makes to what is perceived as the inner call of God."[4] Ministry in spirituality then means much more than tending to the "spiritual" needs of individuals. Rather such ministry demands the articulation of God's call to service for all Christians to all peoples and the fashioning of responses to that call from the depths of people's hearts and minds. The minister serves here as "cosmic match-maker," summoning individuals and communities to respond in love to the invitation to be loved and to love others. In this peculiar role between "lovers," the minister in spirituality must interpret God's call in understandable words of loving summons and then help the individual and community respond according to the fullness of their gifts and capacities in understanding and commitment at that time. In this "matching-making" the faith development approach offers the minister a powerful measure for gauging an appropriate and adequate response in assisting others while charting the varied terrain, now rugged and dry, now bountiful and life-giving, of his or her own path.

Inasmuch as a contemporary spirituality and worship expressions are communal at heart, "relating us to our God in and through other believers," then "(s)pirituality consists not in becoming more and more responsible in the fulfillment of a duty, but in becoming more and more faithful in a love relationship."[5] As in the understanding of justice as fidelity to the demands of a relationship, so the communal, relational and faith-filled dimensions of spirituality reveal the developmental nature of the spiritual journey. When spirituality and faith development combine in the wealthy tapestry of each person's life, the rich unfoldings of a lively response to God's call emerge. And as we shall see, in many ways the spiritual life today is a journey in imagination, perspective-taking and participation. In this journey we attempt to describe our life with God and God's creation in terms of our life-giving images, our abilities to see the world as God sees it, and our resultant capacities for action. Thus, Fr. Benedict Groeschel quotes the remarkable words of an elderly monk when asked to share the secret of his deep prayer life:

> Well, my secret, if you want to call it that is not much. It is just sort of . . . *imagination* that comes to me when things aren't just up to the mark. It's come to me since I got sick as a lad, and it comes now often in the day. Whenever I stop to think about it, it seems to me that I have spent my entire life *sitting in the place* of St. John at the Last Supper.[6] [author's emphasis]

The pluralism of spiritual forms among Christian traditions and even within a particular tradition means that we cannot take any one approach and chart its developmental course. Rather we will look at the general characteristics of spirituality at each faith level regardless of whether one is Roman Catholic or Quaker, following Francis or Ignatius, utilizing techniques of east or west. For the same dynamics should apply to each particular form.

One caution before we begin involves the distinction between spirituality and faith development. It might seem at first that the higher stages offer the only genuine spiritual expression since union with God seems most related to the kinds of comprehensive knowing described at those levels. However, faith stages remain primarily formal categories and measure capacities in merely formal terms. A spiritual path, however, is always particular, sustained by powerful symbols such as love, compassion, the heart of Jesus, and involves methods and techniques of prayer and meditation foreign to the abstract structures of the faith development theory.

> The faith stages, rather than describing a normative spiritual path within a particular tradition, have as their focus a developmental sequence of systems of structurally integrated operations of thought and feeling. . . . [For example], (W)hile it is true that a person who is best described by Stage 6 is most likely to have strongly developed, disciplined mystical [spiritual] sensitivities, it is not true, conversely, that strongly developed, disciplined mystical [spiritual] sensitivities necessarily indicate Stage 6.[7]

The minister in spirituality, then, must be sensitive to the unique promptings of the Spirit in each person's or group's spiritual style but can use the faith development theory to discern what methods, techniques and guidance are appropriate in a variety of situations. Such ministry might involve leading prayer groups, developing retreats or liturgies, directing others in prayer, times of crisis and moments of discernment, and a variety of other activities or reflections. Regardless of the particular setting or approach for this ministry, however, the dynamics of discernment and guidance will enrich participants' lives when the appropriate spiritual discipline and method best match the particular faith understanding of each person.

Spiritual Development in Faith ──────────

One spring day as I looked at the old rosary resting in my desk drawer, I reflected on the different meanings those colored beads had at different times in my Roman Catholic life. In grade school, the rosary had to be prayed in a certain set form with great attention to the words. One wrong word or missed bead, and I had to start over. And usually I used the rosary to help win the football game. Gradually this instrumental outlook changed to a view of the rosary as one part of a general routine of prayer; the words became familiar patterns and a backdrop for reflecting on the "sorrowful" or "joyful mysteries" of Jesus' life. Then for a long period, especially in view of the liturgical reforms in today's Roman Catholic Church, the rosary became meaningless, a sign of rote, programmed, conventional spirituality—in short, a relic of the past. Now, although perhaps seldom used, the rosary serves as a tool to develop a reflective atmosphere, a Western "prayer wheel," inducing a state of relaxation and openness to meditation.

This discursion on the stages of "the rosary" from two through five illustrates how particular prayer forms exhibit varying understandings at different developmental levels. In the following discussion we will examine how the minister might use different forms and techniques of spirituality depending on the faith development level present.

The child at stage one lives in a world in which all of reality is awe-*inspiring*. In his or her daily encounters with the natural and human worlds, the child experiences reverence and wonder with marvelous ease. One task of the adult "minister," the parent, guardian, teacher, involves the continual nurturance of that sense of wonder and delight; the second task involves helping the child name the source of that wonder and awe as God.

In the child's more explicit understanding of God, God often takes the shape of a super-parent. Hopefully the actual parental and authority figures reflect a playful and supportive posture in the midst of their "awe-inspiring" or even terrifying qualities of authority, power, or size. Images of God in scripture as caring parent are more appropriate than the more dominating and demanding images found in the historical sections of the Hebrew scriptures. In the New Testament, images of Jesus as master story-teller and healer who cares for children help promote the sense of order and assurance which the child needs. The Arch Books from Concordia Press develop Jesus' parables in a marvelously creative fashion.[8]

This story-telling quality becomes even more important as the child moves from the imitative spirituality of stage one into the narratizing mode of stage two. Here stories tell the child something "about us" and reveal character models of ways in which people engage the world. Acquainting the child with the special heroes and heroines of the faith imparts a sense of what it means to be Christian and exemplifies the character and virtues of Christian life. Not long ago comic books and stories of early Christian saints served as important counterparts to the superheroes of the secular culture. While some exciting work is being done in this area, ironically much of this "formation" work was dropped along with other methods of popular piety in the renewals following the Second Vatican Council. Children at this age still need some such expression of Christian heroes and heroines, whether in the form of video-tapes, films or comics.

Since the child's understanding of God at this stage tends to be anthropomorphic, God appears as someone whose reality is beyond even that of the superheroes and heroines. Yet that understanding reveals the importance of superhero and superheroine characters. In their powers, hopefully for the good, and their virtues, the adult minister can explore the character of God. Jesus then takes on some of the majesty, mystery, and power of the superhuman in the child's life, especially in the stories of his healings and miracles. The sense of other powers, traditionally called "angels," and the powers of saints or even relatives who have died may help the child feel more secure against the powers of evil that he or she hears and reads about or even experiences. Prayers to these "good powers" and to God will reflect the child's focus upon meeting his or her needs, but the minister with these older children can now begin to extend their concerns to the needs of other people and groups as well.

Up to this point the spiritualities of children have centered on their own needs and imaged a fascination with "superpowers" imaginatively projected beyond their own sense of powerlessness. The movement into stage three faithing involves an attentive transformation of these images, stories and needs. The fantasy world of the superpeople surrenders to the world of real or fictional people. The identification with the virtues and characters of superpeople yields to models of values and behavior who inhabit a real world which the young person will also inhabit. Stories now become paradigms of relationships and ways of handling relationships, while the images of God as father, provider and Jesus as brother, friend dominate the faith life. At this point in the faith development scheme the central dynamic of spirituality as "response to God's call" begins to take shape in view of the developing capacities to form relationships.

At this point the minister in spirituality serves as the "director" or "guide" in relation to each person's growth in faith. The key questions which nurture the spiritual life from now on are "What is God's will for me?" and "How do I respond in faith?" The conventional faither will answer in light of the authority of those trusted people surrounding him or her or in conformity to a spiritual tradition. The minister or director plays a key role, then, both as listener to each person's story and as interpreter of the spiritual tradition.

At the conventional level the central images of God and Jesus appear as realities separate from the individual and the community. The faither views God as an authority figure, father or mother, to whom obedience is due, or as an intimate friend, son, brother, who is trustworthy, loving, receptive.[9] God and Jesus are the "someone" I address, entreat, praise, even curse. The conventional prayers used at this stage reflect this image, and even the gospels of Mark, Luke and Matthew can mirror this perception of God. The heart of spirituality here rests in a deep, moving dialogue with God whether as a response to God's love, in obedience to God's will or in intimacy with Jesus.

The minister can strengthen this relational dimension by providing a coherent explanation and interpretation for faith. In the very person of this spiritual guide, the conventional faither finds a model of faith in practice which sustains the fragile, emerging spiritual identity. In addition, the minister can begin to draw the "disciple" into forms of prayer, such as meditation, which explore the rich interior life of the growing self. These initial movements in reflection or meditation begin with set forms and methods, such as the *Spiritual Exercises of St. Ignatius,* which employ the imagination and perspective-taking in asking the person in prayer to view oneself in the Gospel stories. And certainly centering prayer, role-playing and aesthetic participation can help as well. The fruit of such prayer is to discern the will of God or achieve intimacy with Jesus through dialogue, as in the "colloquy" of the *Spiritual Exercises:* "The colloquy is made by speaking exactly as one friend speaks to another, or as a servant speaks to a master, now asking him for a favor, now blaming himself for some misdeed, now making known his affairs to him, and seeking advice in them."[10]

At this point, the minister must take care in discerning the initial and subsequent dependence of the "disciple" upon the *minister's* form of prayer, the *minister's* insights, the *minister's* answers to problems in prayer, worship or belief. The notion that whatever worked for the minister will work for everyone else is all too familiar to those who entered religious life or ministry education in the past. In addition, the minister must examine how prayer and other forms of spiritual expression match the questions of suffering, death, love, justice and sexuality as these issues emerge at stage three. For example, the minister can foster a justice dimension to this form of spirituality by interpreting intimacy and life with Jesus as solidarity with the poor and oppressed.

The communal expression of stage three in prayer and worship looms as an important aspect of spirituality as well. At various places across the country, certainly on several college campuses, traditional patterns such as rosaries, Mary devotions and benedictions have re-emerged recently. One possible explanation rests upon a concern that as these popular forms of spirituality found less favor in the years of the late 1960's and the 1970's, a more verbal, intellectualized spirituality emerged which reflected more of an individuative, stage four mode of faithing. Liturgies have lost their "mystery," their sense of "awe" as they become more focused upon the growth of the community. It could be that the reforms of Vatican II and the more cognitive approaches to prayer and worship have passed the conventional faithers by. And perhaps many young people respond to the exotic appeal of cults and eastern spiritualities precisely in response to the symbolism around candles, incense and costume and the conventional, even authoritarian, demands these experiences embody.

In the transition from stage three to stage four, the minister nourishes a faith response rooted in the self-understandings and new awakenings to the inner life of the individuating faither. In Fowler's view, the master/mistress-disciple relationship "can be the context for powerfully centering allegiances and affiliation, providing goals, models, and ideal self-images as well as a coherent and powerful world-view."[11] With great care the minister must discern the movement for more independent and self-chosen aspects of spirituality. If the director is truly a "frontier guide" rather than a "director of the settlement," then he or she should rejoice in this expressive freedom precisely as a movement toward prayer which is "at base, a growing interaction with our own life in and through the Life who is God, an interaction that is 'response' because God initiates and sustains the process."[12]

Prayer and meditation for the individuative faither become a part of the very questioning and self-conscious expressions about life evidenced at this stage. As with other aspects of daily living the spiritual life centers around the growing awareness of inner depth and strength. Prayer no longer depends upon formal expressions and structures of dialogue but becomes a service of the heart rather than a religious duty, a reflective process which brings insight and clarification.

God becomes a personal presence within, united to the world and to the self within the world. Yet often God may be perceived as the wholly other, light and love in tension with darkness and hatred. The gospels become as much a story about the self as about Jesus. And Jesus is no longer seen as "the answer" but as the one who supports our very questions. The vision of God's love, the kingdom, God's justice and righteousness become the criteria by which the individual and the community can evaluate thought, action and society. The very power of these images tends to set up strong dichotomies between the "spirit-filled" or "observant" and the "lukewarm" or "tepid." At this point, the apparent vision of a "universal" kingdom has not yet peered into the ambiguities of suffering and pain or the operation of the demonic *within* the self and society.

The minister serves as a resource, support and listener who helps the seeker elucidate in clearer terms the insights which emerge through encounter with others and with different ideas and perspectives. Through a rhythm of support and challenge the minister demands greater efforts and questions in a continuing attempt to move the seeker to express and take responsibility for his or her own feelings, attitudes and movements of growth.

Not only does the minister serve as listener, but he or she becomes an interpreter now for the various routes along the spiritual path. And at this point in our culture, the very indwelling which becomes the focus of individuating faithing must lead to a sense of renewed responsibility and engagement with the surrounding world as well. Prayer at this stage "eventually always invites us to become, in our own unique way, in our history and culture, a prophet."[13]

As the minister in the role of spiritual guide leads the faither into more deeply contemplative modes of prayer and action, he or she can sculpt the forms of contemplation which blend justice with spirituality. First, such contemplation involves new visions: "Contemplation refreshes human imagination and enables it to develop the artistic creativity needed to envision and fashion new patterns of relations in a never-ending process of entering into the mystery of the life of the Holy Trinity."[14] Second, such contemplation roots justice in resistance to the demons of our culture

> . . . that has invested its soul in getting and selling, whose critical spirit is systematically dulled and whose religion is blindness. . . . Contemplation in such a culture as our own is thus an act of resistance. . . . Resistance and contemplation are ultimately simply aspects of a confident seeking in hope, a faith in God and in persons.[15]

Such a mode of contemplative prayer sustains active resistance, political or otherwise, over a long period of time and fights the burn-out which invariably inflicts people in service to others. At this point the minister can provide invaluable help by guiding the individuative faither, joined in various justice and peace issues, toward a spirituality which accepts limits, defeats and discouragement while celebrating relationships over achievements. Already the minister is preparing the faither for a more developed form of spiritual energy and justice expression.

The transition from stage four to stage five faithing involves the incorporation of personal experiences of suffering, defeat, loneliness, injustice and other dimensions of inner struggle into the conscious understandings of daily life. For some the transition begins with personal experiences of suffering, brushes with the unromantic banality of evil or empathy with the injustices of the oppressed yet sympathy with the plight of the oppressor. For others the patterns of personal intimacy spread outward toward a more inclusive community. The role of the minister here calls for guiding the faither toward greater understanding of the areas of the secret self, one's blind side and the motivation of the subconscious. Far from denying these realities, the faither must be guided to transform these very limitations into the vulnerabilities which provide empathetic understandings of others. The revolutionary prophet becomes the wounded healer who joins transformation of unjust structures with transformation of peoples as well.

Fowler describes the transition to stage five in spirituality and the role of the minister/guide in this manner:

> [A] person's serious turning to a spiritual path will have to do with the need for integration into consciousness and action of that within the

self, in one's past, and within one's near and far environment, which
is discordant, repressed, or threatening. . . . For Stage 5 the need is
for permeation of boundaries—self-other, subjectivity-objectivity,
conscious-unconscious. . . . [S]piritual disciplines for this transition
must be attuned to paradox and to the silence beyond concepts, language, and other symbols.[16]

For the Christian in this "conjunctive" stage the paschal mystery of
death and resurrection becomes embodied in the recognition of one's own
weaknesses and of the partiality of one's "vision" of God's justice. In
addition, the discovery of the "hidden demons" within one's intentions
and actions brings a greater willingness to be vulnerable, to let go of relationships, ideas, fantasies. Consequently as the focus shifts from con-
structing one's "armor of self" to "breaking through" the walls, the
faither becomes more able and willing to serve others and become a sponsor of other's growth and development.

In the Christian tradition, Paul is one spokesperson for this form of
spirituality. The imagery of light and darkness of John's gospel gives way
to Paul's themes of death *and* life, power *and* weakness. "Faith is letting
go of one's own power, so as to be taken over by the gift of God's power
available in and through Christ Jesus, who dies on the cross and was raised
from the dead."[17]

The minister no longer resembles a model of spirituality but rather
supports the conjunctive faither in walking through a world of sin *and*
grace, finding strength in weakness. Most of all, as the clear insights and
revelations of an earlier spirituality give way to the murky ambiguities and
puzzling paradoxes of stage five, the minister brings the faither into a
faithful reading of his or her "autobiography" rather than the "biographies" of spiritual people, "the saints," which might have been appropriate earlier. With the minister's help, the *seeker* of visions at stage four
becomes a *listener* to the silence of God through discernment of movements within the self and the world. Moving, in this manner, out of one's
own spirit, the conjunctive faither becomes a spiritual guide for others
along the path of deeper understanding and global compassion.

The mode of contemplation changes at the conjunctive stage as well.
As the willingness to explore the dark side of self and the unconscious
increases, the reality of the paschal mystery of death/resurrection becomes
a more evident rhythm of life. A dying to self or loss of self becomes a
part of the spiritual path: "Gradually I must pass from an active life in
which I am the centre to an active life in which Christ is the centre."[18] Or

in Paul's words, "I live, now not I, but Christ lives in me." This gradual loss of the self proves to be an agonizing experience, and the minister's task here is one of support, guidance and interpretation of the inner movements of the Spirit in these struggles.

> Within us are two personalities. Number one is the personality we show to the world . . . the personality which becomes a doctor or a businessman or a teacher—our self-image derives from this personality. But much deeper than this slumbers another personality. . . . Scarcely visible in early life, it is so smothered up by external things that only one who loves and understands us deeply can get a glimpse of it. We are not yet ourselves. But as life enters its middle period this deeper personality awakens, begins to assert itself and to rise to the surface of conscousness. It is now that conflict begins. . . .
>
> [N]umber one is captain of the ship and does not wish to lose control or be dislodged. And yet certainly, if vaguely, I realize that number one must die if number two is to emerge into life. My old self must die if my new self is to be born.[19]

This "death to self" also transforms the method of contemplative prayer. The conjunctive faither is drawn ever deeper into the "silences" within. The insights and understandings "discovered" in this inward journey erupt forth less in verbal discourse than in imagery, symbols, stories, poetry or the arts. Even resistance takes on a new meaning:

> Resistance has come to mean much more than a symbolic act of protest such as pouring ashes at Lockheed. . . . Resistance implies a way of life in which I am challenged to conform and creatively respond to my own darkness as well as the world's. . . . Perhaps, then, to resist the depths of my own violence is to build Christian community where human value is seen in a different light. . . .
>
> Contemplation is a process of stripping ourselves of all pretenses and adornments so that we may allow God to be fully God, and humans to be fully human. It is in that place that we may more fully recognize our connectedness with other women and men, even those towards whom we feel great alienation.[20]

For theologian Anthony Padavano such a spirituality involves: (1) a resistance to the greed of compulsive complaining, (2) a movement toward the pain of others, (3) a resistance to the arrogance of power, (4) a willingness to express one's own needs, and (5) an asceticism of unpretentiousness, doubt, vulnerability, magnanimity, acceptance of undeserved blame and a dying to the self.[21] In whatever form, the spirituality of stage five faithing supports the faither *and* the minister in working with the dark side of the self and of the world to draw good out of evil, to allow the weeds to grow with the grain and allow the Lord to separate the chaff from the wheat.

At the point of transition to a stage six "universalizing" spirituality, any account of such a transition fails to do justice to the "giftedness" operating here. The minister acts more as witness than as "sponsor" of such a spirituality. Here the dynamic reality of God's empowering grace seems most graphically illustrated in the transition from autobiography to gospel story. In this sense faithers at stage six become symbols themselves of the nature of God's transcendent presence. Patterns of dependence, independence and interdependence yield to an intradependence which embodies the challenging love of the God who is Love: "Love will come to its perfection in us when we can face the day of judgment without fear; because even in this world we have become as God is" (Jn 4:16–17).

Eugene Bianchi grasps the heart of this form of spirituality in the following words:

> As we become more transparent to ourselves and universal in our sentiments and concerns, we will experience a new faith in God. . . . What counts is the gradual acceptance of an ultimately benevolent presence in our psychic depths and in the outer world. This God, whether named or not, will at times be distant and disappointing. . . . The God that is glimpsed and experienced in mature faith needs no justifying rationale. Rather, we experience this divine presence as a sustaining, challenging benevolence, as a suffering fellow traveler . . . in the very inward and outward dimensions of mature faith.[22]

Or as Fowler himself notes when describing stage six in relation to the kingdom of God as our future possibility, a spirituality at stage six is "best" precisely because it "incarnates and makes visible [in actual persons] the Power of the future in its faithful liberation and fulfillment of the futurity of being."[23]

Our review of the implications of faith development theory for spirituality comes to a close on this note. We have seen that each stage develops successive openness and response on the part of the faithing person. The minister in spirituality faces the formidable task of guiding, supporting and nurturing people on their way along the paths open to them. Hopefully, the faith development scheme enables the minister both to understand his or her own promptings by the Spirit as well to foster the child, the adolescent, the young person and the mature adult in the realities of God's presence in their lives and the structures of the world.

Worship: The Center of a Justice Spirituality

Our look at ministry in justice and spirituality has now come full circle. Necessarily, we must now reflect on the ways in which these central dimensions of Christian faithing manifest themselves in the life of the community sustained in the Spirit. Worship is faith's ritual form and our encounter as community with God's presence in time and space. The centrality of images, symbols and participation in worship focuses our attention as a summary of the dynamic relation of faith development to ministry.

In worship the "forms of imagination serve to transform the ways participants see themselves and, correspondingly, the ways in which they enter into relationships with others."[24] In that sense, then, the modal faith levels of the community shape, modify and transform its worship. For in worship the community finds the end result of what faith seeks, and in turn the modes of worship feed and nurture the faith understandings of the community. When we realize that most of us gain our knowledge of Christian living and experience our meaning and motivation as Christians through our worship, then the relationship between worship and daily life for Christians becomes a central focus of ministry in spirituality, indeed of all ministry.

Furthermore, in view of the interrelation among faith, justice and spirituality our celebrations in worship demand that we worship our God in view of our own needs and the needs of all our brothers and sisters. "There is an essential link between the liturgy and life . . . between the celebration of the eucharist by the Church and the mission of the Church in the world for the kingdom of God." Particularly in relation to the eucharistic celebration,

> . . . the real presence of Christ in the eucharistic community is pure gift offered to humanity for the saving purposes of healing, reconciling, liberating and unifying all "in Christ". . . . At the same time it must be remembered that this Christ who is really, truly and "substantially" present in the eucharist is the same Christ who is also personally present in the poor and downtrodden of this world. These two

presences of Christ must be kept together and understood as complementing each other.[25]

As we explore this intimate relationship between liturgy and life, we find
our worship as much more than relief from the hustle of daily living.

Most fundamentally, worship comprises those experiences in which
we become most human and thus most Christian. Rooted in the reality of
God's presence and our presence to each other and to all our brothers and
sisters, worship should challenge, sustain and nurture us all through its
invitation to our imaginative participation. We are literally invited to "ec-
stasy," to "step outside" of ourselves in order to experience not an altered
state of consciousness but the "mind of Christ," which centers on the liberating transformation of people and structures. *How* we thus become
more human and *how* we put on the mind of Christ Jesus will depend in
large part on the ways in which faith is structured and developed in the
community.

Because of the reflections drawn earlier, we only need to mention a
few perspectives on worship and faith development as the center of ministry. We begin with the realization that in worship we are imaginatively
participating in the re-creation of events calling us to take the perspective
of Jesus himself, and as these symbolic, perspectival and participative dimensions of faith development find or fail to find full expression in worship, our worship succeeds or fails not just in dramatic impact on our lives
but in fostering our basic sense of God's presence in our world.

In the earliest stages of the child's development, worship performs
the foundational tasks of ordering the child's confused understanding of
church and of providing a language, verbal and non-verbal, to grasp God's
presence in our lives. The images, rituals and prayers learned in those
years serve as the basis for new awarenesses later. Yet how foreign and
certainly boring for many children of stages one and two our worship must
be! When we as parents, teachers and ministers have felt the obligation to
take the children to our adult liturgies so they will learn by example or in
order that the family might pray together, we have completely overlooked
the developmental nature of faith and of children's growing patterns, not
only in faith development but in other developmental schemes as well.
Although we admit that we are bored at children's movies and that our
movies are not suited for them, in the case of worship we somehow assume
that they are "little adults" and look at that worship service the same way
we do. Rather we must adopt worship to suit the children's levels of faith
development, celebrating gospel as story and worship as imaginative and

participative. Little wonder that so much of our adult worship seems un-inspiring when we were never allowed to express our own "worshipings" in our own manner as children, rich in imagination and ready for the "awesome" power of stories.

While children at stages one and two need liturgies appropriate to their understandings, imagery and lively spirits, people at the conventional adolescent and adult levels need worship which calls them into a com-munity of believers and celebrates a personal God who responds to human needs and refreshes us to respond to those around us. This worship world depends upon unconscious symbols which evoke powerful feelings of rev-erence and awe while inviting participation along conventional patterns. Here the minister faces a challenge brought on by the very changes meant to renew the liturgical life of the church. As mentioned earlier, in the movement toward a more "understandable" form of worship, a more "reasonable" manner with emphasis upon the understanding of the Word, the symbolic element of mystery which supports a stage three faithing has diminished. Not that incense, candles and vestments ever constituted the heart of worship, but those elements did situate the *experience* of worship in the emotional and symbolic experiences of the people. "In the quest for clear *understanding* and easy participation, our liturgy has become ex-cessively verbal. . . . Many believers today have a good point when they complain that awe and mystery have gone out of our liturgy."[26]

The minister must understand the conventional faither's worship needs. Centered around an interpersonal world and around the expecta-tions of a "good Christian," the faither at this stage will "catch" his or her Christianity through worship in which symbols, story and structure play a large role.

> People learn who they are and who they are becoming before God by their very physical positions and their assigned roles in sacred assem-blies, by what they themselves do and say, by what is said and done to them and for them, by the transactions in which their participation is either prescribed or proscribed. This learning, because it is ritual learning, is preconscious, not consciously available to the ritual sub-jects, but nevertheless taken into their identity and formative of their world view from which their behaviors will flow.[27]

The minister can work with the symbols in various ways, such as the meaning of Eucharist as sharing bread with others around the world, as sacrifice for liberation from sin. But the minister must remember that the faither will interpret the worship event in terms of the conventional structures of faithing. Likewise, the very structure of the worship service at this stage will support a growth toward more individuative faithing modes of reflection and participation or will restrict growth through passive involvement and unchallenging routines.

In relation to the dynamics of stage four worship offers both a more reflective tone and a more powerful call for action as a consequence of worship itself.

> [A]n essential element in the celebration of the eucharist should be raising the consciousness of those who worship to their responsibility for effecting a liberating change in the world around us. . . . The authentic celebration of the eucharist should inspire some form of action for justice in the world, and genuine action for justice in the world must be rooted in the paschal dynamics of the eucharist community. Participation in the eucharistic mystery carries with it a serious obligation to share with others.[28]

At this level of faithing, the worship expression involves an articulation of these relationships between the reality of the suffering world around us, the celebration of God's liberating presence in the world and in the worshiping community, and the support for personal commitment as a consequence of participation in worship. In addition, precisely inasmuch as worship becomes participative by members of the community and invites relationships between personal stories, social stories and the gospel story, that worship supports and promotes stage four faithing modes.

As we enter into the world of the latter stages of faith development, worship must take on yet another dimension, the liberation of worship from the avalanche of words which usually surrounds our Sunday expressions. At these levels of faithing, the minister must attend to the dramatic impact of symbols upon the participant's imaginative powers and the ways in which those symbols evoke meaning and motivation which link promise with limitation, prophecy with vulnerability, justice with mercy. First, such worship experiences must provide people with encouragement to articulate and share their sufferings, pain and loss as well as joy through readings, homilies and reflections on sacred texts. But just as importantly, the worship must name and expel the dark side, the personal and social demonic forces of reality and thus bring true liberation to individuals and peoples.

Finally, such worship expressions will center upon the profound understandings of the paschal mystery and human experience. Death and resurrection are the living metaphor through which the adventures of daily living find expression and meaning. The reality of the paschal pattern most certainly leads to a different expression of worship at stage five: "How can one create an authentic ritual for Good Friday and Easter if the pattern of the paschal mystery does not merge and mesh with his or her life as its unifying and interpreting form?"[29] Turned around this question means that the profound experiences of loss and suffering will lead to a different understanding of "dying" than at stages two or three, for example, where the "dying" and "rising" patterns are externalized in such Lenten practices as "giving up" candy or movies. And yet even that kind of "dying" expression serves as an important ritual in helping conventional faithers "catch" a sense of the paschal pattern.

While the central, eucharistic symbols of bread and wine will evoke different meanings at stages three and four such as Jesus' sacrifice, meal of love, and sharing with all peoples, the meaning of "bread as broken" and "blood poured out" has compelling significance at stages five and six. The broken bread signifies the reality of the minister and faither as "wounded healer," vulnerable and so all the more sensitive to others' wounds and needs for healing. Similarly, the "blood poured out" reflects an awareness that drinking of the cup "activates the memory that suffering for the life of the world is a blessing for those who drink deeply." For the conjunctive and universalizing faither, this paradoxical nature of the cup also "witnesses to the human capacity for self-transcendence by the imbibing of spirits, that promises transformation and joy in the loss of self to the power of the Holy Spirit of Jesus."[30] In this way suffering is not eliminated but transformed; evil is not vanquished but encountered and used for good.

Suffering as blessing, transformation, joy in the loss of self—these phrases become realities for individuals and whole peoples through worship most appropriately at the levels of stages five and six. We celebrate the *memory* of the passion, death and resurrection of Christ Jesus in the eucharistic liturgy and thus truly enter into the mystery of Christian living. Then ministers *to* and *with* people at the higher stages can support such faithing through the full exploration of these symbolic dimensions of bread broken and blood poured forth—patterns for personal redemption and "the redemption of the whole human race and its liberation from every oppressive situation."[31]

Summary —————————————————————————————

Worship is the heart of Christian experience and thus of ministry. The life-blood of meaning and motivation should flow through the Christian community, the body of Christ, enliving the community and so the world because of the central events celebrated in worship. But worship is also the gathering together, the "return" of life-flow for renewal and remembrance. And so newness of life in justice and spirituality begins for all members and for all ministry in and through worship.

In whatever form such worship takes, the three dimensions of faith development serve to strengthen worship at every faith level. For through our imaginative participation in the "mind of Christ Jesus," we become a fully alive Christian people. Worship as a deeply symbolic reality fosters life only through our images of the reality toward which faith points. And worship, as opposed to theater or film, *is* participatory, or it fails in its very purpose. It must draw forth, evoke the very reality of God's presence which it celebrates. Finally, worship demands that all members step aside from their own views and put on the mind of Jesus, sharing bread and wine together only after they have set aside their differences and joined together in mind and heart. The faith development scheme attempts to delineate the shapes which those imaginative, perspectival and participative dimensions might take at different moments in people's lives and among different members of the community.

Thus in this chapter we have examined the ways in which ministers and others can use the faith development scheme to build up the community and foster personal growth. Yet we have filtered the discussion through an emphasis upon "the signs of the times" (Mt 16). That is, the increasing understanding of the church's mission for justice work and the calls for sustaining spiritualities reflect the most poignant struggles of our day. These thrusts must find their sustenance and expression in the Christian community's worship if they are to nurture the whole community and not just those in ministry or in leadership roles in the community.

Finally in the last section of this chapter we hope to have given the minister who works in the area of liturgy some hints for forming the community around its worship experiences. Although much work has been done in liturgical renewal, a major undertaking looms ahead, namely, the development of worship which expresses the real experiences of the people worshiping and the expression of those experiences in ways which capture the imagination and thus the hearts of us all.

If spirituality and especially worship prior to the Second Vatican Council reflected a conventional, non-participative, hierarchial faithing and if liturgical reform after the Council has tended toward a more reflective, participatory and individuative mode, then perhaps the next burst of ritual expressions will plumb the symbolic, paradoxical and creative mode of synthetic faithing while utilizing imaginative rituals which draw in, nurture, and challenge faithers at all developmental levels.

As Fr. Patrick Collins suggests, the theologian and theoretician among us have begun the task but the artist who engages our imagination must now lead the way: "Choreographing liturgy toward imagination will be . . . our prime agenda. The task of making ritual an art which allows assemblies to experience Presence and Mystery is breathtaking."[32] And for that ministry, with its focus upon our imaging of reality as central to our faith expressions, the faith development approach can serve as a creative guide toward worship experiences leading to God's justice in the full life of the Spirit.

NOTES

Chapter 1   "Ministry, Faith and Imagination" ————

[1]*The Jerusalem Bible.* New York: Doubleday & Co., Inc., 1966. All scriptural quotations will be taken from *The Jerusalem Bible.*

[2]Quoted in Lucretia B. Yaghjian, "Omission of Imagination Causes Revelation Stagnation," *National Catholic Reporter,* April 4, 1986, 14.

[3]William F. Lynch, S.J., *Images of Faith* (Notre Dame: University of Notre Dame Press, 1973), pp. 50–51.

[4]Edward Schillebeeckx, O.P., *The Church with a Human Face* (New York: Crossroad Publishing Co., 1985), p. 60.

[5]William J. Bausch, *Traditions, Tensions, Transitions in Ministry* (Mystic, CT: Twenty-Third Publications, 1982), p. 19.

[6]Schillebeeckx, *The Church,* pp. 73, 120–21; Thomas O'Meara, O.P., *Theology of Ministry* (New York: Paulist Press, 1983), p. 185.

[7]Schillebeeckx, *The Church,* p. 254.

[8]O'Meara, *Theology of Ministry,* p. 142. O'Meara's definition reflects a much broader and historically grounded sense of "ministry" than does the narrow understanding adopted by the National Council of Catholic Bishops which restricts the term "ministry" in all their future documents to mean either the ordained ministry or what is called "designated lay ministry," such as acolyte and lector, who perform a designated function within the church. Cf. *Today's Parish,* October 1986, for a discussion of the issue.

[9]Urban Holmes, *The Future Shape of Ministry* (New York: Seabury Press, 1971), p. 91.

[10]Dennis Geaney, O.S.A., *Emerging Lay Ministries* (Kansas City, MO: Andrews and McNeil, Inc., 1979), pp. 12–13.

[11]Urban Holmes, *Ministry and Imagination* (New York: Seabury Press, 1981), p. 8.

[12]Elizabeth J. Koenig, "Imagination and the Face of God in Julian

of Norwich,'' *New Catholic World,* Vol. 225 (Nov./Dec. 1982), No. 1350, 263.

[13]Geaney, *Emerging Lay Ministries,* p. 11; Holmes, *Future Shape,* pp. 220–22.

[14]Walter Brueggemann, *The Prophetic Imagination* (Philadelphia: Fortress Press, 1983), p. 110.

[15]O'Meara, *Theology of Ministry,* p. 200.

[16]Bausch, *Traditions,* p. 39.

[17]Alfred C. Hughes, *Preparing for Church Ministry* (Denville, N.J.: Dimension Books, 1979), p. 19 as quoted in Bausch, *Traditions,* p. 115.

[18]For an excellent discussion of these qualities, cf. James D. Whitehead and Evelyn Eaton Whitehead, *The Emerging Laity* (New York: Doubleday & Co., Inc., 1986), esp. chs. 5 and 6.

[19]Gregory Baum, *Faith and Doctrine* (Paramus, NJ: Newman Press, 1969), pp. 11, 17.

[20]Karl Rahner, S.J., ''Faith,'' in Karl Rahner, ed., *Encyclopedia of Theology, Concise Sacramentum Mundi* (New York: Seabury Press, 1975), p. 496.

[21]James W. Fowler, *Stages of Faith* (New York: Harper and Row, 1981), p. 14.

[22]Lynch, *Images of Faith,* p. 35.

[23]Fowler, *Stages of Faith,* pp. 93ff.

[24]Lynch, *Images of Faith,* p. 17.

[25]Fowler, *Stages of Faith,* p. 33.

[26]Baum, *Faith and Doctrine,* pp. 14–28.

[27]James Fowler, ''Future Christians and Church Education,'' private circulation (Atlanta: Emory University, 1982), pp. 17–19.

[28]*Ibid.,* p. 17.

[29]Holmes, *Future Shape,* pp. 196–200; Holmes, *Ministry and Imagination,* pp. 8, 240.

[30]Holmes, *Ministry and Imagination,* p. 88.

[31]Sharon Parks, *The Critical Years* (New York: Harper and Row, 1986), p. 109.

Chapter 2   ''The Transformation of Faith'' ─────────

[1]A fictional account of a Cub Scout meeting from the author's experience as Cub Scout Den Leader. The oath is taken from *Wolf Cub Scout Book* (Irving, TX: Boy Scouts of America, 1978), p. 27.

[2]A personal interview conducted by the author, March 1977, with a twenty-five year old, white, male, college student.

[3]James Fowler and Sam Keen, *Life-Maps* (Waco, Texas: Word Books, 1978), pp. 86–87.

[4]Parks, *The Critical Years*, p. 109.

[5]For a fuller development of cognitive developmental theory in relation to faith development, cf. Fowler, *Stages of Faith*, pp. 98–107.

[6]Cf. Lawrence Kohlberg, "The Claim to Moral Adequacy of a Highest Stage of Moral Judgment," *The Journal of Philosophy*, Vol. LXX (October 25, 1973), No. 18, 632–36, "Stage and Sequence," in D. Goslin, ed., *Handbook of Socialization Theory and Research* (New York: Rand McNally, 1969), pp. 347–48 and "From Is to Ought," in T. Mischel, ed., *Cognitive Development and Epistemology* (New York: Academic Press, 1971), pp. 167–74; and Fowler, *Life Maps*, p. 34.

[7]Jean Piaget, *Six Psychological Studies* (New York: John Wiley & Sons, 1970), pp. xxii and 3–8, and Herbert Ginsberg and Sylvia Opper, *Piaget's Theory of Intellectual Development* (Englewood Cliffs, N.J.: Prentice-Hall, 1969), ch. 1.

[8]Here Fowler has relied upon the work of social psychologist Robert L. Selman in "Social Cognitive Understanding," in Thomas Lickona, ed., *Moral Development and Behavior* (New York: Holt, Rinehart and Winston, 1976), pp. 299–316.

[9]Kohlberg, "Stage and Sequence," pp. 347–480. See also Lawrence Kohlberg, "The Child as Moral Philosopher," *Psychology Today* (September 1968), 25–30, and Lawrence Kohlberg, "Moral Stages and Moralization," in Lickona, ed., *Moral Development and Behavior*, pp. 31–53.

[10]Holmes, *Ministry and Imagination*, pp. 46–48.

[11]Fowler, *Life-Maps*, pp. 68–69.

[12]Cf. Erik Erikson on basic trust vs. mistrust in *Identity, Youth and Crisis* (New York: W. W. Norton, 1968).

[13]George Eliot on childhood as quoted by George F. Will, *Newsweek*, December 11, 1977, p. 116.

[14]Mr. Rogers, "Scarey Bad Wishes Don't Make Dreams Come True," from "A Place of Our Own" (Woodbury, NY: Pickwick International Inc., 1970).

[15]Harper Lee, *To Kill a Mockingbird* (New York: Popular Library, 1960), p. 34.

[16]Cf. Erikson for further discussion of identity in *Identity, Youth and Crisis*, pp. 128–29.

[17]Fowler, *Stages of Faith,* p. 185.

[18]Charles Schultz, *Peanuts,* as illustrated in Robert L. Short, *The Gospel According to Peanuts* (Richmond: John Knox Press, 1965), p. 111.

[19]Fowler, *Stages of Faith,* pp. 200ff.

[20]Malcolm Muggeridge, *Something Beautiful for God* (New York: Ballantine books, 1971), p. vi.

[21]James W. Fowler, "Faith Development, Futurity and the Kingdom of God" (Boston College: unpublished paper for private circulation, 1976), and Fowler, *Stages of Faith,* pp. 204–11.

Chapter 3   "Religious Education and the Growth of Faith"

[1]Thomas Groome, *Christian Religious Education* (New York: Harper and Row, 1980), p. 25.

[2]Mary Boys, "A Word about Teaching Justly," in Padraic O'Hare (ed.), *Education for Peace and Justice* (New York: Harper and Row, 1983), p. 98.

[3]Gabriel Moran, *Interplay* (Winona, MN: St. Mary's Press, 1981), p. 19.

[4]James Fowler, "Faith Development Theory and the Aims of Religious Socialization," in G. Durka and A. Smith, eds., *Emerging Issues in Religious Education* (New York: Paulist Press, 1981), pp. 187–211.

[5]John Elias, *The Foundations and Practice of Adult Religious Education* (Malabar, Florida: Krieger Publ. Co., 1982), p. 163.

[6]Cf. John Westerhoff, *Will Our Children Have Faith?* (New York: Seabury Press, 1976) and James Michael Lee, *The Flow of Religious Instruction* (Birmingham, Ala.: Religious Education Press, 1973).

[7]For a beautiful and moving expression of such "child-like" faithing, cf. *Mister God, This Is Anna,* by Fynn (New York: Ballantine Books, 1974).

[8]Holmes, *Ministry and Imagination,* p. 104.

[9]Elias, *Foundations and Practice,* p. 70.

[10]Erikson, *Identity, Youth and Crisis,* p. 124.

[11]Holmes, *Ministry and Imagination,* p. 173.

[12]Ronald Goldman, *Readiness for Religion* (New York: Seabury Press, 1976).

[13]Daniel Csanyi, "Faith Development and the Age of Readiness for the Bible," *Religious Education* (September–October 1982), 521.

[14]Holmes, *Ministry and Imagination*, p. 169.

[15]Erikson, *Identity, Youth and Crisis*, p. 129.

[16]Elias, *Foundations and Practice*, referring to the work of R. Potvin and Associates, *Religion and American Youth* (Washington, D.C.: United States Catholic Conference, 1976).

[17]Margaret Gorman, "Moral and Faith Development in 17 Year Old Students," *Religious Education* (September–October 1977), 491–504.

[18]Cf. Michael Warren, *Readings and Resources for Youth Ministry* (Winona, MN: St. Mary's Press, 1987) and *Youth, Gospel, Liberation* (New York: Harper and Row, 1987).

[19]Gorman, "Moral and Faith Development," pp. 499–500.

[20]Eugene J. Mischey, "Faith Development and Its Relationship to Moral Reasoning and Identity Status in Young Adults" (Ph.D. dissertation, Department of Educational Theory, University of Toronto, 1976), pp. 203–06.

[21]For a sample of Kohlberg's work on the just community concept, cf. Lawrence Kohlberg, "High School Democracy and Educating for a Just Society," in Ralph Mosher (ed.), *Moral Education* (New York: Praeger & Co., 1980); Clark Power and Joseph Reimer, "Moral Atmosphere: An Educational Bridge Between Judgment and Action," in W. Damon (ed.), *Moral Development* (New York: Praeger and Co., 1980); entire issue, *Moral Education Forum,* Vol. 6, No. 4 (Winter 1981).

[22]For a fuller discussion of ministry in the high school setting, cf. Gary L. Chamberlain, "Faith Development and High School Campus Ministry," *Religious Education* (May–June 1979), 314–24.

Chapter 4   "Religious Education for Maturing Faith"   —

[1]Parker J. Palmer, *To Know as We Are Known: A Spirituality of Education* (New York: Harper and Row, 1983), p. 113.

[2]Elias, *Foundations and Practice*, p. 177.

[3]Francis L. Gross, Jr., *Passages in Teaching* (New York: Philosophical Library, 1982), pp. 169–70.

[4]Mische, "Faith Development . . . " pp. 202–09.

[5]Gary L. Chamberlain, personal interviews with ten young adults over a year's period, all of whom had been part of a Christian living community since their college years; St. Louis, MO, 1977–78.

[6]Elias, pp. 76–77.

[7]*Ibid.*, p. 78.

[8]Lawrence Kohlberg, "Continuities in Childhood and Adult Moral Development: Revisited," Chapter 6 in Lawrence Kohlberg, *The Psychology of Moral Development*, Vol. II (New York: Harper and Row, 1984), pp. 466ff.

[9]For a lively and thoughtful study of these issues, cf. Gross, *Passages in Teaching*.

[10]Erikson, *Identity, Youth and Crisis*, p. 157.

[11]To examine that diversity, cf. Fowler, "Appendix B: Research Results," in *Stages of Faith*, pp. 313–23.

[12]Elias, *Foundations and Practice*, pp. 55, 139.

[13]General Catechetical Directory, as quoted in B. L. Marthaler, *Catechetics in Context* (Huntington, Ind: Our Sunday Visitor Press, 1973), p. 50; United States Catholic Conference, *Sharing the Light of Faith: National Catholic Catechetical Directory* (Washington, D.C.: USCC Publications Office, 1979), art. 188.

[14]Erikson, *Identity, Youth and Crisis*, pp. 138–39; cf. also Erik Erikson, *Childhood and Society* (2nd ed.) (New York: W. W. Norton, 1968), pp. 266–68.

[15]Elias, *Foundations and Practice*, p. 191.

[16]John C. Haughey, S.J., "Jesus as the Justice of God," in John C. Haughey (ed.), *The Faith That Does Justice* (New York: Paulist Press, 1977), p. 265.

Chapter 5   "Family and Parish: Faith Nurturers" ———

[1]Pope John Paul II, Apostolic Exhortation, "On the Family," December 15, 1981 (Washington, D.C.: USCC Publications Office, 1981), p. 19, #21.

[2]Philip J. Murnion, "The Parish as Source of Community and Identity," in Evelyn Eaton Whitehead (ed.), *The Parish in Community and Ministry* (New York: Paulist Press, 1978), p. 102.

[3]John Shea, "The Religious Mission of the Parish," in Whitehead, *The Parish*, p. 69.

[4]David M. Thomas, *Family Life and the Church* (New York: Paulist Press, 1979), esp. ch. 9, "Family Life and Parish Renewal."

[5]Cf. for example the research by Charles Glock and Gerhard Lenski in Charles Y. Glock, Benjamin R. Ringer, and Earl R. Rabbie, *To Comfort and To Challenge* (Berkeley: University of California Press, 1967), esp. Part I, "Sources of Church Involvement"; Gerhard Lenski, *The Religious Factor* (New York: Doubleday and Co., 1961).

[6]Thomas, *Family Life*, p. 107.

[7]Most Rev. Howard J. Hubbard, as quoted in "For Your Information," *Today's Parish*, March, 1984, p. 5.

[8]Pope John Paul II, "On the Family," p. 15, #17.

[9]"Death of the Family," *Newsweek*, January 17, 1983, 26ff; "Portrait of Divorce in America," *Newsweek*, February 2, 1987, 78.

[10]"Listening to America's Families, A Summary of the Report to the President, Congress and Families of the Nation," November 1980 (Washington, D.C.: US Government Printing office, 1980).

[11]Dolores Curran, "Family Ministry and the Parish: Barriers and Vision," in Gloria Durka and Joanmarie Smith (eds.), *Family Ministry* (Minneapolis: Winston Press, 1980), pp. 12–13.

[12]Brennan and Marie Hill, "The Family as Center of Ministry," in Durka and Smith, *Family Ministry*, pp. 205–07.

[13]*Sharing the Light of Faith*, art. 226.

[14]Bernard Cooke and Pauline Turner, "The Family, Heart of Liturgy," in Durka and Smith, *Family Ministry*, p. 187.

[15]Kohlberg, "Moral Stages and Moralization," in Lickona (ed.), *Moral Development and Behavior*, p. 50.

[16]John Elias, "The Christian Family as Moral Educator," in Durka and Smith, *Family Ministry*, p. 51.

[17]James W. Fowler, "Perspectives on the Family from the Standpoint of Faith Development Theory," *Perkins Journal* 33:1, 1–19.

[18]*Ibid.*

[19]*Ibid.*, p. 22.

[20]William J. Bausch, *The Christian Parish* (Mystic, CT: Twenty-Third Publ., 1980), p. 73.

[21]Shea, "Religious Mission of the Parish," p. 56.

[22]Murnion, "The Parish as Source of Community and Identity," pp. 108–09.

[23]Robert R. Newsome, *The Ministering Parish* (New York: Paulist Press, 1982), p. 25.

[24]Shea, "Religious Mission of the Parish," p. 69.

[25]Evelyn Eaton Whitehead, "The Structure of Community," in Whitehead (ed.), *The Parish*, p. 48.

[26]Newsome, *The Ministering Parish*, p. 79.

[27]*Ibid.*, pp. 57, 61.

[28]Msgr. John J. Egan, "Forward," in Whitehead (ed.), *The Parish*, p. 1.

[29]Thomas, *Family Life*, p. 103.

Ch. 6 "Ministry with the Sick" ―――――――――

[1]This was the author's own experience during preparation for minor surgery.

[2]Gerald Niklas and Charlotte Stafanics, *Ministry to the Hospitalized* (New York: Paulist Press, 1975), p. 113.

[3]National Association of Catholic Chaplains, *The Apostolate to the Sick* (St. Louis: Catholic Hospital Association, 1967), p. 14.

[4]Thomas Kelly, "Catholic Health Care Institutions and Social Justice," in *The Ministry of Healing* (St. Louis: Catholic Health Association, 1981), p. 89; Edweward F. Bobihal and Charles Wm. Stewart, *When a Friend Is Dying* (Nashville: Abingdon Press, 1984), p. 15.

[5]Bobihal and Stewart, *When a Friend Is Dying,* p. 10.

[6]John Burke, O.P., "Eucharistic Health Care Facility Transcends Professionalism," in *The Ministry of Healing,* p. 40.

[7]Kelly, "Catholic Health Care," p. 88; *Apostolate to the Sick,* p. 12.

[8]Steven S. Ivy, "*Stages of Faith:* The Psychology of Human Development and the Quest for Meaning," *The Journal of Pastoral Care* XXXVI (December 1982), 273.

[9]David Thornasma, "The Basis of Medicine and Religion," in *The Ministry of Healing,* p. 33.

[10]James L. Empereur, *Prophetic Anointing* (Wilmington, Del.: Michael Glazier, Inc., 1982), p. 199.

[11]*Ibid.,* p. 196.

[12]*Ibid.,* pp. 141, 200.

[13]Bobihal and Stewart, *When a Friend is Dying,* pp. 67–70.

[14]George Paterson, "Death, Dying, and the Elderly," in William M. Clements, ed., *Ministry with the Aging* (New York: Harper and Row, 1981), p. 221.

[15]Bradford Smith, as quoted in Bobihal and Stewart, *When a Friend Is Dying,* p. 75.

[16]Pierre Teilhard de Chardin, *The Divine Milieu* (New York: Harper and Row, 1960), cf. especially Part Two, "The Divinisation of Our Passivities," ch. 3, "The Passivities of Our Diminishment," pp. 52–68.

[17]George Paterson, "Death, Dying, and the Elderly," in William C. Clements, ed., *Ministry with the Aging* (New York: Harper and Row, 1981), p. 225.

[18]Dobihal and Stewart, *When a Friend Is Dying,* p. 35.

[19]*Ibid.,* p. 16.

[20]*Ibid.,* p. 43.

[21]Thornasma, "The Basis of Medicine and Religion," p.32.

[22]*Ibid.,* p. 33.

[23]*Ibid.,* p. 34.

[24]Catholic Chaplains, *Apostolate to the Sick,* p. 11.

[25]Kelly, "Catholic Health Care," p. 87.

[26]Empereur, *Prophetic Anointing,* p. 190.

[27]*Ibid.,* p. 210.

Chapter 7   "The Elderly and Ministry" ————————

[1]"The Fall Campaign," *Newsweek,* November–December 1984, p. 109.

[2]Maggie Kuhn, quoted in Martin J. Heinecken, "Christian Theology and Aging: Basic Affirmations," in William M. Clements, ed., *Ministry with the Aging* (San Francisco: Harper and Row, 1981), p. 89.

[3]Michael Harrington, *The New American Poverty* (New York: Holt, Rinehart and Winston, 1984), p. 225.

[4]Quoted in Bartholomew J. Laurello, *Ministering to the Aging: Every Christian's Call* (New York: Paulist Press, 1979).

[5]Allen J. Moore, "The Family Relations of Older Persons," in Clements, *Ministry with the Aging,* p. 180.

[6]Harrington, *New American Poverty,* p. 224.

[7]P. S. Timiras, *Developmental Physiology and Aging* (New York: Macmillan & Co., 1972), p. 465, quoted in Douglas C. Kimmel, *Adulthood and Aging* (New York: John Wiley and Sons, Inc., 1974), p. 350.

[8]Robert Katz, "Jewish Values and Sociopsychological Perspectives on Aging," in Seward Hiltner, ed., *Toward a Theology of Aging* (New York: Human Sciences Press, 1975), p. 144.

[9]Eugene C. Bianchi, *Aging as a Spiritual Journey* (New York: Crossroad Publ. Co., 1982), p. 171.

[10]Erikson, *Childhood and Society,* pp. 268–69.

[11]Bianchi, *Aging,* p. 179.

[12]James and Evelyn Whitehead, "Retirement," in Clements, *Ministry with the Aging,* pp. 132ff.

[13]*Ibid.,* p. 134.

[14]Chardin, *The Divine Milieu,* p. 46.

[15]Bianchi, *Aging,* p. 182.

[16]Katz, "Jewish Values," pp. 148–49.

[17]Urban Holmes, "Worship and Aging: Memory and Repentance," in Clements, *Ministry with the Aging*, pp. 91, 94.

[18]Don Browning, "Preface to a Practical Theology of Aging," in Hiltner, *Toward a Theology of Aging*, p. 171.

[19]Ann Belford Ulanov, "Aging: On the Way to One's End," in Clements, *Ministry with the Aging*, pp. 121–22.

[20]Bianchi, *Aging*, p. 210.

[21]*Ibid.*, pp. 205, 297.

[22]*Ibid.*, p. 208.

[23]*Ibid.*, p. 161.

[24]Lecture by Dr. Kathleen Fischer, "Story Telling and Aging," Seattle University, July 21, 1984; cf. also Kathleen Fischer, *Winter Grace* (New York: Paulist Press, 1985).

[25]John C. Bennett, "Ethical Aspects of Aging in America," in Clements, *Ministry with the Aging*, p. 141. For an excellent discussion of these conditions and an analysis of some of the factors involved, cf. Mary Adelaide Mendelson, *Tender Loving Greed* (New York: Alfred A. Knopf, 1974).

[26]For an excellent set of the kinds of questions involved here, cf. Kimmel, *Adulthood and Aging*, p. 462.

[27]Bianchi, *Aging*, p. 143.

[28]Richard N. Shulik, *Faith Growth Among the Aging* (Unpublished Ph.D. dissertation, Harvard University, 1980), Ch. 3, p. 40.

[29]Bianchi, *Aging*, p. 209.

[30]Catholic Bishops of the United States, *Society and the Aged: Toward Reconciliation* (Washington, D.C.: United States Catholic Conference, 1976), p. 8, quoted in Laurello, *Ministry to the Aging*, p. 29.

[31]Shulik, *Faith Growth*, Ch. 5, pp. 10–11.

[32]*Ibid.*, pp. 7–9.

[33]For a fine listing of organizations and publications of interest to elders see Sara and Richard Reichert, *In Wisdom and the Spirit* (New York: Paulist Press, 1976), pp. 84–85.

[34]For further elaboration of this developmental, interactive model, cf. Allen J. Moore, "Family Relations of Older Persons," in Clements, *Ministry with the Aging*, p. 181.

[35]I am indebted again to Dr. Kathleen Fischer for her personal comments on this section and her insights into the dynamics of family interaction from her work in the area.

[36]Donald Miller, "Adult Religious Education and the Aging," in Clements, *Ministry with the Aging*, pp. 244–45.

³⁷*Ibid.*, quoting National Interfaith Coalition on Aging's 1976 survey, p. 169.

³⁸Elbert C. Cole, "Lay Ministries with Older Adults," in *ibid.*, p. 257. For a thorough discussion of the Center, cf. pp. 256–63.

³⁹Empereur, *Prophetic Anointing,* p. 157, quoting Leonard Bowman, *The Importance of Being Sick* (Wilmington: Consortium Books, 1976), p. 212.

⁴⁰Holmes, "Worship and Aging," in Clements, *Ministry with the Aging,* p. 106.

⁴¹Empereur, *Prophetic Anointing,* p. 170.

⁴²Henri Nouwen and Walter Gaggney, *Aging* (Garden City: Doubleday and Co., 1974), p. 51, quoted in Empereur, *ibid.,* p. 201.

Chapter 8   "Ministry to the Imprisoned" ——————

¹Quoted in Gerald A. McHugh, *Christian Faith and Criminal Justice* (New York: Paulist Press, 1978), p. 195.

²Quoted in Renny Golden, "Crime and Prison: A Socio-Economic Reflection," *To Proclaim Release for Prisoners* (Chicago: National Federation of Priests' Councils, 1981), p. 43.

³Quoted in *ibid.,* p. 48.

⁴Cf. discussion of this difference in Hans Toch, *Men in Crisis: Human Breakdowns in Prison* (Chicago: Aldine Publishing Co., 1975), pp. 145–46.

⁵Jeffrey H. Reiman, *The Rich Get Richer and the Poor Get Prison,* 2nd ed. (New York: John Wiley & Sons, 1984), pp. 16, 20–21, 109.

⁶Mark Umbreit, *Crime and Reconciliation* (Nashville: Abingdon Press, 1985), pp. 57–58.

⁷Golden, "Crime and Prison," p. 45.

⁸"Opinion Page," *The Seattle Times,* February 4, 1986.

⁹"American Correctional Association Winter Conference," *The Chap-lett,* Vol. 30 (October 1984), No. 3, 37.

¹⁰Michael E. Endres, *The Morality of Capital Punishment* (Mystic, Conn.: Twenty-Third Publications, 1985), p. 2; "Death Watch," *National Catholic Reporter,* October 9, 1987, 24.

¹¹Umbreit, *Crime and Reconciliation,* pp. 41–42, 51.

¹²Reiman, *The Rich Get Richer,* p. 78.

¹³*Ibid.,* p. xii.

¹⁴McHugh, *Christian Faith,* pp. 103, 112, 121.

[15]D. Marrero, "Spatial Dimensions of Democratic Prison Reform," *Prison Journal,* 1977, 57 (2), 38, as quoted in Joseph E. Hickey and Peter L. Scharf, *Toward a Just Correctional System* (San Francisco: Jossey-Bass Publishers, 1980), p. 24.

[16]McHugh, *Christian Faith,* pp. 83–84.

[17]Reiman, *The Rich Get Richer,* pp. 40–41.

[18]Toch, *Men in Crisis,* pp. 6–7, 145ff.

[19]Julian Roebuck, "The Short 'Con Man,' " *Crime and Deliquency* (July 1964), 243, as quoted in McHugh, *Christian Faith,* p. 77.

[20]Mchugh, *Christian Faith,* pp. 97–98.

[21]Umbreit, *Crime and Reconciliation,* p. 83.

[22]In the 1950's and 1960's Fr. Dismas Clark, S.J. expressed his successful ministry in jails and prisons and built his halfway house in St. Louis upon the image of Dismas, the thief crucified at Jesus' side. From the author's own observations at Fr. Clark's halfway house, the image had a powerful attraction for the ex-prisoners who stayed there.

[23]For more information about these and other programs, see Umbreit, *Crime and Reconciliation,* esp. pp. 61ff.

[24]McHugh, *Christian Faith,* p. 168.

[25]George M. Anderson, "Prison Labor" in *The Chap-lett,* Vol. 30 (October 1984), No. 3, 28.

[26]Hickey and Scharf, *Toward a Just . . . ,* pp. 51, 57, 62.

[27]*Ibid.,* pp. 164–65.

[28]South Carolina Department of Corrections, *Correctional Industries Feasibility Study* (Columbia, S.C.: South Carolina Department of Corrections, 1973), p. 1, as quoted in Hickey and Scharf, *Toward a Just . . . ,* p. 178.

[29]Hickey and Scharf, *Toward a Just . . . ,* pp. 172–75.

[30]*Ibid.,* pp. 188–89.

[31]McHugh, *Christian Faith,* pp. 170–71.

[32]Joseph Mulligan, S.J., "A Theology of Prisons," in NFPC, *To Proclaim Release for Prisoners,* p. 7.

[33]Hickey and Scharf, *Toward a Just . . . ,* p. 143.

[34]Cf. Umbreit, *Crime and Reconciliation,* pp. 103ff. for a description of these programs.

[35]Hickey and Scharf, *Toward a Just . . . ,* p. 136.

[36]Cf. Umbreit, *Crime and Reconciliation,* pp. 60ff., 88, and McHugh, *Christian Faith,* pp. 229–31 for listing of programs.

[37]McHugh, *Christian Faith,* p. 5.

[38]Umbreit, *Crime and Reconciliation,* p. 133.

Chapter 9   "Transformations in Justice" ————————

[1]Quoted in November 1981, mailing from the Institute for Peace and Justice, Jim and Kathy McGinniss, Directors, St. Louis, MO.

[2]Quoted in Paul VI, "On the Development of Peoples," in David J. O'Brien and Thomas A. Shannon, eds., *Renewing the Earth* (New York: Image Books, 1977), p. 321.

[3]Letty M. Russell, *Human Liberation in a Feminist Perspective* (Philadelphia: Westminster Press, 1974), p. 153.

[4]Paul Steidl-Meier, S.J., *Social Justice Ministry* (New York: Le Jacq Publishing Inc., 1984), pp. 149–60.

[5]Synod of Bishops, "Justice in the World," 1971, in *Renewing the Earth,* p. 391.

[6]Steidl-Meier, *Social Justice Ministry,* p. 126.

[7]John R. Donahue, S.J., "Biblical Perspectives on Justice," Haughey (ed.), *The Faith That Does Justice,* p. 69.

[8]Richard P. McBrien, S.J., *Catholicism,* (Minneapolis: Winston Press, 1980), p. 986.

[9]Richard R. Roach, S.J., "Tridentine Justification and Justice," in *The Faith That Does Justice,* p. 203.

[10]Survey of pre-Vatican II Sunday reading by William G. Thompson, S.J., as indicated to author; see also notes by William G. Thompson, S.J., "Images of God and Styles of Prayer," private circulation, Institute of Pastoral Studies, Loyola University, Chicago, Summer 1979, p. 4.

[11]Dermot A. Lane, *Foundations for a Social Theology* (New York: Paulist Press, 1984), p. 124.

[12]John C. Haughey, S.J., "Jesus as the Justice of God," in *The Faith That Does Justice,* pp. 265ff.

[13]Roach, "Tridentine Justification and Faith," p. 191.

[14]Dorothy G. Singer and Jerome L. Singer, "Is Human Imagination Going Down the Tube?" *The Chronicle of Higher Education,* April 23, 1979, and "Come Back, Mister Rogers, Come Back," *Psychology Today,* March 1979, 56–60.

[15]Charles F. Kemp, *Pastoral Care with the Poor* (Nashville: Abingdon Press, 1972), esp. ch. 8, pp. 64–71.

[16]Lane, *Foundations,* p. 131.

[17]Cf. Carol Gilligan, *In a Different Voice* (Cambridge, MA: Harvard University Press, 1983), esp. ch. 5, pp. 128–50.

[18]Albert Camus, *The Plague* (New York: Modern Library, 1948).

[19]James Fowler, "Faith, Liberation, and Human Development," The Thirkield-Jones Lectures, Gammon Theological Seminary, February 26–27, 1974, 28.

Chapter 10   "The Spirit in the World" ————————

[1]Quoted in Jan Balles, "The Challenge of Living Humanly," *Catholic Radical,* February–March, 1980, 3.

[2]Eugene C. Bianchi, *On Growing Older* (New York: Crossroad Publ. Co., 1985), pp. viii–ix.

[3]Quoted in Patrick W. Collins, *More Than Meets the Eye* (New York: Paulist Press, 1983), p. 7.

[4]Benedict J. Groeschel, O.F.M., *Spiritual Passages* (New York: Crossroad Publ. Co., 1984), p. 4.

[5]Katherine M. Dyckman, S.N.J.M., and L. Patrick Carroll, S.J., *Inviting the Mystic, Supporting the Prophet* (New York: Paulist Press, 1981), p. 18.

[6]Groeschel, *Spiritual Passages,* p. 188.

[7]James W. Fowler, "Stages in Faith: The Structural-Developmental Approach," in Thomas Hennessy, S.J., ed. *Values and Moral Education* (New York: Paulist Press, 1976), pp. 32–33.

[8]Cf. the Arch Book series, published by Augsburg Publishing Company, Minneapolis, MN.

[9]I am indebted in this analysis of faith development and scripture to the work of William G. Thompson, S.J., especially his article, along with Mary Sharon Riley, R.C., "Images of God and Styles of Prayer," private circulation, Loyola University, Institute for Pastoral Studies, Summer 1978.

[10]*The Spiritual Exercises of St. Ignatius of Loyola,* Annotation 54.

[11]Fowler, "Stages in Faith," p. 34.

[12]Dyckman and Carroll, *Inviting the Mystic,* pp. 37, 43.

[13]*Ibid.,* p. 83.

[14]Steidl-Meier, *Social Justice Ministry,* p. 47.

[15]William O'Neill, "Resistance and Contemplation," *Catholic Radical,* February–March, 1980, 4.

[16]Fowler, "Stages in Faith," p. 34.

[17]Thompson and Riley, "Images of God," p. 9.

[18]William Johnston, S.J., *The Inner Eye of Love* (New York: Harper and Row, Publ., 1982), p. 28.

[19]*Ibid.*, p. 147.

[20]Balles, ''The Challenge of Living Humanly,'' p. 3.

[21]Anthony T. Padovano, ''Our Vulnerability Needs Ministry,'' *National Catholic Reporter*, October 23, 1981, 18.

[22]Bianchi, *On Growing Older*, p. 81.

[23]James W. Fowler, ''Faith Development, Futurity and the Kingdom of God,'' private circulation, Boston College, 1976, p. 14.

[24]Collins, *More Than Meets the Eye*, p. 54.

[25]Lane, *Foundations for a Social Theology*, pp. 154–55.

[26]Collins, *More Than Meets the Eye*, p. 12.

[27]Mary Collins, O.S.B., ''Eucharistic Praxis, Justice, and Ministry,'' Catholic University, private circulation, delivered at ''Justice and Ministry Conference,'' Boston College, Nov. 15–16, 1983, pp. 14–15.

[28]Lane, *Foundations for a Social Theology*, p. 144.

[29]Collins, *More Than Meets the Eye*, p. 86.

[30]*Ibid.*, pp. 18–19.

[31]Roman Catholic Bishops, ''Justice in the World,'' in O'Brien and Shannon, eds., *Renewing the Earth*, p. 391.

[32]Collins, *Move Than Meets the Eye*, p. 149.